# SPORT AND PHYSICAL ACTIVITY
# IN THE MODERN WORLD

D1737540

# SPORT AND PHYSICAL ACTIVITY IN THE MODERN WORLD

## J. RICHARD POLIDORO

*The University of Rhode Island*

**ALLYN AND BACON**

Boston ■ London ■ Toronto ■ Sydney ■ Tokyo ■ Singapore

**Vice President, Editor-in-Chief:** Paul A. Smith
**Publisher:** Joseph E. Burns
**Editorial Assistant:** Tanja Eise
**Marketing Manager:** Richard Muhr
**Production Administrator:** Deborah Brown
**Editorial-Production Coordinator:** Marret Kauffner
**Text Design/Electronic Composition:** Karen Mason
**Composition Buyer:** Linda Cox
**Manufacturing Buyer:** David Repetto
**Cover Administrator:** Jenny Hart

Copyright © 2000 by Allyn & Bacon
A Pearson Education Company
160 Gould Street
Needham Heights, MA 02494

Internet: www.abacon.com

Between the time Website information is gathered and then published, it is not unusual for some sites to have closed. Also, the transcription of URLs can result in unintended typographical errors. The publisher would appreciate notification where these occur so that they may be corrected in subsequent editions. Thank you.

**Library of Congress Cataloging-in-Publication Data**
Polidoro, J. Richard (John Richard)
    Sport and physical activity in the modern world / J. Richard
Polidoro.
        p.    cm.
    Includes bibliographical references and index.
    ISBN 0-205-27158-8 (alk. paper)
    1.  Sports--History.    2.   Physical education and training--History.
3.  Sports Cross-cultural studies.      4.   Physical education and
training Cross-cultural studies.    I.   Title.
    GV571.P65   2000
    796--dc21                                                    99-38056
                                                                    CIP

Printed in the United States of America
10 9 8 7 6 5 4 3 2 1    04 03 02 01 00 99

# CONTENTS

**CHAPTER TWO**

# Sport and Physical Activity in Nationalistic Europe     25

CHRISTIAN BECKER, WOLFGANG BUSS, LORENZ PEIFFER

**CHAPTER THREE**

## Sport and Physical Activity in Modern America    54

J. RICHARD POLIDORO

## CHAPTER SEVEN

# Global Issues in the Profession of Physical Education and Sport    157

EARLE F. ZEIGLER

# PREFACE

Most introductory books on the history of sport and physical activity provide a general overview of developments from the beginning of civilization until the present day. They usually review sport and physical activity in primitive and early societies, developments in ancient Greece and Rome, events of the Middle Ages, developments during the Renaissance and the Age of Enlightenment, and, in conclusion, nineteenth and twentieth century developments in Europe and the United States. Although certainly of historical value, most of these books do not provide sufficient analysis of modern and current developments from a global perspective, particularly in terms of programs, issues, and concerns.

This book, on the other hand, is designed to provide a concise and comprehensive review of major developments in sport and physical activity from the end of the eighteenth century to the twenty-first century. Most of the material is devoted specifically to events and developments from 1800 to the year 2000, viewed from an international perspective. The text pays considerable attention to the identification and analysis of major issues confronting sport and physical education in a global context. A distinctive feature of the book is the chapter contributions from an array of internationally known scholars and sport historians.

In Chapter 1, Uriel Simri (Israel) reviews the development of sport and physical activity in ancient Greece. One may wonder why a chapter on sport in ancient Greece should be included in a book that is devoted primarily to an analysis of sport in modern times. The answer, however, is quite simple. It was in ancient Greece that the seeds of modern-day sports and physical activity were planted. In this chapter, the origins of Greek sport are reviewed, with particular attention to the development of its competitive program of athletics and the ancient Olympic Games.

The scene then jumps to sport developments in modern Europe, during the time when many countries were experiencing a rising sense of nationalism. In Chapter 2, three noted German historians—Christian Becker, Wolfgang Buss, and Lorenz Peiffer—review major developments in sport and physical activity in nineteenth- and twentieth-century Europe. Developments in four different countries—Germany, England, Ireland, and the German Democratic Republic (East Germany)—are reviewed to illustrate the relationship of sport to political and nationalist elements. The material presented by Becker, Buss, and Peiffer clearly illustrates the role that sport played in achieving national political goals.

In Chapter 3, J. Richard Polidoro (United States) reviews the development of sport and physical activity in the United States. This chapter makes the point that the forms of sport and physical activity found in a given society are largely a reflection of the social structure and culture of that society. Events in the United States from colonial times to the present are reviewed, to illustrate the changing nature of America's perceptions and values. The chapter concludes with a scathing analysis of the present status of sport and physical education in the United States.

Uriel Simri (Israel) traces the development of modern international sports in two chapters. Chapter 4, entitled "The Genesis of International Sports," reviews the development of international sport during the nineteenth century, culminating with the emergence of the modern Olympic Games in 1896 and the development of world championships. Significant twentieth-century developments in international sports are analyzed in Chapter 5. The chapter also discusses major problems and concerns associated with these developments. Particular attention is paid to the politicization of international sports as well as to the problems of doping.

In Chapter 6, Joanna Davenport (United States) provides an overview of major global developments in women's sports during the nineteenth and twentieth centuries. Her review shows that women's increasing participation in the sport arena parallels society's gradual but increasing acceptance of competitive sports for women. One will also see that advances in women's participation were often held back by major obstacles. Although women today have more opportunity to participate in a variety of sports than at any other ime in history, complete gender equity in sport has yet to be realized.

In Chapter 7, Earle Zeigler (Canada) discusses current worldwide issues and concerns confronting the profession of physical education and sport. Physical education in the schools is facing a severe uphill struggle for acceptance and recognition. At the same time, sport-related problems of violence, drug use, gambling, commercialization, and unethical behavior abound. Zeigler argues that competitive sport and physical activity should be so organized and administered that they make a positive contribution to society. To this end he offers several recommendations for improvement.

The ethical problems associated with sport are specifically addressed in Chapter 8. In this chapter, Zeigler stresses the urgent need for those involved in programs of physical activity and competitive sport to improve their approach to ethics. Specifically, he proposes a cross-cultural application of an applied ethics model that is based on a merger of Toulmin's "jurisprudential argument" with Kant's, Mill's, and Aristotle's tests of consistency, consequences, and intentions.

Chapter 9 is, quite frankly, a plea for reform. After a brief summary of the issues confronting physical activity and sport, it points out the need for change in both attitude and practice. It especially proposes that the competitive sports "establishment" should be held more accountable for its actions.

As one reads through the various chapters, numerous questions will no doubt arise. The Study Questions at the end of each chapter are designed to help students refine their thinking about controversial issues. Answers to questions may also be explored through the rich resources of the Recommended Readings at the end of each chapter.

All the writers hope that the book will help readers gain awareness and better understanding of the current state of sport and physical activity in the modern world. They further hope that the book will make a difference by encouraging sport and physical activity professionals to deal with the many problems and issues in this vital aspect of modern society.

## ACKNOWLEDGMENTS

I wish to thank all the writers who contributed chapters to this book. Without the contributions of Christian Becker, Wolfgang Buss, Joanna Davenport, Lorenz Peiffer, Uriel Simri, and Earle Zeigler, this book would never have come together. Their willingness to share their vast knowledge and expertise is most appreciated.

A special thank you is extended to Uriel Simri, who, in addition to contributing three chapters, helped considerably in the planning and developmental stages of the book. His insightful input and willingness to provide a critical review of the manuscript gave me the necessary encouragement to see the book through to completion.

I also wish to thank the reviewers, who include Doris Corbett, Howard University; Stephen Cone, Keene State College; and Synthia Snydor, University of Illinois.

I am also indebted to the editorial staff at Allyn & Bacon, especially Suzy Spivey, Sara Sherlock, Pat Wakeley, and Marret Kauffner for their willingness to support this endeavor from the beginning stages to completion. Their belief in the book and their assistance are most appreciated.

Finally, without the encouragement and support of Jolene, this book would not exist.

J. Richard Polidoro

# ABOUT THE CONTRIBUTORS

**Christian Becker** (M.A.) was born in 1967 in Berlin, Germany. As of 1998 he was a scientific assistant and doctoral student at the Institute for Sport Sciences at the University of Göttingen (Germany). He has studied both history and sport sciences in Berlin and Göttingen, and has published in the area of nineteenth and twentieth century European sport history. At the present time, Mr. Becker is working with a team researching the sports movement in the German Democratic Republic.

**Wolfgang Buss** (Ph.D.) was born in 1944 in Germany. He is currently an akademischer oberrat (the equivalent of an associate professor) at the Institute for Sport Sciences of the University of Göttingen (Germany). Dr. Buss has studied history, political science, and sport sciences. His research and publications have focused on the contemporary history of sports and sport politics. At present, he is chair of the research team investigating the sport system of the German Democratic Republic.

**Joanna Davenport** (Ph.D.), now professor emeritus, was until June 1997 a professor in the Health and Human Performance Department at Auburn University, Alabama, where she served as director of women's athletics from 1976 to 1985. A former president of the National Association for Girls and Women in Sport, she was also a member of the Education Council of the United States Olympic Committee. She has been three times an American delegate to the International Olympic Academy in Olympia, Greece. A sport historian, Dr. Davenport has written extensively on women's sports and the Olympic Games.

**Lorenz Peiffer** (Ph.D.) was born in 1947 in Germany. He is currently serving as a professor of sport pedagogy, specializing in social and contemporary history at the Institute for Sport Sciences of the University of Hanover (Germany). Dr. Peiffer's research and publications have been in the areas of contemporary German sport history and the Olympic movement. At the present time, he is chair of a research committee investigating the political relations between the Federal Republic and the Democratic Republic of Germany.

**J. Richard Polidoro** (D.P.E.) was born in the United States. He is currently a professor of physical education and exercise science at the University of Rhode Island. A graduate of Springfield College, Dr. Polidoro has studied extensively in the areas of sport history, sport pedagogy, and international sport and physical education. Besides numerous publications, he has delivered approximately fifty professional papers on the state, national, and international levels. His recent research and publications have centered on topics pertinent to ancient and contemporary sport history. He has also conducted a number of sport history study tours throughout the world for students and athletes.

**Uriel Simri** (Ed.D.) was born in 1925 in Vienna, Austria. He moved to Israel in 1934 and has studied in both Israel and the United States. He received his doctorate from the University of West Virginia. Dr. Simri served as a senior staff member at the Wingate Institute for Physical Education and Sport and the Zinman College for Physical Education (Israel) from 1961 until 1991. He has published thirty-one books and over one hundred fifty scientific articles. An internationally known sport historian, Dr. Simri has served as a guest professor and guest lecturer at universities in the United States, Canada, Great Britain, Belgium, and Germany.

**Earle F. Zeigler** (Ph.D.) is professor emeritus of kinesiology at the University of Western Ontario (London, Canada). He received his doctorate from Yale University and has recently completed his fifty-seventh year in the profession. A dual citizen of the United States and Canada, Dr. Zeigler has published thirty-three books and monographs and approximately four hundred fifty articles throughout his extensive career. He has taught and coached at Yale and has held administrative and teaching positions at the University of Western Ontario, the University of Michigan, and the University of Illinois. Dr. Zeigler is best known for his studies in sport history, sport philosophy, and ethics.

# SPORT AND PHYSICAL ACTIVITY IN THE MODERN WORLD

# CHAPTER ONE

# SPORT AND PHYSICAL ACTIVITY IN ANCIENT GREECE

## URIEL SIMRI

You may wonder why a chapter on ancient Greece appears in a text that deals primarily with the development of sports and physical activity in modern times. The answer is simply that ancient Greece is considered by most historians as the fatherland of modern sports, or at the very least a major source of inspiration. It was ancient Greece that developed the roots of many of the present-day Western values and concepts that permeate modern sports and physical activity programs. Thus, in spite of limited space, a review of sport and physical activity in ancient Greece is essential for understanding and appreciating modern developments.

To begin, we must first examine the environment in which Greek sports developed. It is important to realize that Greece did not become a unified nation until the year 338 B.C., when it was united by Philip, king of Macedonia and father of Alexander the Great. Prior to that time, ancient Greece consisted of loose confederations of various city-states. The city-state, or *polis* as it was known in antiquity, developed between 900 and 700 B.C. and consisted of an urban center and its agricultural surroundings. For its citizens, the city-state created a feeling of social belonging, local patriotism, and political responsibility. However, the population consisted of both citizens and slaves. As the slaves often far outnumbered the citizens, an urban elite came into being, an elite very similar to the wealthy leisure class of citizens in more modern times. The major forces that brought the city-states together were worship of the same gods and adoption of a common language. Some historians, in addition, believe that the ancient Greeks' inherent love and passion for competition, which was expressed particularly in their sports, may have been a minor unifying factor.

Once developed, the city-states frequently formed leagues with each other, often on the basis of treaties for a particular purpose. The leagues and treaties, however, did not prevent frequent intercity wars. The wars between the city-states came to an end only in 338 B.C., when the Macedonians created the so-called Hellenic League. This league was open to anyone who accepted Greek culture. Those who belonged to the league were "Hellenists," while those who did not belong were "Barbarians."[1]

In early historic times, the Greek people belonged primarily to one of two stocks, either the Dorians or the Ionics. The Dorians were concentrated on the Peloponnese, having subdued Mycenae soon after 1200 B.C. The Ionics settled primarily in the southern part of the Greek mainland and on the islands in the Aegean Sea. Of the two groups, the Dorians, who invaded Greece from the north, made by far the greater contribution to the development and spread of sports in ancient Greece.

## THE ORIGINS OF GREEK SPORTS

It has been well documented that throughout the history of ancient Greece, the Greeks participated in a highly organized and sophisticated program of competitive sports that they called *agonistics*. The agonistics were part of a much larger system of physical training called *gymnastics*. To the Greeks, the term *gymnastics* literally meant "actions performed in the nude," and the term was adopted because the males did indeed perform physical activity in the nude. Why the Greeks developed such an intense and sophisticated program of competitive sports and gymnastics is open for interpretation and considerable discussion.

For the origins of sports in ancient Greece, we look first to the Minoan culture, located on the island of Crete and various Aegean islands, and then to the Mycenaean period of settlement on the mainland. Although historians agree that the roots of sport in ancient Greece can be traced to these two early Greek cultures, opinions are divided as to whether the sporting activities were indigenous to these cultures or were imported from Egypt and other cultures in the Middle East.

Ruins on Crete provide clear evidence that activities like tumbling, leaping over bulls, wrestling, and boxing were prevalent in the Minoan culture (3000–1400 B.C.). A boxing fresco originating on the island of Thera (Santorini) can be traced to the same era.[2]

By the middle of the fifteenth century, Knossos, the great capital of the Minoan civilization on Crete, had fallen into the hands of the Mycenaeans. The Mycenaeans enjoyed their greatest prosperity during the fourteenth and early thirteenth centuries B.C. As the Peloponnese and other parts of southern Greece became settled, the inhabitants of Mycenae imported not only gold but also ideas for physical activity to the Greek mainland.

The Mycenaeans were a warlike people, and it was the Mycenaeans who waged war on Troy in Asia Minor. The Trojan War became the theme of Homer's most famous works. In the *Iliad*, Homer relates the story of this war and in particular gives a detailed account of sport activity and games that were held at the funeral of the dead hero Patroclus. The games mentioned by Homer included competitions in chariot racing, boxing, wrestling, running, armed combatives, discus and javelin throwing, and archery. In his second book, entitled the *Odyssey*, Homer describes several sporting activities held in honor of the wandering Odysseus, who triumphs over formidable foes through superior intelligence rather than brute strength. The date when the Homeric epics were written is still under discussion; estimates range from the tenth century to the sixth century B.C.

Although the writings of Homer provide a detailed account of early forms of sports competition, opinions differ widely as to the primary impetus for sport in ancient Greece. To date there are four prevailing theories. Two of the theories are influenced heavily by a religious cult perspective while the other two theories are primarily secular.

The first theory, widely accepted, is that the games developed as part of a cult honoring the dead. This concept of competitions being held as a funeral celebration is reinforced by Homer's account of the games held in honor of the slain Patroclus. We find similar customs in a variety of cultures throughout the world, with the accompanying belief that participation in physical activities will assist in the resurrection of the dead.

A second view holds that sport developed in ancient Greece in conjunction with the cult of fertility. The followers of this view point primarily to the important role that Demeter, the mythical goddess of fertility and agriculture, played in the ancient Olympic Games. Since the priestess of Demeter was the only woman legally allowed to attend the Olympic Games, many historians believe the games were held in celebration of fertility. Although Demeter was indeed the goddess of fertility, she also maintained a close relationship to the dead. In Greek mythology, her husband Hades was king of the underworld and her daughter Persephone ruled the kingdom of the dead. Since the basic premise of this theory is the belief that the gods will repay physical efforts performed in their honor, the relationship between Demeter and the underworld provides an interesting connection with her position at the games and the games' connection with the celebration of the dead.

One of the secular views explaining the development of sport in ancient Greece is that it was organized simply as training for military purposes. The great philosopher Plato advocated this theory. He was a strong supporter of Greek gymnastics and felt that they were important for the development of a strong military. Supporters of this theory also point to the success of the militaristic city-state of Sparta in the early days of the ancient Olympic Games.

The fourth theory pertaining to the etiology of sport in ancient Greece is that the Greeks had an inherent urge for competition and enjoyed competitive contests of all kinds. The development of a program of sports and physical activity is thus seen as a natural competitive activity. It is important to note that while this theory has historical roots in Homer's *Odyssey,* modern-day supporters of this theory tend to be primarily British historians who have been influenced heavily by the development of organized English sports in modern times.

Most recently, Sansone (1988) has expressed a unique theory that relates the beginnings of sport to both the cult of the dead and the cult of fertility. Sansone's theory is that sport evolved primarily as a ritual sacrifice of physical energy.

## THE PRINCIPLES OF ARETE AND KALOKAGATHIA

*Arete* is an ancient Greek term that embodies the cultural ideal of excellence. This concept permeated the entire ancient Greek culture. The earliest reference to it is found in the epics of Homer. Arete has been frequently misunderstood mainly because of attempts to translate the term literally, its closest translation being "virtue." What was intended by Homer, it is believed, was not the ideal of virtue but the ideal of excellence—the drive to excel, to be victorious, to be first and best in one's category, and to perform deeds of heroism.

The concept of excellence was, however, often interpreted differently by different city-states. For instance, the Dorian citizens of Sparta narrowed the concept of excellence to pertain almost exclusively to excellence in military strength and skill, especially in the seventh and early sixth centuries B.C. The focus on a strong military no doubt was a major factor in the success that Sparta enjoyed in the early Olympic competitions. The French historian Marrou (1956), however, points to an interesting change in the attitude of the Spartans. Sparta supplied more than half the Olympic champions until the year 576 B.C.; after that date, only sporadic victories by the Spartans were recorded. Marrou believes that the Spartans felt that involvement in agonistics was now too time consuming and they directed their youth to concentrate instead on premilitary education and training. Also, Sparta, which was relatively small in population, ruled over an enormous area.

The early Ionic Athenians adopted a different view of arete, or excellence, expressed in a cultural ideal called *kalokagathia*. Kalokagathia stressed the importance of developing mind and body in harmony with each other. The Athenians viewed the fine arts (music)[3] as a way to develop the mind and viewed gymnastics as integral to the development of the body. Needless to say, tensions between those in charge of gymnastics and those in charge of music often presented an obstacle that was not easy to overcome.

Following the Athenians' defeat of the Persians in the second half of the fifth century B.C., teachers and philosophers called sophists became the major intellectual power in Athens. They placed a strong emphasis on intellectual development, and topics such as reasoning and rhetoric were added to the growing list of educational pursuits. These intellectual activities were added at the expense of physical activities.

The philosopher Plato (427–344 B.C.) has often been credited with the later revival of gymnastics in Athens, though his role may be overemphasized. In any case, Plato viewed physical activity as a means to achieve a greater end and not as a goal in itself. To Plato, the moral values of gymnastics and competitions far outweighed their mere physical value, and he was firmly committed to the view that a healthy body could better serve a healthy soul or mind.

Despite their very different views of excellence, both Sparta and Athens focused primarily on the development of the individual. This is clear in all their cultural and educational ideals and values. This emphasis on the individual helps explain why we find no team activities in the program of Greek agonistics.

## THE ANCIENT OLYMPIC GAMES: MORE THAN A MERE SPORT EVENT

The role played by the ancient Olympic Games in ancient Greece was much more important than that of just a major sporting event. The games were undoubtedly one of the most important religious and social events of their time. Held in honor of the supreme god Zeus, they were considered "sacred games." Further, the games held at Olympia were only the first of four *crown games* in which the victor received a garland.

## Origins of the Games

The origin of the Olympic Games is shrouded in mystery. The date of 776 B.C. has been widely accepted as the year of the first games primarily because of the availability of recorded evidence beginning in that year and the lack of an alternative exact date. Doubts about this date, however, were already being voiced in antiquity. Many have accepted the date suggested by the historian Phlegon (A.D. 138), who claimed that the games were revived (not initiated) in the year 888 or 884 B.C. Such a date is plausible if we believe that the famous lawmaker Lycurgus of Sparta was one of the initiators of the games, together with Iphitos (king of Elis) and Kleisthenes (king of Pisa). Some historians further point to evidence which claims that the original games may have taken place as early as 1501 B.C. Others credit Zeus personally with the foundation of the games at an even earlier date. It should be noted that the date of 776 B.C. is further doubted since it was first mentioned by Hippias, a sophist from Elis, only around the year 400 B.C.

Despite the uncertainty of the exact date of the first Olympic Games, there is little disagreement among historians that the sacred games were associated with the notion of *ekecheiria*.[4] This concept of a sacred treaty or pact among the Greek city-states is often misinterpreted. The agreement among the city-states guaranteed the sanctity of the temple area of Olympia, as well as free passage to and from Olympia for everyone participating in or attending the Olympic Games.[5] For example, Sparta in 420 B.C. was excluded from the games for waging war that endangered the people on the road to Olympia. The guarantees associated with the ekecheiria have often been interpreted to mean that all wars did in fact stop during the Olympic Games, but this was not the case. A war actually took place inside the temple area of Olympia during the games of 364 B.C.

Throughout the history of the ancient games, the control of the temple of Olympia was cause for continuous fighting between the city-states of Elis and Pisa. Evidence shows that Pisa controlled the games of 748, 644, and 364 B.C., but Elis maintained domination and control over the majority of the Olympic Games. It is for that reason that the "official" history of Olympia is derived from sources connected to the city-state of Elis and may be biased in that direction.

## Organization and Development of the Games

The games were organized and refereed by local officials called the *hellanodikae,* who were citizens from the city-state of Elis (or Pisa). Only one hellanodike was used at each of the games until 584 B.C. Thereafter, the number of officials gradually grew to twelve. It seems that as long as there was a single official, that person assumed the role that the *agonothet* (president of the event) held in other competitions in Greece. In Olympia, only two people were ever honored with the title of agonothet. The first was Herod, the king of Jerusalem, who is thought to have saved Olympia from bankruptcy in 8 B.C. when on his way to Rome to arrange an inheritance with Emperor Augustus, who was a great fan of the Olympic Games.

The officials at Olympia had far more rights than do officials today. In addition to being the sole organizers and developers of the games themselves, the officials could impose fines on participants, coaches, and even spectators. They were also empowered to administer corporal punishment to participants who did not abide by the rules.

Hippias (400 B.C.) tells us that the first games consisted of only one event, the *stade* race, which was a footrace to the distance of one stade, or approximately 600 feet. Because this race was the only event included in all of the Olympic Games throughout their history, each game was named after the winner.

Originally the games were completed in a single day. A second day was added in the games of 680 B.C. Gradually, as more events were added to the program, the games were prolonged to five days beginning in the fifth century B.C. During the five-day program, much of the time was occupied by religious ceremonies.

The ancient Olympic Games were also events of great social significance, presenting a rare occasion on which a congregation of 40,000 people from all over Greece and its overseas colonies would gather in one place. The games were frequented by top artists, politicians, and members of the ruling classes.

The games were held during the second full moon following the summer solstice, thus taking place either in the second half of July or in the month of August. In certain years, an intercalary month was introduced in order to catch up with the solar year. In those years, the games were held about four weeks later. The games were scheduled every fourth year, and the interval between games became known as the *Olympiad*. From the days of Hippias (400 B.C.) until the end of the fourth century A.D., the Olympiads served as a means of counting the years in ancient Greece.

Estimates of the number of athletes and officials in any of the ancient Olympic Games ranged up to a maximum of 300 participants. In the earlier games, participation was open only to free Greeks who had no blood on their hands. In those days most if not all of the participants seem to have been from the Peloponnese. However, a competitor from Smyrna in Asia Minor competed in the games of 688 B.C. Participants from other overseas colonies followed soon thereafter. In later years individuals from bordering nations, such as the Macedonians, were given the right to participate. King Philip of Macedonia, for example, was a legitimate Olympic victor. At the time of Philip, all Hellenists were allowed into the games. After the Roman conquest of Greece, which was completed in the year 146 B.C., the Romans forced their way into the Olympic Games.

All participants in the games had to appear at Olympia one month before the beginning of the games for final preparation under the supervision of the hellanodikae. The hellanodikae were allowed to give the participants training instructions. Coaches, however, were not allowed in Olympia during this month of preparation.

The prize for each Olympic victor, at least as of 752 B.C. consisted of a garland from a holy olive tree that stood near the temple of Zeus in Olympia. Red ribbons were also tied around various parts of the winner's body. The origin and significance of the ribbons has never been explained. In earlier years, the victor of the stade race was honored by being given the right to light the fire under the sacrifice on the altar of Zeus.

Although the prizes awarded at Olympia were modest, a winner at Olympia was showered with gifts of all kinds on his return home and handsomely rewarded for the prestige and honor he had brought to his native city-state. In retrospect, it appears that mere participation in the games was of no importance and winning at Olympia was everything. The Greeks had a saying that "the second goes home in shame." Further, it is clear that the ancient Greeks were not amateurs in the sense of amateurism as it developed and became widely accepted in the nineteenth and twentieth centuries.

As of the sixth century B.C., the winners at Olympia were allowed to erect a *stele,* or statue, inside the temple area as a memorial to their victory. Pausanias claimed in the second century A.D. that the number of these steles reached over 3,000.[6] This figure is obviously incorrect because the number of Olympic victors could not have been that many at that point in time. Other steles were erected in the temple area as well. *Zanes* also were erected. These were statues built to memorialize the shame and dishonor of some participating Olympians. They were built as a punishment for breaking the rules. Only thirteen zanes seem to have been erected near the vaulted entrance from the temple area to the stadium.

As of 720 B.C. the participants in the Olympic Games competed in the nude. A variety of reasons have been advanced for this practice, but only a few of them allude to the reason that seems most logical. Without question, the ancient Greeks were extremely proud of the beauty of their bodies, and the games provided an opportunity for public display of excellence of physique. In the fifth century B.C., coaches also were required to appear in the nude at the stadium. The reason for this decision appears to relate to the story that at one of the games a woman disguised herself as a male coach in order to see her youngest son become an Olympic victor.[7]

The training and competitive facilities in Olympia included the classical Greek facilities, namely the *stadium,* the *gymnasion,* the *palestra,* and the *hippodrome.* The stadium in Olympia was among the largest in Greece, with the stade measuring approximately 210 yards.[8] The gymnasion and the palestra were both training facilities where individuals practiced the various events. The hippodrome was the facility where the horse and chariot races were held. Whether a permanent hippodrome existed at all is still under discussion. No trace of such a facility, which according to different sources was between 600 yards and a mile in length, has been found. Some historians believe that for each of the Olympic games, agricultural land was specifically prepared for the chariot and horse-racing events

By 724 B.C. a two-stade race called the *diaulos* was added to the program, and in 720 B.C. a long-distance race called the *dolichos* was added. The dolichos varied in length from eight to twenty-four stades. Throughout the history of the games, several other activities were added to the program, as shown in Table 1.1. Then, from 200 B.C. until the end of the games approximately 600 years later, the program remained unchanged.

TABLE 1.1    **The Development of the Olympic Program**

| | |
|---|---|
| 776 B.C. (?) | The stade race |
| 724 B.C. | The diaulos (2 stades) |
| 720 B.C. | The dolichos (8–24 stades) |
| 708 B.C. | The pentathlon and wrestling |
| 688 B.C. | Boxing |
| 680 B.C. | Chariot racing with four horses |
| 648 B.C. | Horse racing and the pankration (combination of boxing and wrestling) |
| 632 B.C. | The stade and wrestling for youth |
| 628 B.C. | The pentathlon for youth (included a single time only) |
| 616 B.C. | Boxing for youth |
| 520 B.C. | The hoplite race (race in armor) |
| 500 B.C. | Chariot race with two mules (canceled 56 years later) |
| 496 B.C. | Horse races on mares (canceled 52 years later) |
| 408 B.C. | Chariot race with two horses |
| 396 B.C. | Competitions for announcers and trumpeters |
| 384 B.C. | Chariot race with four foals |
| 268 B.C. | Chariot race with two foals |
| 256 B.C. | Horse race with foals |
| 200 B.C. | Pankration for youth |

The people of Elis, who controlled a majority of the games, seem to have been quite conservative in regard to the program of Olympic events. At no time were more than eighteen events included in any of the games. The Elisans also resisted the introduction of contests in the fine arts and included only two such events, competitions for announcers and trumpeters, at a relatively late time (396 B.C.). Competitions in the fine arts played a much more important and significant role in the other crown games.

## Decline of the Games

Two major theories have been cited by historians for the decline and the ultimate end of the Olympic Games: the professionalization of the games and the influence of the Roman Empire. There was, however, no distinction between amateur and professional in ancient Greece. To assert that the influence of professionalism was a major contributing cause of the decline of the games is misleading and open to considerable question.

The assertion that the influence of the Roman Empire was a major contributing factor is equally questionable. Recorded history shows that the games were held for well over 500 years under Roman rule. In fact, it was the interest and favor shown by most Roman rulers that allowed the games to continue for so long. For example, after his decisive victory over the Greeks at Corinth in 146 B.C., the Roman commander Mummius rushed to Olympia and donated an enormous gift to the temple. This is the same Mummius who is said to have introduced Greek agonistics to Rome.

Gaius of Rome was the Olympic victor in the dolichos race in 72 B.C. The Roman emperors Tiberius and Germanicus were legitimate Olympic winners in chariot races in the years 4 B.C. and A.D. 17, respectively. The last known Roman Olympic champion was Lucius Minucius in A.D. 129.

Roman emperor Nero established an Olympic record when he was declared the winner in five events, three of which were never included in the official Olympic program. To show his admiration for Olympia, Nero sent an army unit to hold up the games of A.D. 65 until he could arrive and compete. Then he threatened everybody with death if they dared to compete against him. The five events, which after his death were declared to be against the spirit of the games, were playing the lyre, a competition for heralds, performing a tragedy, a chariot race for four foals, and a race for ten horses.

In A.D. 86 Emperor Domitian initiated the Capitolia Games in Rome. These games were held in honor of the Roman god Jupiter and were given the status of a crown game. The Capitolia Games lasted until the fourth century A.D.

The Romans encouraged the organization of similar games throughout the Roman Empire. Approximately 300 games followed the Greek pattern, and girls and women participated in many of them. The Romans also developed the *spina*, a narrow spine that divided the track into two separate parts. The spina prevented participants from crashing into each other as they moved back and forth in competition. It was especially important in the chariot and horse races.

It is thus misleading to blame the Romans for the decline and eventual end of the Olympic Games. On the contrary, the Romans were instrumental in preserving the program of Greek agonistics for over 500 years.

The decisive factor contributing to the decline and end of the Olympic Games of antiquity was the rise of Christianity. Christianity viewed the games as sacrilegious because of the worship of pagan gods. The early Christians also condemned many customary practices associated with the games as outside the realm of Christian morality. Although many historians credit the Christian emperor Theodosius I, ruler of Byzantium, with ending the games in A.D. 393, others question the accuracy of this conclusion. Perhaps it was Theodosius II, the grandson of Theodosius I, who brought the games to a close thirty years later. But this lack of precise information about the last games is of minor importance. It is believed that either emperor would have ended the games because of his Christian convictions, since Christianity became the religion of Byzantium around A.D. 330.

Whatever was not destroyed by the Christian rulers of Byzantium was destroyed by two tremendous earthquakes that shook the entire Peloponnese in A.D. 522 and 551. Those earthquakes have made the task of modern archaeologists much more difficult. Systematic digging at Olympia began in 1875, and after 125 years of excavation much still remains to be uncovered. What has especially fascinated archaeologists is the search for what was considered one of the seven wonders of the ancient world, namely, the statue of the sitting Zeus in the temple at Olympia. This statue, twenty-three feet in height, was completed by the noted sculptor Phidias in 420 B.C. No remnant of this magnificent piece of art has ever been found.

## THE CROWN GAMES AND OTHER SPORTS COMPETITIONS

Almost 200 years after the first recorded games at Olympia, other major competitions and festivals developed throughout ancient Greece. In addition to the games held at Olympia every four years, three other major games known as the Crown Games were developed and held in temples near Delphi, Corinth, and Nemea. Like the games in Olympia, the other crown games were considered holy.

### The Pythian Games

The Pythian Games were held in the temple of Apollo near Delphi. They were considered the second most important of the crown games, second only to the games at Olympia. The quadrennial Pythian Games originated in 582 B.C. following a victory by a league of city-states over the city-state of Kirrha. The war, considered a sacred war, was fought to gain control of the site of the famous Delphic oracle, who was called Pythia. The original festival at Delphi was a musical festival, but it was replaced by a quadrennial festival that included both music and sport. The physical activities followed the model of Olympia. The Pythian Games were controlled by a league of city-states, the so-called Amphictyonic League, of which both Ionic (including Athens) and Dorian city-states were members.

The Pythian Games, held in the late summer of the third year of the Olympiad, were dedicated to the god Apollo. Among his other functions, Apollo was the god of the fine arts. In the early years of the games, the prize for victory was merely an apple, a symbol of Apollo. In later years, a garland of laurel was added as the prize.

Although many events were staged at the stadium in Delphi, the hippodrome was in the nearby valley of Krisa because the mountainous terrain around Delphi was not suitable for chariot and horse racing events.

The Pythian Games differed from the games of Olympia in at least two other aspects besides the inclusion of fine arts. Unlike the games held in Olympia, women were allowed to participate, at least in later years. Second, the division of youth and adults was different. There was an obvious distinction made in ancient records between "Olympic youth" and "Pythian youth."

### The Biennial Crown Games at Corinth and Nemea

The first of two biennial crown games to appear were the Isthmian Games, which were held at a temple outside Corinth. The Isthmian Games were held in honor of the god of the sea, Poseidon. They were first held in 581 B.C. and were then held every other year. The games were therefore held in the year immediately following and immediately preceding the Olympic Games.

After the battle of Corinth in 146 B.C., which completed the Roman conquest of the Greek mainland, the games were moved to the town of Sykion. Later, at an unknown date, they were returned to their original site. Emperor Julian mentions the games being held in Corinth in the fourth century A.D., so the games must have returned at least by that time.

The competitive program of the Isthmian Games did not differ much from the program of the Olympic Games. The major differences were that the competitions were held for three age groups and not two as in Olympia. Women also participated in the Isthmian Games, at least in Roman times, and artistic competitions played a much bigger role than at Olympia. The victor in the Isthmian Games was crowned with a garland of pines.

Eight years after the beginning of the Isthmian Games, the Nemean Games were held at a temple for Zeus in Nemea, which is located about twenty miles south of Corinth. The games were established as a religious and political reaction to the Isthmian Games. Whereas the Isthmian Games had a *Panhellenic* (all Greek), if not an Ionic character, the games at Nemea clearly had a Dorian flavor. The city-state of Athens, for example, had some say in the Isthmian Games but none whatsoever in the Dorian culture reflected in the games at Nemea. The competition between the Isthmian and the Nemean Games is evident in that they were both held in the same year. Political differences caused frequent upheavals in the Nemean Games and changes in locale. The games were often moved to the town of Argos or placed under the control of that city-state. Argos, however, was a major ally of Athens. For many years control of the games moved back and forth between the towns of Kleonai and Argos, but the games ended up in the hands of Kleonai and were still being organized in the fourth century A.D. It was during this period that Emperor Julian praised the games at Nemea for preserving the true spirit of Greek agonistics.

Like the Isthmian Games, competitions in the Nemean Games were held in three age groups, and women were admitted to the games in Roman times. The victor in Nemea was crowned with a garland of wild celery.

As the Pythian, Isthmian, and Nemean Games developed, the circle of the four crown games became known as the *periodos,* and the competitors trained and competed at each of the sites to complete the four-year cycle. The victor in any event in all six competitions during the Olympiad became known as a *periodonike.* The title of periodonike was the most important and prestigious title given in Greek agonistics.

In the era of Augustus, who ruled Rome for forty-two years until A.D. 14, the circle of the crown games was enlarged by edict of the emperor. Three more games were given the status of crown games: the games held in Rome, the quadrennial games held in Actium near the town of Nicopolis, and games held in Argos. The Argos games were obviously held at a time in which the Nemean Games were under the control of Kleonai.

## Other Sports Competitions

The crown games were not the only competitions in Greek culture. In fact, these games were only a few of all the competitions held. Most of the other competitions were called *athletic* competitions. The term *athletics* had a specific meaning in ancient Greece. According to the ancient Greeks, an athlete was one who competed for a prize, and the word *athlon* meant prize. The prizes awarded to athletes in athletic competitions in ancient Greece went far beyond the award of a garland as in the crown games.

In the beginning, the prizes consisted of shields and amphoras of oil, but they were soon replaced by monetary awards. The amounts paid to the winners of athletic competitions varied from competition to competition. In most cases it depended on the wealth of the organizing city-state. The amounts also varied from event to event. Usually, the prize allotted to the chariot race exceeded all other events.

Certain athletic meetings allocated prizes not only to the winner but also to those who placed second in the competition. This was obviously done as a means of attracting more competitors to the events. The second-place prize rarely exceeded one-fourth of the prize for the winner.[9] We know of only one case in which prizes were also given to third-place athletes. This happened outside Greece when Herod, the king of Jerusalem, held an athletic meet in honor of Emperor Augustus in Caesarea Maritima in Palestine in 12 B.C.

Since it would be almost impossible to count all the athletic competitions held in ancient Greece, only a few of the most important ones are mentioned here. Beginning in the middle of the sixth century B.C. Athens organized the Panathenian Games. These games were held annually on a small scale and, on a much larger scale, once every four years. The major Panathenian event took place in the third year of the Olympiad. This schedule put the games directly in competition with the Pythian Games. Because it had few political allies in Greece, particularly among the Dorian city-states, Athens could not achieve the status of crown games for these competitions. Many city-states organized more than one athletic competition. Athens, for example, also organized the Theseia and Eleusinia games.

The more important athletic games were the ones held on a quadrennial basis such as the Asklepieia in the town of Epidaurus. The Asklepieian Games were held in honor of Asklepios, the god of health. Other games in honor of this god were held on the island of Kos, which was the home of Hippocrates, father of Greek medicine. Athletic contests in honor of the goddess Hera were held in the city-state of Argos. As indicated earlier, these games were granted the status of crown games in the days of Emperor Augustus, but that was a unique event in the history of Greek agonistics.

It is interesting to mention that the victors in the crown games were not excluded from participating in the various athletic competitions, nor did they shy away from receiving monetary rewards for their victories in those games. Even Olympic champions who were members of the upper social class often collected handsome rewards as victors in athletic competitions. This fact further supports the view that the concept of amateurism in Greek agonistics should be considered an anachronism.

## THE PROGRAM OF GREEK AGONISTICS

### Footraces

The first and only event of the Olympic Games for over fifty years was the *stade* race, a 600-foot footrace. This race was performed on the straight length of a flat surface.

The *diaulos* race was a footrace equal to two stades. Because the distance of the stade race varied from city-state to city-state, the same naturally held true for the diaulos and for longer races. The length of the stadium or other facility never exceeded the length of one stade. For distances greater than that, runners had to turn around at some point. There is still discussion among historians as to whether all the runners had to turn back around a single turning point or whether each runner made the turn at a point in his own lane.

The *hippios* was a race equal to the distance of four stades. Four stades would have been a distance of a little less than one-half mile. This race was never included in the Olympic program, yet it can be found in the programs of the crown games at Isthmia and Nemea. The hippios was also a popular event in many of the major athletic competitions. The name of this race has led some to believe that it may indicate the length of the hippodrome, but there is no proof for this, and contradicting evidence exists.

The *dolichos* was the most popular long-distance race in ancient Greece. An interesting aspect of the race was that it was not performed to a constant distance but varied from eight to twenty-four stades. Most sources mention a distance of twenty or twenty-four stades at the games held in Olympia. This would be equivalent to approximately three miles. In any case, the dolichos race was the longest race in Greek agonistics.[10]

The *hoplite* was a footrace with arms. In most cases, the hoplite race was performed to the distance of a diaulos. In some cases, though, it extended to the distance of a hippios. The hoplite race was first introduced into the Olympic program in the last quarter of the sixth century B.C., approximately 200 years after the introduction of the dolichos. The introduction of the hoplite event seems to coincide with a time when the Greek city-states were forced to create a large army based on infantry.

The *torch relay*, a footrace that has become quite popular in modern times, was never included in the agonistic program of ancient Greece. Although the torch relay was common at that time, it was considered only a part of certain cultic festivals.

The ancient Greeks also invented a starting device for their footraces. To prevent false starts, an error for which competitors could be flogged, a starting gate called the *husplex* was introduced. The husplex put a wooden bar in front of each runner that was lowered when the starter pulled on ropes connected to the bars. Since up to twenty runners often competed at one time, this invention made the work of a starter much easier.

### Wrestling

The style of wrestling in ancient Greece resembled the modern freestyle and not the so-called Greco-Roman style, which is clearly a misnomer. Disagreement exists among historians as to how a wrestling match was decided. While some claim that three falls were needed in order to win, others speak of the best of three falls. Further, we have no clear understanding of what constituted a fall. It may have meant one knee touching the ground or both shoulders touching the ground.

The wrestling competition was organized in a single weight class and the loser of a bout was eliminated from further competition. Special honors were given to a wrestler who won a competition without any sign of dust on his oiled body.

## The Pentathlon

The pentathlon was a competition consisting of five events: the long jump, the discus throw, the javelin throw, the stade race, and wrestling. Little is known about the order of these events, but wrestling was probably the final one. There is little agreement among historians as to how the winner of the pentathlon was decided, but most agree that the pentathlon could have been won in just the first three events. One hypothesis claims that only those who had won in one of the first three events were allowed to participate in the fourth event. This view further holds that the two who excelled in the fourth event wrestled for the crown.

Very little is known about the number of attempts each participant was allowed in the long jump and the two throwing events. We do know that even though the pentathlon required a diversity of skills, the winner of this event was not held in high esteem. This assertion is based on the relatively small prize given to the winner.

## The Long Jump

The long jump was performed in ancient Greece with the participants carrying weights. These weights, known as *halteres*, weighed up to eight pounds. The reason for the weights is not fully understood. One popular theory contends that the halteres helped increase the length of the jump, but this has been proven false. Other details about the mechanics of the jump are equally obscure. We do not know whether the event consisted of a single jump, a double jump, a triple jump, or even a fivefold jump. The reason for this uncertainty is based on the lack of any available evidence as well as the record held by Phayllos of Croton, reported to be a jump of fifty-five feet. Nor do we know whether a run-up was used for the jump or whether the ancient Greeks used take-off boards. One interesting observation, reported by Philostratus, is that the long jumper could be assisted by a flute player who provided musical accompaniment to the performance.[11]

## The Discus Throw

Although the discus throw is mentioned in the writings of Homer, doubts about the origin of the event have been expressed. It may have originated in the Middle East. The mechanics of the throw in ancient Greece are unknown to us. We do not know whether the discus was thrown from a standing position or following a rotational movement of the arm. Also unknown is the exact weight of the discus used in competitions. Disci weighing from three to fifteen pounds have been uncovered. The diameter of these disci ranges from 6.5 to 13.5 inches. It has been reported that Phayllos of Croton (the long jumper) threw the discus a distance of a little over thirty yards, a distance which sounds reasonable.

## The Javelin Throw

The Greek javelin was a pointed shaft five to six and one-half feet long made from elderwood. A thong was wrapped around the middle of the shaft. The competitor would loop the thong over the first finger or first two fingers of his throwing hand, perhaps to provide leverage and help make the javelin travel in a straight line. This was of great importance since the event was held in long, narrow facilities. Unfortunately, we have no recorded evidence of the distance of any javelin throw in ancient Greece. Many drawings depict athletes carrying two javelins, but we do not know whether this means that each thrower was awarded two attempts in the event. Throwing a javelin at a target, rather than for distance, was a common practice among teenage boys in ancient Greece, but it was never included in competitions.

## Boxing

Even though Philostratus and Pausanias both tell us that the first rules of boxing were formulated by Onomastus of Smyrna in 688 B.C., neither of them, nor any other source, gives details about the rules. We do know, though, that a match continued until one of the participants surrendered (by raising his hand) or was declared unfit to continue the fight. This observation is supported by the fact that the Spartans, who considered it unseemly to participate in a sport in which a contestant could surrender, never took part in a boxing event. In ancient boxing, there were no weight classes and no intermissions between rounds as in modern times.

The boxers did not fight barefisted but wrapped leather thongs around their knuckles. In the beginning, the thongs were made of soft leather. By the fourth century B.C., the soft thongs were replaced by a much harder material. In Roman times, the *caestus* was introduced, a piece of equipment in which the thongs were hardened by inclusion of metal pieces. The introduction of the caestus was responsible for turning boxing into a murderous event.

## The Pankration

The *pankration* has been described by Philostratus, writing in the third century A.D., as a mixture of boxing and wrestling. We do not know what restrictive rules may have governed this sport, but one aspect of the event is clear: the fight lasted until one of the participants surrendered. Again, as with boxing, the Spartans refrained from participating. Unlike wrestling and boxing, the bout of pankration was continued on the ground. The opponents were determined by means of a lottery and the loser was eliminated from further competition. That pankration gained in prestige in the Roman era can be seen by the size of the prize allocated to this event in athletic competitions.

## Chariot and Horse Racing

Chariot and horse races were sports of the aristocracy in ancient Greece and remained so, while other events were open to lower social strata. This can be seen by the fact that the owner of the chariot or of the horse was declared the winner in the race and not the driver or jockey, who remained anonymous. Whereas chariot races played an important role in the epics of Homer, it was not until 680 B.C. that the first chariot race was introduced into the Olympic program. The horse race followed thirty-two years later. Six of the seven events added to the Olympic Games after 500 B.C. were events of either chariot racing or horse racing. Four of these events remained in the program until the end of the games in the fourth century A.D.

The size of the hippodrome is a topic under discussion to this day. Estimates range from a length of two stades (420 yards) to eight stades (a little less than a mile). We also know very little about the length of the races, but they seem to have ranged from two miles to as much as eleven and one-half miles. Most historians agree that the distance of a race was not constant and varied from race to race. At the Olympic Games no more than six events in chariot and horse racing ever appeared in the program. On the other hand, the number of races reached twenty-five in certain athletic competitions.

## Marginal Agonistic Activities

Additional physical activities were popular in ancient Greece, even though they did not occupy a major role in competitions.

**Swimming.** Although Greece is surrounded by water and has hundreds of islands within its territories, swimming was not considered a major sport. Some historians attempt to explain this fact by noting that the major crown games were held some distance from major sources of water. This theory, however, does not hold for the games held at Isthmia. It is more reasonable to accept the view that the ancient Greeks considered swimming as primarily a safety measure, far more important than a mere sport. They considered it the duty of a father to teach his son reading, writing, and swimming at an early age. A man who did not know how to swim was considered uneducated.

**Ball Games.** Ball games were very popular in ancient Greece. In fact, the claim has been made that they were so popular that nobody considered it necessary to describe them in detail. We thus have only a list of the names of ball games and a manuscript describing the virtues of "the game with the small ball" written by a leading medical authority, Galenos, in the second century A.D. A small number of sculptures depict ball games but do not provide any details of how the games were played. One reason for the lack of records and written rules may be that the educational system of the ancient Greeks always emphasized the development of the individual. There was no place for team games in their "agonistics."

**Archery.** Although archery played an important role in the *Iliad* and the *Odyssey*, this activity never gained a parallel role in Greek agonistics. We can find written evidence of archery competitions in ancient Greece, but none of these competitions was of major importance. Two goals are mentioned in the written sources about archery; shooting toward a target and shooting for distance. Plato was one of the most important supporters of archery in Greek antiquity; he valued its contribution toward military training, which he saw, in turn, as the primary object of Greek gymnastics.

**Rowing.** We have scattered reports about competitions in rowing. The most significant competition took place at the quadrennial games of Actium, which were held at Nicopolis from the third decade B.C. These games eventually gained the status of a crown game by order of the Roman emperor Augustus. The Athenians also included rowing in the curriculum of the *ephebeia*, an educational institution for late teenage boys. The ephebeia was established in the second half of the fourth century B.C. Further, some evidence exists of boat races held in Hermione on the Peloponnese and on the island of Kerkyra (present-day Corfu).

## COACHES AND COACHING

Specialized coaching made its appearance in ancient Greece no later than the fifth century B.C. Before this, a *paidotribe* fulfilled the role of coaching. The paidotribe was similar to a modern-day all-around physical educator. Although the paidotribe continued to perform his functions throughout ancient times, the role of the specialized coach, known as the *gymnastes*, became more and more important as the number of sporting events increased. The gymnastes provided specialized training for athletes.

Pindar, in his famous forty-four odes to the victors of the fifth century B.C. crown festivals, celebrates the work of gymnastes. In both the Nemean Ode No. 6 and the Olympic Ode No. 7, he praises the wrestling coach Melesias from the island of Aegina. The pupils of Melesias had won thirty crowns in four great agonistic festivals. Some of the victories were gained in the pankration, an event that combined boxing and wrestling.

The most complete description of the work of a coach in ancient Greece is given by Philostratus, writing in the third century A.D. In his critical treatise on developments in Greek gymnastics, he provides considerable detail about the training program of coaches. This program included diet, heredity, and health science, among other topics. Philostratus also describes in detail the most prevalent method of coaching, called the *tetrad*. The tetrad was a four-day cycle of varying efforts of training. According to Philostratus, the ancient Greek gymnastes adhered religiously to this system and did not take into account either individual differences or the condition of the athletes.

The only individuals who systematically objected to the tetrad system of training were the hellanodikae at Olympia. Since the rather conservative representatives of Elis had full power over the training of athletes for one month prior to the Olympic Games, they were able to suppress, to some extent, the use of the tetrad system.

The coach had practically unlimited power over the athlete in ancient Greece. He could even cause the death of an athlete without being punished. For example, Philostratus justifies a coach who killed his athlete with a sharpened scraper because the athlete did not exert himself to win. Philostratus further stated that coaches should wield even more authority than they already had, despite his generally critical view of coaching as a profession.

In addition to the gymnastes, other sport specialists performed a number of ancillary duties in Greek agonistics. The duty mentioned most often is that of the *aleiptes,* whose duties resembled those of a modern masseur. Thus the preparation of an athlete might be considered a matter of teamwork. The paidotribe provided basic training, the gymnastes provided specialized training, and the aleiptes was in charge of keeping the athlete's body fit.

## FACILITIES FOR PHYSICAL TRAINING

The traditional facility for physical training in ancient Greece was the *gymnasion.* The literal meaning of this term is a place where people are active while naked. The gymnasion was a public facility that rose to prominence in the second half of the seventh century B.C. Later, it was considered an essential facility if a community wished to gain the status of polis, or city-state. The gymnasion always contained a covered running track or path called the *dromos.* The usual length of a dromos was one stade. In addition to the dromos, there was an open space for practicing activities such as throwing the javelin and the discus. In Roman times, baths were added to the facility.

In the sixth century B.C., another facility appeared on the scene. The *palestra* was originally a school for wrestling that was considered a part of the gymnasion. At certain locations, however, the palestra became an independent institution, devoted primarily to the physical training of younger children. According to the architect Vitruvius (circa 27 B.C.) the palestra consisted of a rectangular or square area that measured one diaulos. The outer part of this facility provided a covered area for running events, while the inner part served as a training area for the combative sports of wrestling, boxing, and pankration. The palestra was considered a private school, as opposed to the gymnasion, which was a public facility.

## HERO WORSHIP IN GREEK AGONISTICS

It is understandable that when an event occupies the central stage of a nation's life for over a millennium, as the Olympic Games did in ancient Greece, a number of outstanding heroes become the source of legend and even of worship. Following are the stories of four such heroes whose activities bordered on the legendary. In one instance, the individual was even believed to be a demigod by his city-state.

*Arrhichion of Phigalia* is the only man in the history of sports who has been declared an Olympic champion after his death. Arrhichion had won crowns in the pankration in Olympia in 572 and 568 B.C. In the final of the same event in 564 B.C., his opponent choked Arrhichion to death. Arrhichion had succeeded, however, in breaking his opponent's toe prior to his death, and the opponent, who could not endure the pain, had even lifted his hand as a sign of surrender. Although choked to death by his opponent, Arrhichion was declared the Olympic champion, in accordance with the rules of the competition.

*Milo of Croton* won six Olympic crowns in wrestling in the years 540 to 520 B.C. He became the commander of the army of Croton and according to one account was also the son-in-law of the famous mathematician Pythagoras. The heroic deeds of Milo are too numerous to relate here, but one of his exploits, it is said, is that he killed a four-year-old bull after carrying it around the stadium of Olympia and then consumed the bull all by himself within one day. He is also said to have insisted on carrying his own statue, a very heavy object, into the shrine of Olympia. It is even claimed that the city-state of Croton decided to tear down its defensive city walls, saying that a town in which Milo lived needed no additional defenses. Another tale is that Milo befriended the Persian king Darius after his own son-in-law, Democedes, was taken prisoner by the Persians. Democedes was freed by the Persians after promising to bring his famous father in-law, Milo, for a command performance before the king. Milo's death is also a matter of legend. As an old man, Milo walked into a forest, where he decided to try his strength by splitting the trunk of a tree with his bare hand. His hand got stuck in the tree, and Milo could not remove it before being eaten by hungry wolves.

*Phayllus of Croton* joined the ranks of the immortals even though he never won an Olympic crown. He did, however, win three Pythian crowns in the pentathlon. Phayllus became a legendary hero when, nearly 150 years later, Alexander the Great proclaimed him to be a wonderful example to the youth of the country. What excited Alexander's admiration was the fact that Phayllus had left the Olympic Games of 480 B.C. to join the Greek navy with his own vessel in order to help defeat the Persian navy in the decisive battle of Salamis. Alexander expressed his esteem for Phayllus by sending a great part of the spoils of the battle of Issus as a gift to Croton.

*Theagenes of Thasos* was considered a juvenile delinquent in his youth after removing the statue of a god from the marketplace in Thasos. Instead of putting him to death, the judges decided to place him in a severe training program. This decision was destined to bear good fruit. Theagenes won two Olympic crowns, one in boxing in 480 B.C. and the other in the pankration in 476 B.C. In addition, he won three crowns at the Pythian Games, ten crowns at the Isthmian Games, and nine crowns at the Nemean Games. Ancient sources credit him with as many as 1,400 victories in various competitions, including a victory in a dolichos race. Statues of Theagenes were erected in Olympia as well as in his hometown of Thasos.

Following his death, one of his unsuccessful opponents started to flog his statue in the marketplace. The statue of Theagenes collapsed and killed the man, whereupon it was sentenced to be thrown into the sea as a place of exile. When a severe drought followed this event, the people of Thasos went to the oracle in Delphi for advice. She advised them to return the statue to its original place. When this was done, the drought suddenly ended. Theagenes was thereafter considered a demigod by the citizens of Thasos.

## THE ROLE OF WOMEN IN GREEK AGONISTICS

Because married women, if not all females, were forbidden to enter Olympia during the Olympic Games, many historians have overlooked the role of women in the gymnastics of ancient Greece. The more accurate picture, however, is that women were never excluded from physical activities.

Reference to the participation of women in physical activity is found in both Greek mythology and in historical documentation. Greek mythology tells of the fleet-footed Atalanta, who swore to marry only a suitor who could beat her in a footrace. After many had failed in the challenge, Hippomenes succeeded with the assistance of Aphrodite, goddess of love. She aided the lovelorn suitor by putting three golden apples on the track. Atalanta could not withstand the temptation. During the race she bent down to pick up the apples, and Hippomenes was able to overtake her.

Frescoes from the early Minoan civilization, which flourished on the island of Crete, also provide evidence of women participating in physical activities. Of particular importance is the fresco of women engaging in the traditional sport of bull-leaping. It has been reported that Lycurgus, the famous lawmaker of Sparta, ruled that girls should share in the physical activities of boys. In a later period, Plato is among those repeating this recommendation. The Spartans followed Lycurgus' ruling for centuries. In A.D. 70–79 Emperor Vespasian expelled Palfurius Sura from the Roman senate for participating in a wrestling match against a Spartan woman, an action by which Palfurius was thought to have degraded himself. Although the results of the contest are unknown, the event is considered the first of many pieces of evidence that women participated in wrestling in Roman times.

Even at Olympia, there was a place for women to compete. Every four years, races were held for women in honor of the goddess Hera in the sacred site. These races were completely separate from the Olympic Games. While the origin of these races is not known, the most widely accepted view is that they began in the sixth century B.C. The races for women were held in three age groups and were for a distance of five-sixths of a stade, or approximately 175 yards. Information is lacking about the scope of participation in these races, which were called *Heraea*. The prizes for the victors were similar to those of the Olympic Games. Unlike the men, who competed in the nude, the women competitors wore tunics that laid only the right shoulder and breast bare. The games were administered by women only, with all the officials being citizens of Elis.

Although women were excluded from the Olympic Games, a number of women are nevertheless listed as winners in the games. These women were winners in the chariot race, where victory was ascribed to the owner of the chariot and horses, and not to the charioteer. There was no law prohibiting women from owning either the chariot or the horses. Cynisca of Sparta is the first recorded victorious woman (380 B.C.) and was in fact the first absentee woman victor in the history of the Olympic Games.

Other crown festivals in ancient Greece were more liberal than the Olympic Games. Female victors are found in the games at Delphi, Nemea, and Corinth in the Roman era. Quite naturally, women played an even larger role at games and competitions other than the crown games.

Of special interest is an inscription from Delphi dating to the middle of the first century A.D. In it Hermesianax from the town of Tralles praises the victories of his three daughters, Tryphosa, Hedea, and Dyonisia for their victories at Delphi, Corinth, Nemea, Athens, Sykion, and Epidaurus. Seven of the victories were in the stade race. We do not know whether these victories were gained in competitions against men or in separate competitions for women.

## GREEK AGONISTICS UNDER ROMAN OCCUPATION

Greece was ruled by Rome from 146 B.C. until the fall of the Roman Empire. As previously indicated, the Romans maintained a very positive attitude toward the Olympic Games. In fact, Greek agonistics flourished in the Roman Empire to an extent unheard of in earlier times. Despite the positive influences, relationships between Rome and Greece often became strained. From 82 to 80 B.C. the Roman dictator Sulla not only plundered Olympia but attempted to transfer the Olympic Games to Rome. As an extreme nationalist, Sulla considered Rome to be the only place worthy of organizing the games.

Over 100 years earlier, Fulvius Nobilior had become the first to introduce Greek-style games into Rome. His attempts, as well as similar ones, turned out to be sporadic. It was not until Emperor Domitian started the Capitolia Games in A.D. 86 that the games became a permanent fixture in Rome. The Capitolian Games lasted at least until the fourth century A.D.

The gladiatorial games that provided blood-thirst entertainment for the Roman public had no connection whatsoever to the various programs of Greek-style physical activity. The athletic contests took place in the *ludi circenses* (circus games), which offered a program quite similar to that of Greek agonistics. The circus games often included footraces, boxing, wrestling, and horse and chariot races. The extent of these games can be judged from a fourth century A.D. document that lists 176 games a year in Rome. Of the 176 games, 102 were theater shows, 64 were ludi circenses, and only 10 were considered gladiatorial games.

The greatest Roman admirer and benefactor of Greek culture was Emperor Hadrian (A.D. 117–138), who is often credited with the revival of Greek physical activities. Hadrian was honored by the people of Athens by the establishment of special games held in his honor. These games were called the *Hadrianeia*. Through these games, Hadrian and his successors brought Greek agonistics to a point that reminded the Greeks of their glorious past.

In A.D. 227 Alexander Severus legalized exemptions from the military for victors in the sacred Olympic festivals. This exemption was also found in the code of Justinian in the sixth century A.D. It is interesting to note that when armed combat was introduced into a number of agonistic events in the Roman Empire, the Greeks were greatly displeased. They complained that athletics were emphasized in those events at the expense of religion.

Unlike the Greeks, the Romans never competed in the nude. The Romans were never proud of their bodies and even considered the Greek goal of harmonious development of the body and mind as effeminate in nature.

The extent of Greek agonistics in the Roman Empire resulted in the creation of an athletes' guild as early as the first century B.C. The guild negotiated a suitable timetable for the various events and established the structure of prizes to be awarded to winners. The guild also made sure that the athletes met their commitments to appear at the various competitions.

While many historians are of the opinion that the Romans brought on the eventual destruction of the Greek agonistics, just the opposite appears to be true. Significant historical evidence suggests that the modern world owes a debt to the Roman Empire for preserving Greek agonistics for a period of well over half a millennium.

## SUMMARY

Hundreds of studies and books have been devoted to the history of sports in classical antiquity. This chapter should therefore be considered but a brief overview of the development of sports in ancient Greece.

Despite the numerous articles, books, and studies on this topic, many questions remain unanswered. One major uncertainty revolves around the origin of Greek sports. We do not have a firm concept of *why* sports originated or *when*. With reference to the Olympic Games, dates are controversial. Historians' concerns range from uncertainty about the date of the first games to disagreement about the date in which the games were terminated.

One of the major reasons for this uncertainty and disagreement among historians is that most of the available sources of information stem from a relatively late period in time, primarily in the second and third centuries A.D. For example, the traditional dating of the Olympic Games (776 B.C.) is completely based on information derived from individuals writing 400 years later.

Despite the uncertainty and unanswered questions, the available information is sufficient to provide a vivid picture of the nature and scope of sports in ancient Greece. Systematic study and analysis of existing information leads to the conclusion that, despite many differences between sports in ancient Greece and those in modern times, ancient Greece was without doubt the leading precursor of modern organized sports. Many consider it the fatherland of modern sports.

## STUDY AND DISCUSSION QUESTIONS

**1.** Discuss the similarities and differences between the ancient Olympic Games and the modern Olympic Games.

**2.** What aspects of Greek agonistics have been absorbed into modern sports?

**3.** Compare and contrast the role of women in the agonistics of ancient Greece with the role of women in the modern world of sports.

**4.** Compare the role of gymnastics in the educational system of ancient Greece with the role of modern-day physical education. What role should physical education play in the educational system of the twenty-first century?

## RECOMMENDED READINGS

Douskou, I., ed. *The Olympic Games in Ancient Greece*. Athens: Ekdotike Athenon, 1982.

Finley, M. I., and H. W. Pleket. *The Olympic Games: The First Thousand Years*. London: Chatto and Windus, 1976.

Harris, H. A. *Greek Athletes and Athletics*. London: Hutchinson, 1964.

Harris, H. A. *Sport in Greece and Rome*. London: Thames and Hudson, 1972.

Homer. *Iliad*. Chicago: University of Chicago Press, 1951.

Marrou, H. I. *A History of Education in Antiquity*. London: Sheed and Ward, 1956.

Miller, Stephen G. *Arete*. Chicago: Ares, 1979.

Pausanias. *Guide to Greece* (vol. 2; trans. P. Levi). London: Penguin Books, 1971.

Philostratus. "On Gymnastics," in R. S. Robinson (ed.), *Sources for the History of Greek Athletics*. Ann Arbor: University of Michigan, 1955.

Pleket, H. W. "Games, Prizes, Athletics and Ideology," *Arena-Stadion* 1, no. 2 (Cologne, 1975): 49–89.

Polidoro, J. Richard, and Uriel Simri. "The Games of 676 B.C.: A Visit to the Centenary of the Ancient Olympic Games," *Journal of Physical Education, Recreation and Dance* 67, no. 5 (1996): 41–45.

Robinson, R. S. *Sources for the History of Greek Athletics*. Ann Arbor: University of Michigan, 1955.

Romano, D. G. *The Origins of the Greek Stadion*. Philadelphia: American Philosophical Society, vol. 206, 1993.

Sansone, D. *Greek Athletics and the Genesis of Sport*. Berkeley: University of California Press, 1988.

Simri, Uriel. "On Coaching and the Coaching Profession in Ancient Greece," in U. Simri (ed.), *The Art and Science of Coaching*. Netanya, Israel: Wingate Institute, 1980.

Swaddling, Judith. *The Ancient Olympic Games*. London: British Museum, 1980.

Tzachou-Alexandri, O., ed. *Mind and Body—Athletic Contests in Ancient Greece*. Athens: Ministry of Culture, 1989.

Young, David C. *The Olympic Myth of Greek Amateur Athletics*. Chicago: Ares, 1984.

## NOTES

1. To this day, the official name of Greece is Hellas.

2. The findings on Crete can be seen at the museum in Heraklion, Crete, while the fresco from Thera is displayed in the National Archeological Museum in Athens.

3. In ancient Greece, music was the comprehensive term used for all the fine arts.

4. In later years, the crown games held at Corinth, Nemea, and Delphi claimed that the ekecheiria pertained to those games as well.

5. Olympia was never a town or city-state. It was considered the holiest and most sacred site in ancient Greece.

6. Pausanias, *Guide to Greece: Vol. 2* (London: Penguin Books, P. Levi, trans., 1971). Two long chapters are devoted to the history of Elis and the Olympic Games.

7. The punishment for a woman attending the games was death according to the existing law. The woman in this instance was pardoned because she was a member of a family of many Olympic champions.

8. The stade at Delos measured only 175 yards, and other stadia built throughout ancient Greece varied in length. Measurements differed because each polis apparently had its own measurements. The people of Elis explained that the reason why Olympia had such an enormous stade was that it was measured by the giant demigod Heracles.

9. The practice of awarding medals to first and second place athletes can be considered the reason why the organizers of the first modern Olympic Games in 1896 allocated medals only for the first and second place.

10. The marathon race, encompassing a distance of over twenty-six miles, is a modern event. It was introduced in 1896 during the first Olympic Games of the modern era.

11. See Philostratus, "On Gymnastics," in R. S. Robinson (ed.), *Sources for the History of Greek Athletics* (Ann Arbor: University of Michigan, 1955).

# CHAPTER TWO

# SPORT AND PHYSICAL ACTIVITY IN NATIONALISTIC EUROPE

## CHRISTIAN BECKER, WOLFGANG BUSS, AND LORENZ PEIFFER[1]

Throughout history, at various times and within differing social and political systems, a variety of terms have denoted the cultural phenomenon that we today call sport. The ancient Greeks used the term *gymnastics* for their system of physical training. Toward the end of the eighteenth century, this Greek term was adopted by Johann Guts Muths in Germany. Similarly, the term *gymnastics* was adopted by the founder of the health-oriented Swedish system of physical activity, Pehr Henrik Ling. At the beginning of the nineteenth century, Friedrich Ludwig Jahn introduced the term *Turnen* to designate the German system of physical activity. Jahn's system clearly manifested a nationalist character. In the United States, a commonly accepted sport term is *athletics*. In other countries, however, the term "athletics" is used only for track and field activities. In developing its program of sport and physical activity, the Soviet Union introduced the term *physical culture*, not only within its boundaries, but in all socialist states that came under its direct political influence.

The word *sport* comes from Latin words meaning to divert, amuse, or frolic. The meaning of the word evolved, however, primarily in the nineteenth century in the English language, as a result of the development of organized programs of physical activity in Great Britain. Since its introduction in this sense in England, the term has spread throughout the world. Today, it has international acceptance, particularly in Europe. When we deal with sport history, therefore, it is important to keep in mind the era and the geographical area from which our data derive.

At the same time, we should further remember that sports, and physical education as well, are explicitly connected to the political and social developments of a given society. While few doubt that sport is directly influenced by society, there is considerable evidence that sport is also capable of influencing general social phenomena. We can therefore speak of a reciprocal relationship between modern sports and political and social developments. The modern "sportive lifestyle" in the Western world can serve to illustrate this interrelationship. Structural elements—

symbols, techniques, and contents—are used to achieve goals that are common to both politics and sports, as we can readily see in the playing of national anthems at the beginning of a sport event. Modern society and sports possess many such congruities.

## SPORT AND NATIONALISM

Today, *nationalism* is a universal phenomenon. The term encompasses a multitude of political aspects that center around a political movement maintaining a political entity, such as a state or nation. The term also describes an entity striving to gain independence, or at least a degree of self-rule and freedom from suppression. Within the spirit of nationalism, the individual is thought to owe a feeling of "belonging" to his or her nation and is expected to be completely loyal to it. The individual identifies with the historical and cultural heritage of the nation, even to the point of fighting in its wars and suffering their consequences. To the individual, the nation means not only a place to live but a purpose in life as well.

Hugh Seton-Watson (1977), a leading expert on nationalism, doubts whether a clear scientific definition of *nation* is possible. His doubts are based on the presence of multiple basic elements and obscure definitions. However, he points out three conditions that are always necessary for binding people together into the frame of a nation: a feeling of solidarity, a common culture, and a national perception.

Nationalism combines rather easily with other ideologies, and we can therefore classify it as either a positive or a negative ideology depending on the intentions and goals combined with it. Independence movements as well as anticolonial movements in Europe and the Americas in the eighteenth and the nineteenth centuries are generally thought to be positive. As an example of positive "nation building," we can also look to East Germany, although its attempts to gain independence were long hindered by Cold War tensions between the West and the Soviet Union. On the other hand, the combination of xenophobia (hatred of strangers) and racism, as well as ideologies of territorial expansion found in both German fascism and the Stalinism of the Soviet Union, exemplify destructive, inhuman creeds.

The relationship between sport and nationalism originated toward the end of the eighteenth century. Since then, it has been shown time and again that as a means of communication, organized sports have served as one of the most effective ways for a country to present itself and its nationalism to the rest of the world. This has occurred because of the structural similarity of elements found in both sport and nationalism, or at least of elements that complement each other. A broad base of supporters, as well as the means to reach people through modern media, is a prerequisite for realizing nationalist ideals, as well as a major aim of sports.

Organized sports have played a specific and effective role in the rise of nationalism in several European countries over the past 200 years. In many instances, sport has served as a means of mobilizing the masses for political ends. It also has been an effective means of promoting political education and the goals of physical fitness within a framework of clubs and schools. On the other hand, sports organizations have often attempted to influence political institutions and to use governments either to achieve their own goals or to gain ascendancy over other social subsystems. As one example, consider the present rift between political support for competitive sport and support for physical education in the schools.

The interrelationship between European sports and European nationalism has played an equally important role in the development of sports over the past two centuries. During this period, when nationalism was the dominant political force in Europe, sport experienced continuous growth in social importance and recognition. This is clearly demonstrated in the four examples examined in detail in this chapter: (1) the German "Turnen" movement; (2) the development of sports in England in the nineteenth century; (3) the Gaelic sports movement in Ireland; and (4) the sport system of East Germany, or the German Democratic Republic (GDR), in the second half of the twentieth century.[2]

The German Turnen movement early in the nineteenth century was a combination of the ideals of enlightenment, which formed a basis for the development of all modern sports in Europe, with a romantic concept of nationality. Instead of referring to themselves as a nation, the Germans used the term *Volkstum*, which does not translate easily into other languages. By *Volkstum* is meant belonging to a group on the basis of descent and language, rather than citizenship. This made sense, in a way, because at that time Germany consisted of several small principalities and had not yet become a unified modern state.

The leaders of the initial Turnen movement, including Jahn, were among the frontline fighters for a German national state. At first, their goal was liberation of Prussia from French occupation after the Napoleonic wars. Later they joined the ranks of conservative nationalists fighting for a clear demarcation of a German nation, as well as its territorial expansion. These goals ultimately contributed to the rise of the Nazis in the 1920s and 1930s. Many supporters of the Nazi party had first adopted political attitudes of opposition to internationalism and of aggressive racism in the ranks of the Turners.

During the nineteenth century, attitudes similar to those of the Turners could also be seen in the Sokol movement of the Czech people and in the Union of Gymnastic Clubs after 1873 in France. The Sokol's primary goal was to gain independence from the Austro-Hungarian monarchy, whereas the development of gymnastic clubs in France was more concerned with that country's self-realization.

Sports were also used to advance political and nationalist interests in England, which can be considered the "motherland" of modern sports. The development from the "pastime sports" of the nobility in seventeenth and eighteenth century England to the "gentlemen sports" during the industrial revolution was closely connected to political developments. During the era in which England was the greatest colonial power in the world, sport became a means of educating future leaders in the system of "public" schools.[3] At the same time, the development of sports served as a compensatory instrument for social conflicts in an advanced capitalist society. Further, as England expanded its colonial empire, sports were exported throughout the world and became an integrative element of British culture. Not only did organized sports become a national cultural export of the British, but the English sport system later became the foundation of the modern Olympic movement, which included competition among nations as well as definite nationalist elements.

Our third major example of the connection between sports and nationalism is the development of the modern sports program in Ireland. The major goal of the Gaelic Athletic Association, at its very beginning, was the separation of Ireland from the British crown. This goal still is a factor in Northern Ireland. The Irish example is also of special interest because it includes indigenous physical activities at the expense of activities imported from England.

The development of the sports program in the German Democratic Republic is a clear example of the role played by sport in ideological and national conflicts between East and West in the post–World War II era. After 1945 sports became instrumental in the development and recognition of the German Democratic Republic (East Germany) as a separate nation. Sport in East Germany was viewed in light of its perceived contribution toward integrating the German population as well as providing a way for East Germany to achieve recognition as a state. Within the frame of competition between the major political systems of the East and West, the state-controlled sport program in the German Democratic Republic played a major political role. It was used to help counter the view of a supposedly oppressive socialist culture. In addition, it helped perpetuate the German cultural traditions.

## THE GERMAN TURNEN MOVEMENT AND GERMAN NATIONALISM

The nineteenth century was decisive in the development of German physical education and sports. Traditional concepts associated with physical activity practices and patterns of the past gave way to new thinking. Physicians, educators, and philosophers of the late eighteenth and early nineteenth centuries criticized the lack of physical activity, the pleasure-seeking attitude, and the general physical weakening of German young people. The new leaders called for programs emphasizing the "health of the German youth."

The beginnings of an institutionalized program of German physical education are found in the *Philanthropinums,* which were private schools limited to educating socially elite boys. One of the basic elements in a Philanthropinum education was training for "masculinity." Toward the end of the eighteenth century, a program of physical education called gymnastics was introduced into the curriculum. Johann Guts Muths (1759–1839), a teacher at the Philanthropinum at Schnepfental, concentrated his efforts toward making his program of gymnastics a means of national education. His program, which was similar to the ancient Greek concept of gymnastics, included such physical activities as climbing, jumping, vaulting, tumbling, rope climbing, and exercises using various other apparatus. Guts Muths' work laid the foundation for the development of German physical education.

The defeat of Prussia[4] by Napoleon in the 1806 battle at Jena and Auerstedt served as a major catalyst for the development of German nationalism. That defeat meant not only the end of the First German Reich but also immense territorial losses. It was a military catastrophe that resulted in an enormous need for both political and social rehabilitation. The defeat by Napoleon and the subsequent French occupation of Prussia thus became a driving force behind the development of Prussian-German nationalism at the beginning of the nineteenth century. The fact that a new, strong, and emotional nationalism could develop in Prussia can be explained by a French policy that left considerable control of internal affairs to the occupied peoples. Civil servants in Prussia used those liberties to modernize the structure of the state and to create a climate of reform. The liberation of the peasants, the autonomy granted to the cities, as well as reforms in education and the armed forces, proved to be fertile seeds for the awakening of the German nationalist movement.

## The Beginnings of the Turnen Movement

The carriers of nationalist ideas in early nineteenth century Germany were educated members of the middle class. They made their ideas popular through a variety of speeches, lectures, and publications. One of the most important speakers of the movement was Friedrich Ludwig Jahn (1778–1852). Jahn was to become known as Turnvater Jahn—the father of the German Turnen system. He named his system of physical training "Turnen" out of reaction against all foreign influences, including linguistic ones, on German culture.[5] For the same reason Jahn did not use the word *nation* and spoke instead of the German *Volkstum*.

The activities of the Turnen system involved primarily calisthenics and exercises on a variety of pieces of apparatus such as the horizontal bar, the parallel bar, the rings, the horse, and climbing facilities. Jahn also looked upon Turnen as an educational means through which he could imbue German youth with nationalist ideas. Those ideas were contrary to the educational ideals of the Philanthropinists, whose aim was to develop a harmonious personality through their gymnastics. Jahn linked his concept of a unified German nation directly to the concepts of the Turnen movement by creating a connection between physical activity and nationalist thinking. His nationalist ideas were characterized by the following: (1) the German nation should become a political and cultural entity based on the concepts of independence and a common feeling of citizenship; (2) the German nation should overcome social stratification; (3) the nation should idealize the concept of masculinity; and (4) a unified Germany should have, at the core of its nationalism, hatred of the French. Liberation from the French thus became a prerequisite for the creation of a politically and culturally united German state under the leadership of Prussia.

Aside from the German language, Jahn considered his Turnen as the most effective means of spreading the idea of the German Volkstum. In 1811 he opened his first open-air ground for Turnen in Berlin. This exercise field was to serve as an area to train young men in bravery, courage, and strength, as well as to prepare them militarily for the upcoming war of liberation against the French occupation. This first Turnen society gained influence in the nationalist movement through its organizational structure. With its founding, Jahn left the secret nationalist underground movement and began to make public appearances. The Turnen movement thus initially was a public branch of the political underground, and it became a major instrument in organizing the masses. By 1818 approximately 150 Turnen societies flourished in Germany, with a regional focus in Prussia and northern Germany. There were about 100 societies in those areas but only nine in southern Germany. The rest were scattered throughout the country.

Jahn was intensely active during the creation of new societies. He traveled extensively to inspire people and personally attended the founding ceremonies of new societies. In addition, he trained students for future leadership positions at his home base in Berlin. In turn, those trained by Jahn organized new societies with fervor. Within a few short years, a patriotic German Turners system had been created on the basis of a very effective system of communication. It was that communication system that facilitated the continuous spread of the movement, as well as the ideology associated with it. Newsletters, patriotic songs, and national festivals served as major means of creating a nationalist atmosphere and body of thought.

In 1819 the open-air grounds of the Turners were closed by the government to help subdue the movement's political and revolutionary tendencies. By that time Napoleon had been defeated and, the authorities believed, the movement had served its purpose. The training facilities were to remain closed for twenty-three years, yet the ideas and the spirit of the movement lived on. Moreover, Turnen programs continued in schools and private clubs. The purpose of these programs continued to be physical education, caring for health, and preparedness of youth for military service. And the nationalist political ideas of the Turnen movement were not eliminated when the government closed the facilities. Following the 1848–1849 revolution, which occurred throughout much of Europe including Germany, interest in the Turnen was renewed. Interestingly, the center of the renewed movement was in southwestern Germany, not in Prussia. It was in that geographical area that impulses of recent developments in nearby France were felt, thereby influencing the nationalist movement. It was also in this area that the first democratic German Turnen association was founded in 1848 in Hanau. However, this organization ended after the German revolution of that year.

The German nationalist movement gained momentum again at the end of the 1850s and the beginning of the 1860s. The impetus this time was political developments in Prussia, as well as the influence of the Italian unification movement. The Turnen movement was a major influence in this revival of nationalism, along with the contributions of shooting clubs and patriotic songs.

## The German Turnen Festivals

The first major success of the revitalized Turnen movement was at the third German Turnen Festival in 1863 in Leipzig. Over 20,000 members of the organization participated in that festival.

In his publication *A Model for the Future German National State*, Jahn foresaw the importance of national festivals, which were to be held on historical memorial days.

The early festivals of the German Turnen movement followed that tradition. They were typified by speeches, recitals, and songs expressing opposition to the anti-democratic authoritarian state. In the 1840s the program expanded to include a parade, a banquet, a dance, and festive decorations. The festivals were scheduled for Sundays and holidays to assure maximum participation. Interestingly, mass performances and physical competitions seemed to play only a secondary role at the Turnen festivals until well into the 1860s. Until the creation of the Second German Reich in 1871, the Turnen festivals were primarily political festivals where participants could express their democratic-revolutionary spirit against the state's authority. Democratic rights such as freedom of opinion, of speech, and of the press, as well as other constitutional rights, were demanded in speeches at the festivals.

Another noteworthy incident happened in the early 1860s. An army physical training officer by the name of Major Rothstein attempted to introduce the Swedish system of gymnastics into Prussia. He claimed that Swedish gymnastics were important for developing the health of all the people, a goal not included in the Turnen system. A discussion evolved that was nicknamed "the fight over the parallel bars." In the end, the nationalists and the Turnen held the upper hand, and Rothstein was forced to resign.

## From a Democratic-Revolutionary Movement toward a State-Supported Nationalist Movement

With the creation of the Second German Reich in 1871, following unification of Germany under the leadership of Bismarck, the Turnen movement developed from a democratic-revolutionary movement into a state-supported nationalist organization. In 1868 the Turnen had created a new organizational framework called the Deutsche Turnerschaft (the German Turnen Association). With the creation of this new organization, the movement's national festivals lost their political character. The dominant events at the new festivals became physical competitions and group activities, as well as mass performances by thousands of Turners. Calisthenics, performed with military precision, together with strict discipline and organization, adapted the Turnen to the authoritarian pedagogy of the times.

Toward the end of the nineteenth century, even the male leadership of the Turnerschaft adapted to social change. For the first time women were allowed to participate in the festivals. At the 1896 festival in Hamburg, a thousand women were allowed to participate for the first time. At this festival, female Turners dressed in long dresses with high collars performed mass exercises. It was not until the 1920s that women were allowed to participate in competitive activities. This change came about when the male leadership could no longer withstand the emancipatory efforts of the feminist movement.

As a result of the growing public interest in sports and games, the Turnen program began to incorporate new games such as track and field events. The inclusion of these new activities, however, created a collision between the nationalistic Turnen, which tried to avoid foreign influences, and the sport movement, which was definitely influenced by international tendencies. This conflict was forced upon the Turnen movement by young people who had become fascinated with the principles of competition and records.

Germany's defeat in World War I caused major changes in the country's political, economic, and social situation. In its analysis of the causes for the defeat, the Deutsche Turnerschaft sided with the extreme right wing politicians who were enemies of the young Weimar Republic. The Turnerschaft supported demands for military revenge and even made initial claims of a racist nature. Thus, in the years immediately after World War I, the Turnerschaft lined up with the revisionist forces in Germany. This was a far cry from its original political purpose.

## The German Turnerschaft and the Nazis

Under the pressure of tremendous economic and social problems in Germany in the 1920s, the political position of the Deutsche Turnerschaft began to resemble that of the Nazis. When military training was forbidden in Germany after World War I, Turnen turned out to be an acceptable means of providing for physical training. As the Nazis gained influence, Turnen helped legitimize an ideology focusing on nationalism and racist ideas.

When Adolf Hitler came to power at the beginning of 1933, the Deutsche Turnerschaft openly identified with the goals of the Nazis. With the introduction of the so-called "paragraphs of Aryans," Jewish members were expelled from the organization.[6] The same fate awaited members who did not share the same political ideology. In the early 1930s the primary goal of the Turnen was to ensure that each member was an able-bodied individual of German stock. Thus the Turnen movement, which in its founding days had led the fight for democracy, had degenerated into an antidemocratic, militaristic, and racist organization that served a fascist state. In 1936 the Turnerschaft even had to agree to its own dissolution in order to adjust to the organizational pattern imposed by the Nazis.

## The Years after World War II

Following the liberation of Germany from the Nazi regime in 1945, the Allies at first did not permit the German Turners to reorganize. The close alliance of the movement to nationalism, militarism, and anti-Semitism had brought it too close to the Nazis. However, in September 1950, the Allies agreed to the creation of a new national organization named the Deutsche Turnerbund. There were several reasons why the Allies allowed this. First, a similar organization had been created in the Communist Eastern zone, thus creating an imminent danger that East Germany might gain recognition as the sole representative of Germany in international sports. Second, the Deutsche Turnerbund considered itself the follower of a similar democratic organization that had been founded in 1848 in Hanau. Lastly, the Allies were persuaded that there was no connection between the new organization and the Deutsche Turnerschaft.

Later, Cold War tensions between East and West brought a new form of conflict to Germany sports. The sharp differences between the political system of the

Federal Republic of Germany (West Germany) and that of the German Democratic Republic (East Germany) found their way into conflicting policies and practices in the Deutsche Turnerbund and in its sports organizational counterpart in East Germany. This conflict was not resolved until the reunification of East and West Germany in 1990.

## A Digression: The Slavonic Sokol and French Gymnastics

In the second half of the nineteenth century, associations that modeled their activities on the Turnen started up in neighboring European countries. Two of these associations were the Czech *Sokol* movement and the French gymnastic movement. It should be clearly understood, however, that these two groups were not connected with the establishment of an international Turnen movement. On the contrary, there was enmity between the German and French Turners, as well as a major conflict between the Czechs and the rulers of the Austro-Hungarian monarchy. Like the German Turnen, though, the Sokol and French movements existed to encourage fitness and discipline in order to achieve supreme political and nationalist goals.

The Sokol movement was founded by Dr. Miroslav Tyrs in 1862 in Bohemia (now the Czech Republic). Sokol, which had a clear pan-Slavonic national character, saw its main function as preparing for independence from the Austro-Hungarian monarchy.

The gymnastic exercises of the Sokol were borrowed from the German Turnen but simplified to make mass participation possible. The major symbol of Sokol members was a falcon feather on a black hat, symbolizing freedom.[7] Up to World War I, six national festivals of the Sokol were held. The last one before the war took place in 1912. It boasted 30,000 active participants, including some from nearby Slovakia. Following Czech independence in 1918, the Sokol constructed the Strahov stadium for its 1926 national festival. This stadium became the biggest stadium in the world, with seating capacity for 250,000 spectators.

The idea of the Sokol spread from the Czechs to most other Slavonic nations. Mass immigration from these countries to the United States as well as to Western Europe helped spread the Sokol movement all over the world. The Sokol movement, which had both gymnastic and cultural elements, can thus be seen as the Slavonic archetype of a nationalist sport culture.

The French gymnastic movement in the Third Republic (1871–1914) resulted from the political situation in France after its defeat by Germany in the war of 1871–1872. For France, this defeat was connected with a loss of political influence in Europe, as well as loss of national dignity. Soon after the war, gymnastic societies were formed, especially in Eastern France. These societies, which specialized in paramilitary training, emphasized the development of discipline, courage, and masculinity. The Union of Gymnastic Societies, which was a confederation of individual societies, eventually recognized France's new democratic-republican constitution and accepted national unity and reconstruction of the national image as its primary goals.

Even though the Union of the Gymnastic Societies chose *gymnastics* as the name of its physical activity, its activities resembled the German Turnen much more than the Swedish system of gymnastics. The Union paid special attention to the education of youth, and by 1880, gymnastics and paramilitary exercises had become mandatory for boys in all public schools in France. Former army officers were hired as teachers, with political loyalty regarded more highly than professional qualifications.

The development of the French gymnastic movement can be thus viewed as another example of the formation of a Western European form of sport culture motivated by nationalist and revenge-seeking elements. In the 1890s the French gymnastics system was challenged by supporters of the sport movement, particularly by followers of Coubertin's fledgling Olympic movement. Despite Coubertin's emphasis on international sport, he was at the same time in complete agreement with the goals of the Gymnastic Union.

## ENGLISH SPORTS IN THE NINETEENTH CENTURY

Modern English sports are a product of the nineteenth century.[8] In that era the many organized sports developed by the British spread throughout the world. Although the exported sports often mixed with other systems, they maintained a specifically British national core.

### Social and Political Background

The English system of modern sports began with social and political developments in the seventeenth century. The most significant influences included not only these political changes but economic changes accompanying the industrial revolution at the end of the eighteenth century. As a result of these changes, political and economic power in English society shifted from the dominant peerage toward the gentry, which was a mixture of the old nobility and the rising class of "gentlemen." This transition is readily evident in the field of sport. In the seventeenth and eighteenth centuries, sport served as a pastime for the English leisure class. In the nineteenth century, sport became a means of educating youth, integrating the social classes, and representing British culture around the world.

The rise of the gentry class and its increase in power was made possible through the industrial revolution and through a Bill of Rights passed by the Parliament. It was the industrial revolution, with its mines, railroads, and machine-driven factories, that permitted capitalists to emerge from the ranks of early industry and commerce. These individuals soon replaced the noble landowners as the dominant social and economic class in English society.

The industrial revolution created not only a gentry class based on industry and commerce but also an industrial proletariat: the men, women, and children who toiled in mines and factories. Moreover, in the second half of the nineteenth century, the dynamic and materialistic English society expanded into a major colonial power. The nationalist British Empire soon considered itself as not only a world political power but a world cultural power as well. With imperial awareness, Britain emphasized its universal superiority. At the same time, however, that England was enjoying extraordinary success in international affairs, it was undergoing social polarization at home. As a result of unrestrained economic capitalism and political liberalism, English society faced extreme social tensions caused by the ever-growing gap between the social classes and great differences in their living conditions. The working class suffered from long working hours, low salaries, bad living quarters, and poor health care. A means of integrating the social classes was urgently needed to help prevent civil strife.

The gentlemen of the gentry can be credited with developing a unified system of modern sports that replaced the former system, which completely separated activities by social class. The structure and content of sports were modernized in the nineteenth century, and sports were given a new value system and a revised system of organization. This organizational reform found expression in the development of rules for various sports and in the quantification of sports through competitions, statistics, and records. It is these characteristics that determine to a large extent the nature of sports to this day.

## Sports as a Means of Education, Integration, and Representation

The new system of English sports served as one means of creating the social equilibrium that was needed to overcome growing controversies between the social classes. It also gave the British a means of self-expression. By and large, the activities of the various social classes were integrated into one unified system of sports. Although unified, however, differences in the sporting activities of the various classes did not disappear completely. The upper and middle classes indulged in their "gentlemen sports" within the framework of closed and private clubs for amateurs. Their primary sports included, to a large extent, activities that demanded relatively large investments of money, such as tennis, golf, cricket, and rowing. The lower social classes developed "urban sports," which centered on either active or passive participation by the masses, as in soccer and rugby. In London and in the industrial cities of Northern England, professional clubs emerged. In 1863 ten such clubs combined to create the Football (soccer) Association. Other professional sports organizations also came into being, most notably associations of cycling and boxing enthusiasts. Most members of such clubs were laborers. Soccer, especially, rapidly developed into the game of the working class.

Originally, the educational aspects of participation in sports were considered important only for the leaders in politics, the economy, and the military—and their offspring. It was not until the latter part of the nineteenth century that these purposes of sport were recognized as important for the lower classes. Change occurred with the introduction of compulsory physical education into the general school system. One of the major stated objectives of physical education at that time was "to enhance the discipline of the masses."

As indicated earlier, the three major functions of English sports in the nineteenth century were the educational, representative, and integrative functions. These functions were sometimes entwined, yet each had certain characteristics such as a specific set of rules and an organizational framework, as well as fidelity to the ethical principle of fair play.

The educational function of the British sports system can be considered its most important social function during this era. Sport was used to train middle and upper class boys for future leadership, focusing primarily on the development of proper social skills and attitudes. Until becoming part of the general school system in the later part of the nineteenth century, this character training took place mainly in the so-called "public" schools, which were private boarding schools for sons of the social elite. The introduction of character training through sports into these public schools was initiated by Thomas Arnold, the headmaster of Rugby school for fourteen years (1828–1842). It was Arnold who emphasized values of sport in terms of religious and moral training, as well as the importance of gentlemanly conduct. These values later became associated with the concept of *muscular Christianity*, which stressed the value of sports in developing manliness and in inculcating spiritual and moral virtues. As a result of educators like Arnold, sports started to play an important role in the school curriculum. It was not a coincidence that the still-existing rules for rugby football came into existence in this era, replacing old rules that were wild and violent. While the school at Rugby was inventing its game of rugby, the school at Eton came up with the first version of football in which the ball was not to be touched with the hands.[9] This game was the forerunner of modern soccer.

In 1864 a report of the Royal Commission on Public Schools stated that sports, and especially the games of football and cricket, served not only the purpose of improving the player's health but at the same time developed such virtues as masculinity, self-discipline, cooperation, gentlemanly conduct, and adherence to the principle of fair play.

Besides contributing to the development of educational values, the English system of sports also fulfilled the important function of representing England and its social system to the rest of the world. As the dominant world power of the time, the British considered it of utmost importance to secure their Empire not merely through military and political actions, but through transfer of their cultural system as well. Sports gained in importance in this respect throughout the nineteenth century and can be considered a most important medium for the transmission of English culture. Thus English sports were exported to the colonies abroad, primarily by administrative and military personnel, as an example of the "English way of life."[10]

English sports were also spread around the world by English merchants and students. These individuals carried with them an allegiance to their favorite physical activities in a style that might be considered "missionary fervor." They were not willing to accept non-English programs of physical education and sports, especially those in continental Europe. They were, however, willing to adapt to foreign cultural customs as long as those customs did not contradict the basic essence of English culture. The dominance of English sports over foreign systems was based on British conviction of national superiority, and on the fact that the newly introduced sports were welded to the British taste. This attitude of superiority reached its climax towards the end of the nineteenth century.

Another significant role of the English sports system in the nineteenth century grew out of unstable economic conditions. As mentioned earlier, the growing number of proletarians in urban society created an urgent need for social integration of the poverty-stricken masses. Sports turned out to be an important instrument in the creation of a program of "rational recreation." Social drinking and betting on the results of soccer games and boxing events in the taverns of England were replaced by recreational activities in the so-called "sporting public houses." These sporting houses gave ordinary people an opportunity to participate in healthy and productive leisure-time activities. As a direct result of the Public Health Acts of 1848, 1875, and 1890, public parks opened for recreational activities and sports. In addition, a number of swimming pools were constructed and became very popular.

Even the Church of England supported the development of "rational recreational" activity, and endorsed the philosophy of muscular Christianity. Priests and vicars organized team games for youth. The church initiated the creation of youth organizations such as the Boys' Brigade, and the Church Lad's Brigade. The most influential organization on the international scene, the Young Men's Christian Association (YMCA) was founded by George Williams in 1844 in London.[11]

By the end of the nineteenth century, sports fields and playgrounds had became the central meeting place of younger members of the lower social classes. Sports helped improve the health as well as the moral behavior of wide circles of the population. It also provided a way of relaxing social tensions and of developing political loyalty toward the state.

In summary, the development of sports in England can be characterized by the following quotation: "Pro patria est dum ludere videmur" ("even though it seems that we play, we do it for the fatherland"). This patriotic sentiment, taken from the ancient Romans, was the official slogan of the Jockey Club, which was one of the noblest of the English sport clubs in the nineteenth century. Indeed, this slogan expressed the basic characteristics of English sports. As an outcome of the industrial revolution, the development of modern sports was a central element in England's imperialist politics during the nineteenth century. At the same time, however, the English sport system maintained an ambivalent structure: it retained its pattern as an original phenomenon of English culture, but it was also ready to adopt modern technological influences from the outside though without relinquishing the nationalist claim of English superiority and uniqueness. It was this readiness that enabled English sports to overcome charges of chauvinism and to become the accepted "motherland of modern sports." The basic construction of the modern Olympic movement rests, to a large extent, on the structure of sports in the English upper class as well as on the basic and supreme elements of amateurism and fair play.

## SPORT AND NATIONALISM IN IRELAND

The development of sports in Ireland during the past 120 years is another example of a country experiencing a strong relationship between a system of sport and national development. Although occurring primarily in the late nineteenth and early twentieth centuries, the influence of nationalism on Irish sports is recognizable even today. This is the case especially in Northern Ireland, where the religious, cultural, and social differences of the population have a direct effect on everyday sport activities. At the same time, the connection between sport and nationalism can still be felt in the Republic of Ireland, which gained its independence in 1921. This is quite evident even today, when the greatest sport organization in Ireland states that its primary goal is "to foster an awareness and love of the national ideals in the people of Ireland."

The history of Irish sports at the end of the nineteenth century and beginning of the twentieth century can be considered a paradigm of national movements in modern European sports. Here we see all the elements for creating a national sport culture. These elements include the presence of a dominant foreign (English) model of sports, the creation of a national sport organization, adherence to a supreme political goal, and the "invention" of a national sport tradition.

Even though the history of sports in Ireland can serve as an example of developments in other countries, it possesses a number of unique attributes derived from Ireland's specific historical and cultural situation. In the second half of the nineteenth century, when the modern sports of England started their victorious march throughout the world, Ireland was ruled by the English. The English influence had an overwhelming effect on Irish culture and social life. Sporadic attempts on the part of the Irish to shake off English predominance were unsuccessful.

In the mid-nineteenth century, a broad movement for independence developed. Groups such as the Fenian Movement, the Irish Republican Brotherhood, and the Land League were formed. In addition to political and military strategies used against the British crown, the various movements encouraged the revival of national values and traditions. The rediscovery of Gaelic culture at first emphasized Gaelic language and literature. It later extended to include recreational activities and sports. Thus the spread of an independent Gaelic sport culture, as opposed to the sporting activities imported by the English, became an important element of the Irish national movement in its struggle to separate itself from English dominance in all aspects of life.

### The Gaelic Athletic Association (GAA): Formative Years

During the mid-nineteenth century, various appeals to revive national pastimes appeared in the Irish press. But only in 1884, with the creation of the Gaelic Athletic Association (GAA), was there a breakthrough. This organization formed as the result of a newspaper article, "A Word about Irish Athletics," written by Michael Cusack for the *United Ireland*. In the article, Cusack defined the goals of what would become a new organization. He suggested that the Irish people should take the management of their games into their own hands, to encourage and promote, in every way, every form of athletics that was peculiarly Irish.[12]

Cusack, who a few years earlier had promoted English sports in the college in which he was teaching, now turned vehemently against the English influence. This influence was considerable. The imported English sports of rugby, cricket, tennis, and golf had become very popular in the clubs of the social elite in Dublin. Additionally, track and field meetings, held under the rules of the English Amateur Athletic Association, were widespread in Ireland.

The positive reaction to his article encouraged Cusack to call a meeting on November 1, 1884, which led to the creation of the Gaelic Athletic Association. Although only seven people attended the meeting, a number of important decisions were reached. One was to offer the patronage of the GAA to Charles Stewart Parnell, Michael Davitt, and Archbishop Croke. Parnell was a leader of the Irish members of the House of Commons as well as of the Home Rule Movement. As such, he represented parliamentary opposition to British rule. Davitt was a prominent member of the Land League, which took care of poor Irish farmers. Croke was the most prominent member of the clergy who supported the independence movement. Since all three of these men were willing to extend their patronage, the GAA succeeded in getting the leadership of the three most influential political and social groups on its side.

In immediate reaction to the creation of the GAA, clubs and athletes who practiced or competed in English sports created the Irish Amateur Athletic Association (IAAA). This led to considerable competition between the two organizations. All over Ireland, athletic competitions were organized under the supervision of one or the other of the two associations. Whereas the GAA emphasized sprints and throwing events, the IAAA emphasized middle- and long-distance races. In the summer of 1895, the GAA could celebrate its first important victory: a meet attended by over 10,000 spectators. A parallel meet conducted by the IAAA turned into a fiasco.

In the coming months, the GAA enjoyed significant growth in membership. This growth was helped not only through the support of nationalist political and social circles but also through two important decisions. The first decision gained the support of the Catholic Church by calling for the establishment of one athletic club in each neighborhood parish of the church. This decision helped establish GAA clubs all over the country. The second important decision was to open GAA clubs to members of all social classes. The IAAA, which held its meetings on Saturdays, restricted its membership to "non-labourers, tradesmen, and artisans." The GAA, however, held its meetings on Sundays so that people who had to work on Saturdays could still participate in GAA meetings.

Within a few years, the GAA established more than 1,000 clubs. Members were drawn primarily from agricultural areas, whereas the IAAA tended to attract an urban membership. Thus within a short period the GAA reached its goal of driving back the influence of English sports over the Irish population. It was also successful in gaining control over Irish sports.

## National Pastimes:
## Hurling, Gaelic Football, and Handball

Even though the GAA in its first years focused on track and field activities, it also gave significant support to the "preservation and cultivation of national pastimes." The most important of these were hurling, Gaelic football, and handball. Of these games, hurling best fulfilled the criterion of having a long Irish tradition, and it thus became a national game. To this day, the bat used in hurling remains a symbol of Irish nationalism.[13]

The game of hurling plays an important role in Irish mythology and legends. It was purportedly played for the first time in 1272 B.C. At the beginning, noblemen and even kings participated in the game, and it is mentioned continuously throughout Irish history. In the eighteenth century, hurling experienced a first revival, but economic difficulties, mass emigration, and hunger in the nineteenth century caused a backlash. When the GAA was created, a number of clubs in Dublin played "hurley." However, that game strongly resembled English hockey and had very little in common with the game of hurling. At the initiative of the GAA, the game of hurling then entered a second renaissance. Today it is considered the "cleanest" Irish game.

In contrast to the history of hurling, very little is known about the origins of Gaelic football. Like rugby and soccer, it seems to have begun in a mass game of football, played in villages where there was little concern about the size of the playing field, the number of players, or the playing time. Like hurling, Gaelic football suffered during the wave of emigration in the nineteenth century. Despite this, however, and despite the fact that the English introduced rugby in the 1850s and soccer in the 1870s, Gaelic football managed to become the number-one spectator sport in Ireland. Today it resembles the game of soccer more than rugby.

The history of Irish handball is even more obscure than that of Gaelic football. It is possible that French and English soldiers imported the game into Ireland in late medieval times. If so, then the history of the game goes back about 600 years. Irish handball is a batting game in which the ball is batted by the hand. Under the name of "fives," it became popular for some time in English public schools.

One of the first tasks of the Gaelic Athletic Association was to codify the rules of hurling and Gaelic football. Under GAA leadership, the size of the court and the number of players on a team were defined. Under the new rules, both games became less rough, with Gaelic football bearing little resemblance to its historical forerunner.

National championships in hurling and Gaelic football were first held in 1887. Due to the rule changes mentioned above, the number of active players as well as the number of spectators grew into the thousands. Despite strict adherence to rules of amateurism, a cult of admiration for the star players soon developed. However, despite the popularity of these games in Ireland, neither hurling nor Gaelic football could gain a lasting foothold in any other country. Irish immigrants did introduce the games into the United States, however, and in 1914 an American branch of the GAA was established in New York.

## The Politics of Ban

The history of the GAA is noted for a number of bans that prohibited certain individuals from becoming members. The bans essentially were imposed on the basis of a person's sporting interests or occupation. At first, they served an important role in building up the GAA as well as defending it against competing organizations. However, with time, the bans were applied to everything and everyone associated with the British crown. This pattern clearly supports the view that, for a long time, the GAA practiced a separatist rather than an integrative nationalism.

The first ban against participation was declared in January 1885, a few weeks after the GAA's creation. That ban declared that any athlete competing under laws other than those of the GAA was ineligible to compete in any meeting held under GAA auspices. In 1886 a second ban was imposed in an effort to secure GAA monopoly over Gaelic pastimes. This ban stated that any member of a club in Ireland playing hurling, Gaelic football, or handball under rules other than those of the GAA could not become a member of the GAA. Additionally, it was mandated that members of any other athletic club in Ireland could not become members of the GAA.

Another important purpose of the second ban was to strengthen the GAA in its dispute with the Irish Amateur Athletic Association. The ban resulted in the growth of a number of affiliated clubs. In addition, the second ban included an anti-British stipulation that became openly effective with the establishment of the so-called "police ban." Under the influence of the militant Irish Republican Brotherhood (IRB), it was decided to expel from the GAA all members of the Royal Irish Constabulary and of the Dublin Metropolitan Police. These individuals were thought to have acted against the interests of the Irish population. The police ban, which turned out to be the subject of considerable discussion among GAA members, was changed from time to time according to which side had the upper hand. The changes, ranging from annulment of the ban to more severe restrictions, mirrored prevailing attitudes in Irish nationalism. After the police ban had been annulled for some time, it was given new life in 1906. The new form of the ban, which lasted into the 1970s, stated that soldiers, sailors, and pensioners from the British armed services as well as police personnel could not gain GAA membership.

In addition to the police bans, "foreign game" bans were also imposed. These bans stipulated that anyone who played an imported English game was to be excluded from GAA membership for two years. Later the bans were also applied to any spectator of a foreign game. The "foreign game" bans were a way of resisting English pastimes and the further Anglicization of the Irish people.

## The GAA and Irish Politics

Its stated goals made it clear that the GAA was a political organization from the very beginning. The selection of the GAA's patrons illustrates the political consciousness of its founders. However, in spite of its prominent patrons, the GAA was often marked by political differences among various groups of members. The close relationship of the GAA with the militant Irish Republican Brotherhood caused major difficulties, as the Catholic Church strongly opposed the Irish Republican Brotherhood. At times the GAA maintained a close relationship with militant groups. On the other hand, there were times in which the GAA saw itself as strictly nonpolitical and unsectarian.

In the long run, though, the GAA should be considered a prominent member of the independence movement. It took part at decisive stages in the fight for Irish independence. For example, members of the GAA led the procession at the funeral of Parnell in 1891. Seven years later, thousands of GAA members demonstrated at the centenary of the 1798 uprising in Dublin. In 1913 the GAA put its offices at the disposal of the paramilitary Irish Volunteers to serve as a recruiting office. Thousands of GAA members participated in the Easter Rising of 1916, which was the most important event before the independence of the Irish Republic. The harsh British reaction to this uprising caused the independence movement to become even more radical, a reaction felt in the ranks of the GAA as well. After the uprising of 1916, the GAA refused to pay the amusement tax on sporting events that had been imposed by the British parliament. In 1918 the GAA joined the movement that resisted recruitment of Irish youth into the British army. Further, the GAA did not abide by a British law which forbade the organization of sporting events. On August 4, 1918, the GAA organized the so-called Gaelic Sunday, on which over 1,000 hurling and Gaelic football games were held. The GAA was also involved in the most tragic event in Irish sport history. On November 11, 1920, the British army massacred over a dozen spectators at a GAA-sponsored Gaelic football game. This was a done in revenge for an attack on British soldiers by the Irish Republican Army (IRA).

## After Independence: An Outlook

When the Republic of Ireland (Eire) gained independence in 1921, at the cost of the separation of six counties in Northern Ireland, the GAA could pride itself on having contributed to the elimination of British domination over Ireland. That domination had lasted hundreds of years. The GAA's goals of awakening Irish consciousness and developing Gaelic pride undoubtedly made an important contribution in the battle for independence.

Having played a role in the national rebellion, the GAA now showed its prowess by advocating national reconciliation. The first major GAA activity after independence was organization of the Tailteann Games in August 1924. The origin of these games supposedly dates back to pre-Christian times. The revised games, considered the Irish equivalent of the Olympics, were attended by Irish immigrants from overseas. These games can thus be seen as the first self-expression of a proud and independent Eire.

As an expression of Irish national distinctiveness, the GAA is today active primarily in British-dominated Northern Ireland. In Eire the GAA faces a growing interest in English sports, primarily soccer and rugby. The introduction of professional sports has also reached the Gaelic games and has endangered their existence. This is especially true of Gaelic football, which has suffered as a result of the national soccer team of Northern Ireland and of recruitment efforts by professional leagues in the United States and Australia.

Despite GAA opposition to the British sport model, the association has never been able to completely separate itself from modern sports. In fact, the GAA built its foundation on the British model. Thus the development of indigenous Irish sports does not weaken the thesis that modern sports expanded worldwide in the nineteenth and twentieth centuries. On the contrary, the Irish sports illustrate that in spite of all nationalist overtones, the underlying principles of modern sports remain unchanged.

## THE SPORT SYSTEM OF THE
## GERMAN DEMOCRATIC REPUBLIC

As early as 1980, the Canadian sport journalist Doug Gilbert referred to the sport system of the German Democratic Republic (GDR) as "the miracle machine." Indeed, many spoke of that miracle when they attempted to analyze what was to become the most successful facet of East Germany's social system. In its forty-year existence (1949–1989), the GDR could point to relatively little success in the economic and political arenas. Sport was the great exception.

Sports in the Soviet zone of East Germany, which was to become the GDR, began in 1945 immediately after World War II. Over the next forty-four years, until the collapse of the country in 1989, its sports program reached a very high level of development. In spite of its limited population (17 million), the GDR succeeded in challenging both the United States and the Soviet Union for leadership in world sports. Only in the construction of sport facilities did the GDR fail to reach a position of a leadership.

The leaders of the GDR consistently claimed that their achievements in sports were a direct result of applying the theories of Marx and Lenin and of translating these theories into a socialist social system. According to the East Germans, their achievements in sports served as definite proof of the superiority of their socialist system over the capitalist system of the West. In addition, leaders of the GDR sport program prided themselves on having been able to carry on the democratic traditions of the pioneers in German physical culture, from Guts Muths and Jahn up to the workers' sports movement at the beginning of the twentieth century.

A critical analysis of the GDR sport system, however, points to other factors that may have contributed to its unquestioned success. Such factors can be traced to the radical leadership of the state party, commonly known as the Socialist Unity Party (SED). These factors included the utilization of all possible resources and methods including (1) research into the sport sciences; (2) systematic selection of athletes; (3) employment of a large number of personnel; (4) material advantages; and (5) extreme practices of systematic doping.

Such a great investment by a poor society was justified by the GDR leadership as a pragmatic political goal. With the assistance of its so-called "diplomats in track suits," the GDR would gain international respect. At the same time, it would provide a focus for self-identity. In instrumentalizing its sports program for superior political purposes, the GDR drew upon the previous experiences of both the Nazi regime and the Soviet Union.

## Organization of Sports in the GDR

To understand the above-mentioned instrumentalization, we need a basic understanding of the construction and organization of the GDR sports program. At all times the GDR sport system was totally integrated into the national and social system of the country. As a result, it depended on the directives of the supreme political bodies.

The political development of the GDR as a nation was a result of World War II and its aftermath. After the total submission of Nazi Germany in the spring of 1945, the Allies created four occupational zones, each under the control of one of the Allied powers—the United States, the Soviet Union, Great Britain, and France. According to a decision reached at the Potsdam Conference in 1945, the four allies were supposed to follow similar principles in governing their respective occupation zones. Soon thereafter, however, a split in the allied front occurred, especially between the United States and the Soviet Union, and the decision to seek unified development of Germany became worthless. Differentiated development in the different zones and the split between East and West resulted in the formation of two separate states in 1949, namely the Federal Republic of Germany (West Germany) and the German Democratic Republic (East Germany). This division of Germany continued until the countries were reunified in 1990.

In April 1946 the SED became the official party of the government that was set up in the Soviet zone and later in the GDR. As such, the SED enjoyed the status of being the sole political power in East Germany. At the same time, the Soviets maintained supervisory power over their German "allies" and in fact directed them.

According to the ideological concepts of Marxism-Leninism, all areas of life, including sports, are supposed to contribute to the establishment of the socialist state. As a result, sports automatically maintain a political character and share political responsibility for total social development. On the other hand, the state shares responsibility for the development of the cultural life, including sports.

According to a decision of the Allies in 1945, all German sport clubs were to be dissolved and new sport activities were to be limited to the communal sphere. The communities in the Soviet zone were the first to organize sporting activities, and in March 1946 these were joined by the Free German Youth (FDJ) movement of the SED. In the spring of 1948, the FDJ became the sole body responsible for sports in East Germany. Those interested in sports were forced to join the FDJ. A few months later, the SED decided that trade unions should also play a role in the organization of sports. Thus, in October 1948, the FDJ and the trade unions created the first national sport organization—the German Sports Committee.

Under the supervision of this committee, sports were structured according to a specified socialist system, whereby traditional German sport clubs were replaced by workplace clubs. These clubs were financed by the employers, who had to hire professional personnel for their operation. These workplace clubs were organized into sixteen so-called sport associations, each representing a given area of the state's economy and services. In 1956 these associations were joined by two organizations called Dynamo and Vorwaerts, which represented, respectively, the police and secret service and the armed forces. The major purpose of the workplace clubs was to cater to mass activities. For the development of elite athletes, a number of "sport clubs," each dealing with a limited number of sports, were created in 1954.

All this, however, did not complete the control of the political leadership over the total sports program. In July 1952 the SED decided to establish a body to promote and supervise the state's sports program. A State Committee for Physical Culture and Sports was created, following the model established in the Soviet Union.

The strong influence of the Soviet Union over East Germany lasted until the mid-1950s. Following the death of Joseph Stalin in 1953, the first steps in liberalization could be felt in all countries under Soviet influence and a stronger awareness of independence. In addition, the policies of East Germany changed when West Germany joined NATO; in reaction East Germany became a member of the Warsaw Pact. Earlier proclamations and demands for reunification of the two German states were now replaced by declarations acclaiming the separation and independence of the "Socialist German State." Intensive efforts began in all spheres to gain international recognition of that independent state. These efforts were accompanied by efforts to make the citizens of the GDR feel a sense of identity with their state. For this purpose, national mass organizations, including those in sports, were important.

In the spring of 1957, the SED decided that a newly established German Turnen and Sport Federation (DTSB) should become the supreme body, the unified socialist sport organization, of the GDR. The workplace clubs became the organizational basis of the DTSB. Fourteen of the eighteen national sport associations were dissolved and their functions were transferred to the new organization. The only other national organizations that continued to operate were those of the army (Vorwaerts), the police (Dynamo), the railway system (Lokomotive), and the miners (Wismut). These organizations survived primarily because a large percentage of elite athletes trained in them. At the end of 1989, the DTSB claimed a membership of 3,650,000. The selected teams of the GDR also changed their names in 1957 and were called national teams. The national championships were initially known as German championships but later as GDR championships.

Because it was a frontier state between socialism and capitalism, the GDR put special emphasis on the premilitary training for young men. Following the Soviet model, a Society for Sport and Technique was created in 1952 to encourage such activities as aviation, nautical sports, shooting, and motor sports. This society functioned in parallel to the DTSB.

In 1951 the GDR also established an independent National Olympic Committee. This body gained international recognition in 1955 with the provision that East Germany agreed to participate in an all-German representation at the Olympic Games.

Other state institutions for sports developed over these years. The State Committee for Physical Culture and Sport continued to occupy the top position on behalf of the state and the party. However, in 1970, the State Committee changed its name to the State Secretariat for Physical Culture and Sports. In the academic and scientific areas, the state opened the German University for Physical Culture at Leipzig in 1950, which was to become the largest institution of its kind in the world. The school at Leipzig did not prepare academic professors but concentrated on training coaches and instructors. In addition, it was responsible for advanced studies in the sport sciences. In 1963 the Sport Medical Service was established, followed in 1969 by the Research Institute for Physical Culture and Sport. The sole function of the Research Institute was to provide support for elite athletes. Additionally, the Institutes for Physical Education at the various universities and pedagogical academies were renamed Departments for Sport Sciences. These departments were primarily responsible for teacher training.

In 1962 a special body was created for the planning, development, directing, and supervision of elite sports. The State Committee, the DTSB, the Ministry of Health, and the school in Leipzig were all represented in this body.

By the mid-1960s, the centralization of the planning and direction of sports in the GDR had been completed. All developments in sports were based on decisions reached by the Central Committee of the SED. The Central Committee was the second most important political body in the state following the Politburo. All leaders of the sport movement were at the same time members of the Central Committee.

The central system of the GDR was supplemented by a method for identifying athletically gifted children and adolescents. Besides obligatory classes in the school system, close cooperation existed between schoolteachers and the sports instructors in DTSB clubs. The DTSB had as a major goal the early recognition of talented youth. In many cases, the DTSB even sponsored sport clubs in the schools. Systematic standardized testing of all schoolchildren was introduced in 1973; it was conducted annually in grades one, four, and eight. A system of sport competitions held on the local, regional, and national level was established in 1965. These competitions, which further helped to identify the athletically gifted, culminated in the national Spartakiade. In 1965, some 300,000 young people participated in this series of competitions. In 1988 the number was reported to be as high as 900,000.

As of 1964, the most gifted children and youth were prepared in three stages for participation in elite sports. The first stage called for attendance at a regional training center. The second stage of training took place in the national child/youth schools for sport. The last stage provided for training in the sports clubs of the DTSB under the best available professional circumstances.

The organizational framework of the sports program in the GDR was thus created on a step-by-step and methodical basis. Sports in the GDR became a major instrument for implementing the political directives of the state through the SED. At the same time, the system produced immediate and far-reaching results in sports performance. The GDR used these achievements in sports to enhance its supreme political goals on both national and international levels.

## Nationalization: Three Phases

The manner in which the GDR sport system was structured illustrates the abnormally large influence of the East German government on the development of sports in that country. The GDR rulers recognized at an early stage the great role that sports could play in a modern society, and they decided to use that medium to advance their political goals. Certain historians suggest that the GDR created its image as a state primarily through its developed sports program. From the very beginning of the formation of the country, a core idea was nationalization of sports as part of the building of a socialist state on German soil. This could only be carried out, of course, as permitted by particular social circumstances, scientific developments, and the political state of affairs.

The nationalization of the GDR sports program took place in three phases. Throughout, the functions of the GDR sports program were governed by both internal and external considerations. In the initial stage of its development, immediately following the post–World War II period, the goal of the GDR sports program was to assist in the establishment of communist ideology in the new social system, to orient people toward the political concepts of the Soviet Union and the GDR. At that time, the political goal was reunification of Germany under Soviet hegemony, or at least to establish a neutral state. In numerous instructions and proclamations issued by the state leadership, this policy was preached to all athletes and sport functionaries time and again. Athletes were called to line up behind the "workers" class and its party in the battle for national liberation. The athletes were directed to support the unification of Germany through the battle for the unification and liberation of German sports.

When it became clear that the political target of German reunification according to the communist model could not be achieved, the second phase in the development of the sports program began. This phase called for clear demarcation from the West and an intense focus on the independence of the socialist German state with its own sport system. At SED's fifth party convention in 1958, the slogan of the convention was designed to promote the superiority, within a three-year period, of the socialist system of the GDR over the capitalist powers in West Germany. For the sport leadership, that slogan was intended to encourage major achievements in sports that would prove to the West the superiority of the East German system. According to the leadership of the DTSB, its activities during this stage of development contributed significantly toward the strengthening of the GDR and the whole socialist world. On the international level, however, the GDR was confronted by efforts of the West German government to prevent recognition of the GDR state, on grounds that it was a mere puppet of the Soviet Union. The conflict between West and East Germany developed into an international discussion at the highest level, particularly in reference to the question of which country had the right to represent Germany on the international scene.

The third and final stage of the development of the GDR sports system began in the mid-1960s. Western policies calling for nonrecognition of the GDR had utterly failed. Then the West German government of the social-democrats and liberals, which came into power in 1969, revised long-established policies. In a special treaty, the two German states recognized each other, even though the problem of nationality was interpreted differently by the two. Whereas the West German government spoke of two German states and one German nation, the East Germans referred to two nations in two German states.

In 1965 the International Olympic Committee recognized the independence of the GDR and permitted it to enter its own team in the 1968 Olympic Games in Mexico City. For the East German state, and for the leadership of its sports program, this recognition was confirmation of the improved international image of the GDR.

## The Internal Function of GDR Sports

The Soviet occupation zone, as well as the German Democratic Republic after 1949, had to face constant comparisons to the West. In this respect it was different from the other states ruled by the Soviet Union in Eastern Europe. The social system of the GDR and its population were always confronted with these comparisons for two reasons: the common border with West Germany and the strong relationships between the peoples of the two German states. That situation enabled the people to examine the everyday reality of each other's lives, both through personal contacts and through the media. Repercussions after crises in the GDR, such as the people's revolt in 1953 and the erection of the Berlin wall in 1961, were especially severe because of the GDR's economic inferiority and limitations on personal freedom.

The state leadership of the GDR had to make constant efforts to advertise its social activities in order to protect the political system and improve popular awareness and support of the state. To achieve these goals, the state exploited all the traditional means of sports, including great national festivals that promoted the cultural aspects of sports and served as entertainment and diversion from the limited circumstances of ordinary life. These festivals climaxed in the eight national festivals held between 1954 and 1987, in which top athletes were honored. Beginning in 1956, these festivals were held in the enormous People's Stadium in Leipzig. They included, side by side, top-level athletic competitions and mass performances. These festivals were designed to exhibit a cross section of sports in the GDR and to create a positive national experience. At the same time, the festivals were aimed at demonstrating the close relationship between the athletes and the leadership of the state and the party. The various slogans at the festivals presented a clear set of directives for internal and external politics. In the 1950s, the slogans called for the unification of Germany. In later years, the slogans called for the perfection of socialist society and for improvement of the self-awareness of the young state. The national festivals also celebrated positive historical traditions, from the festivals of the Turners in the 1860s to those of the workers' sports movement in the 1920s and 1930s.

In relation to the German Turnen movement in the nineteenth century, the relationship between the GDR and the founder of the movement, Friedrich Ludwig Jahn, presents a peculiar case. In the latter years of the GDR, Jahn was presented as a German patriot and as a fighter for German unity in opposition to the attitude of the forefathers of the German workers' sports movement. In the view of the GDR, Jahn was an extreme nationalist and, as such, a forerunner of the Nazi movement. The DTSB even named its top honor the Jahn medal.

A personality cult of adulation for athletic stars had been encouraged by the GDR leadership since the very beginning. International success was honored not only by medals but also by material benefits. This was especially so if the athlete happened to be a party member, which helps explain why approximately 70 percent of all top athletes were registered party members in the 1980s. Some top athletes were even elected members of parliament. The party leadership used the top athletes and its close relationship with them to enhance its own image.

At the same time, the party also catered to the masses. During the 1950s, party chairman Walter Ulbricht coined the slogan, "Sports for everyone, in any place, several times a week." Mass testing of physical ability started through the implementation of the "Ready for Labor and for the Protection of Peace" program. This program later changed its name to the "Ready for Labor and for the Protection of the Fatherland" program.

The function of these activities was to persuade the entire population to identify with the state and its political system. Sports were also utilized in the development of a national consciousness, especially at the end of the 1960s, when it became important to distance the East German population from the West German state.

## The External Political Function of GDR Sports

Early in the history of the GDR, its athletes were considered "diplomats in track suits." These sport diplomats had a dual function. They represented the fight against West German efforts to prevent diplomatic recognition of the GDR. They also served as a way of demonstrating the superiority of the socialist state.

The major battle on the international sports scene centered around the recognition of Germany by the International Olympic Committee (IOC). The West Germans considered themselves the only legal representative of Germany. Recognition by the IOC was considered to be the equivalent of full diplomatic recognition. The battle between East and West Germany for this recognition lasted fourteen years. From 1951 until 1965 it was known as the "German quarrel." It began in 1951 when the National Olympic Committee of West Germany was recognized, and the IOC refused recognition "to a second National Olympic Committee of the same nation." In 1955 the IOC granted recognition to the National Olympic Committee of the GDR, but both states were forced to participate within the framework of a single German team. The composition of these teams was determined after bitterly fought preliminary competitions that involved considerable politicking. One major aspect of the quarrel was the different national anthems and flags of the two states. When representatives of the GDR insisted on the presence of their symbols, the Federal Republic of Germany refused recognition, because acceptance of the symbols would have meant recognition of the GDR. Finally, both sides agreed to a decision of the IOC that mandated use of a neutral flag and a neutral anthem, Beethoven's Ninth Symphony.

After GDR athletes gained a majority on the common German team for the first time at the 1964 Olympics, the IOC agreed that both German states should appear with separate teams at the 1968 Olympic Games. The success of the GDR athletes at those games in Mexico City immediately improved the international image of the East German state. Their success meant that the East German athletes had achieved the goal set for them by the political leadership, which was to represent the "first peace-loving German state with honor."

The dispute between West and East Germany became even more rancorous before the 1972 Olympic Games, which were held in the West German city of Munich. According to the GDR, these games were held in the territory of the "German enemy of the working class." Here, on the territory of its major political opponent, the GDR felt it was of utmost importance to demonstrate its athletic superiority to the world.

As a result of the best possible preparations and of the SED decision to concentrate on those sports and events in which the chances of winning were greatest, the GDR team managed to place third behind the Soviet Union and the United States. This enormous success was considered by the general secretary of the SED, Erich Honecker, as a major contribution to the "glory of sport and the honor of our Socialist fatherland." It was his belief that the athletes were the best possible representatives of the physical aspects of the total national culture of the GDR.

The superior position gained in Munich in 1972 was maintained by the GDR athletes until the collapse of the state in 1989/1990. At the 1988 Olympic Games in Seoul, the GDR team managed to achieve second place in the overall standing. In addition to preparing for superior performance, the athletes were also trained to engage in political and ideological discussions with their opponents. The directives published in 1987 for the 1988 Olympic Winter Games stated that knowledge of the image of the enemies, and especially hatred toward imperialists, should serve as the basis for discussion with representatives of different social systems. These actions, it was felt, would help assure the achievement of both superior athletic results and honor for the fatherland.

## A Concluding Remark

The international political goals established by the GDR leadership were achieved almost completely by the athletes. There is little doubt that sport played a major role during the battle for diplomatic recognition of the state of East Germany. However, it is not easy to measure the influence of athletic prowess on the self-identification of the citizens with GDR nationalism. Although younger GDR citizens voiced criticism of the state (though they tended to adapt to the socialist state better over time), their criticism never pertained to sports. To the surprise of many West Germans following the reunification of the two German states, former GDR citizens carried with them admiration for their athletic idols, as well as admiration for the GDR sport system. This attitude still persists.

The development of sports in the GDR clearly represents the utilization of sports for political and nationalist purposes in the second half of the twentieth century. It also clearly reflects the ideological warfare between the East and West, as expressed in the relationship between the two German states.

## SUMMARY

During the nineteenth and twentieth centuries, sports in Europe were closely connected to political and nationalist elements. Both sports and nationalism were developed and promoted through identical driving forces and in the same historical contexts, and they therefore supported each other.

The starting point of this connection began with the economic and technological developments of industrialization, which revolutionized political and social conditions in Europe. Nationalist movements and modern sport organizations both used dominant structures of industrialization to gain popularity. An enormous increase in population, primarily in congested urban areas, along with modern political forms of mass organization and technical advances in communication turned out to be decisive factors in the development of both social phenomena. Both sport and nationalist movements tried to rid themselves of earlier traditional forms. Sport attempted to shake the influence of the nobility. Nationalism tried to move away from the feudal-absolute state system of early modern times. Emancipation from outside control and clear definition of an independent national culture within a limited territory were the characteristic developments of the new European states.

Under these circumstances, national frames of physical activity emerged. The German Turnen, British sports, Gaelic-Irish athletics, the Slavonic Sokol, and French gymnastics appeared at various places in Europe and gradually became integrated into national sport systems by the 1920s. Following World War II, as a direct result of the growing influence of the Olympic movement, an internationalization of the sport movement took place, leading to acceptance of the term *sport* as representative of all physical activity. At the same time, a clear demarcation of nationalist tendencies in modern sports remained. Development of the sport system in the German Democratic Republic between 1945 and 1989 serves as the best example of this. With the East versus West conflict as a background, the GDR succeeded in reaching the pinnacle of international sports. At the same time, the GDR used its success in the athletic arena to achieve diplomatic independence and to build an independent state.

The role of sport as an instrument for achieving overriding political goals can therefore be considered one of the basic elements of the sporting movement in Europe during the past 200 years.

## STUDY QUESTIONS

**1.** Discuss the reciprocal relationships between sports and nationalist political movements in Europe.

**2.** Through Jahn's Turnen movement in its initial phases, as well as through the Sokol of the Czech Republic and the Gaelic Athletic Association in Ireland, sports supplied a legal organizational framework for underground political movements. Can you justify this subordination of sports to such political movements?

**3.** Justify or reject the claim that England was the motherland of modern sports.

**4.** Have English sports really enjoyed a "march of victory" in the twentieth century at the expense of the other systems of the nineteenth century?

**5.** Provided the state's control over sports can produce results like those of the German Democratic Republic, discuss the pros and cons of such controls.

## RECOMMENDED READINGS

Brailsford, Dennis. *British Sport—A Social History.* Cambridge: Butterworth, 1992.

Carr, Gerald. "The Involvement of Politics in the Sporting Relationship of East and West Germany, 1945–1972." *Journal of Sport History* 7 (1980): 40–51.

Gerber, Ellen W. *Innovators and Institutions in Physical Education.* Philadelphia: Lea and Febiger, 1971.

Gilbert, Douglas. *The Miracle Machine.* New York: Coward, McKann and Geoghegan, 1980.

Hardman, Ken. "The Development of Physical Education in the German Democratic Republic" *Physical Education Review* 3 (1980): 121–136.

Hoberman, John M. *Sport and Political Ideology.* Austin: University of Texas, 1984.

Holt, Richard. *Sport and Society in Modern France.* Hamden: Archon, 1981.

Holt, Richard. *Sport and the British.* Oxford: Clarendon, 1989.

Lowe, Benjamin, David Kanin, and Andrew Strenk. *Sport and International Relations.* Champaign, IL: Stipes, 1978.

Mangan, J. Anthony. *The Games Ethic and Imperialism.* Harmondsworth: Viking, 1985.

Mangan, J. Anthony, and Roy B. Small, eds. *Sport, Culture, Society.* London: Spon, 1986.

McIntosh, Peter C. et al. *Landmarks in the History of Physical Education.* London: Routledge, 1981.

Mullan, M. "Opposition, Social Closure and Sport." *Sociology of Sport Journal* 12, no. 3 (1995): 268–289.

Rouse, P. "The Politics of Culture and Sport in Ireland." *International Journal of the History of Sport* 10, no. 3 (1993): 333–360.

Schmidt, Ernst. "Procedure in the GDR for Selection of Athletic Talent." *Track and Field Quarterly Review* 4 (1979): 38–39.

Seton-Watson, Hugh. *Nations and States. An Enquiry into the Origins of Nations and the Politics of Nationalism.* London: Methuen, 1977.

Strenk, Andrew. "Diplomats in Track Suits." *Journal of Sport Sociology* 4 (1980): 34–45.

Sugden, John, and A. Bairner. *Sport, Sectarianism and Society in a Divided Ireland.* Leicester: Leicester University Press, 1993.

Winkler, Klaus. "The End of the Miracle." *Coaching Director* (Belconnen, Australia) 6, no. 2 (1991): 46–47.

## NOTES

1. Upon request of the coauthors, their names are listed in alphabetical order.

2. Pehr Henrik Ling's system of Swedish gymnastics also utilized nationalistic feelings following the 1812 defeat of the Swedes by the Russians. This political slant was exploited only in order to promote acceptance of the system (which was based on health reasoning) by the authorities. As soon as his system had established itself, Ling dropped the nationalistic overtones. It is therefore not included in this chapter.

3. The British used the term "public schools" to denote schools for the wealthy gentry as opposed to earlier schools in aristocratic courts, which served only the children of the nobility. Today, "public schools" such as Eton and Rugby are considered private preparatory schools.

4. Prussia was the most important of the German states before the unification of Germany at the end of the 1860s. It was centered in the northern and eastern parts of Germany.

5. Jahn obviously did not realize that the term *Turnen* had its origin in the Latin language.

6. The independent Deutsche Turnbund in Austria had expelled Jewish members as early as 1889.

7. The word *Sokol* means falcon.

8. Whereas the ancient Greeks favored only individual sports, modern team sports developed in nineteenth-century England.

9. The term *football* referred initially to games played on foot as opposed to games played on horseback.

10. How successful that cultural export has been is illustrated by the fact that Sri Lanka (formerly Ceylon) gained the world championship in cricket in 1996.

11. The YMCA reached the United States in 1851.

12. Michael Cusack. "A Word about Irish Athletics," *United Ireland* (October 1884).

13. The bat used in hurling was carried like a rifle in the paramilitary marches that occurred during the years of the revolt.

# CHAPTER THREE

# SPORT AND PHYSICAL ACTIVITY IN MODERN AMERICA

## J. RICHARD POLIDORO

The sports, games, and physical activities of a given society are largely a reflection of its social structure and culture. Sporting forms evolve out of cultural and societal traditions, influences, and practices. Thus the development of sport and physical activity in modern America closely resembles the social, political, economic, and cultural development of the United States itself.

Swanson and Spears (1995) identify six major themes that have shaped the history of sport and physical activity in the United States.[1] One major theme is the cultural diversity of American society and historical contributions from the customs and practices of numerous countries and societies. A second theme emphasizes the uniquely American expectation of the good life and the ultimate pursuit of happiness. A third theme stems from the perceived ethical values and beliefs that have guided the daily lives of Americans. A fourth theme relates to patterns of social organization in the United States, including gender role expectations and patterns of social stratification. The fifth theme alludes to the intermixing of technology, industrialization, immigration, and urbanization and their effects on the development of sport and physical activity. Lastly, the authors believe that changing concepts and justifications of sport and physical education are a major influence.

In this chapter, the relative influence of each of these themes at various times should be apparent. Further, identification of each of the themes should provide a framework for a clearer and more concise understanding of the history of sport and physical activity in the United States.

## EUROPEAN INFLUENCES IN THE COLONIAL ERA, 1607–1783

From its earliest days, the shaping of the United States was heavily influenced by a variety of cultures immigrating initially from England and then from a host of

European countries. Settlers migrating to the new land brought with them their traditional values and beliefs. The developing colonies in the New World represented a diversity of nationalities and religious groups. Early settlers came in search of religious freedom and of economic and entrepreneurial opportunity. Whereas the first settlers in New England and some of the Mid-Atlantic colonies sought religious freedom in the New World, early settlers in the Virginia colony sought to establish an economic and commercial trading base.

## New England

The Puritan settlers in colonial New England, fleeing religious intolerance in England, were heavily influenced by the philosophy of Protestant *asceticism*. This religious philosophy stressed devotion to hard work, religious discipline, and the development of moral character associated with a virtuous and godly life. Settlers in the Massachusetts Bay Colony set out to build a model community of godly living. To them, free time, idleness, and frivolity were a waste of time and talent. Play, amusement, and leisure pursuits were seen as deviations from approved social behavior. Sports and physical activity were viewed as frivolous, profane and, in many of the colonies, sinful instruments of idleness. These activities were considered major distractions from the principles of work and divine salvation. In several New England colonies, local officials developed regulations that prohibited such sporting activities as sledding, football, dancing, swimming, bowls, ninepins, shuffleboard, and gaming for money. Above all, the New England colonies took a very strong position on the prohibition of all Sunday amusements and pastimes. All the New England colonies imposed severe penalties for participating in any form of pleasurable activity on the Sabbath.

Despite the religious opposition, participation in a variety of forms of play and other amusements became common. Children on the streets in Boston, for example, played football, cricket, rounders, and many other games. Evidence even suggests that the church leaders may actually have encouraged participation in forms of physical activity deemed to be useful and practical. Such activities as hunting, fishing, fowling, and similar activities were often associated with harvest celebrations.[2] Amusements and other pastimes were also common sights in taverns, which developed as major social centers in the colonies. The typical tavern provided a place where people could gather for conversation, food, drink, and other forms of diversion and amusement.

## The Mid-Atlantic Colonies

Early settlers in the Mid-Atlantic colonies represented a diversity of nationalities and reasons for settling in the New World. The original English settlers in the Pennsylvania and Delaware colonies came in search of religious freedom. The Society of Friends, more commonly known as Quakers, were a small group of Protestants, under the leadership of William Penn, who believed in the simple, peaceful, and good life. As news spread about the religious freedom and farming opportunities in the new land, William Penn's territory soon welcomed thousands of settlers from several other European countries including Sweden, Germany, France, Scotland, and Ireland.

Unlike the early settlers in the Pennsylvania colony, the Dutch settlers in the New York and New Jersey colonies came to the New World with a strong commercial spirit. Settlers migrating to these colonies came in search of new world trade routes. Once settled, the town of New Amsterdam rapidly became a major fur-trading post and a seaport for a major trade economy.

Just as the original Mid-Atlantic colonies differed in their reasons for settling in the New World, differences in attitudes toward and participation in sport were also evident. The Quakers of Pennsylvania held a view of sport similar to that of the New England Puritans. In 1682 the Pennsylvania Assembly banned many pastimes and amusements and strictly regulated leisure activity on the Sabbath. It was not until the early 1700s that games and other forms of leisure pursuit became socially acceptable in the Pennsylvania colony.

Dutch settlers in the New York area took a much more positive view of physical activity. Horse racing became very popular. Ninepins (bowling), ice skating, and early forms of tennis and other ball games were particularly popular in the New York area. The Dutch immigrants were noted for strong family and communal values as well as for frugality and diligence. They were also very fond of gambling, and betting became a major part of the sporting scene, particularly in horse racing and ninepins.

## The Southern Colonies

Settlers in the Virginia colony were predominantly Anglicans, following the doctrines of the Church of England. They came to the New World for economic opportunity rather than freedom of religious worship. Although the original colonists suffered extreme hardship, it did not take long before a flourishing tobacco trade developed. With an abundance of land and an entrepreneurial spirit, the colony soon entered a period of prosperity and affluence.

Although in its early days the Jamestown settlement enacted laws as restrictive as those in New England, recreational sports, games, and amusements flourished as the southern colonies expanded. Nearly all the British sports were practiced, and foxhunting became the major sport of the southern gentleman. With the issuance of King James's *Book of Sports* in 1618, followers of the Church of England were encouraged to participate in lawful recreational activities such as dancing, archery, leaping, and vaulting, even on the Sabbath, provided these activities took place after divine service.

As the southern colonies expanded, society was greatly influenced by a rapidly expanding tobacco trade, the implementation of slavery as an economic system, and the development of a class structure that was firmly in place by the beginning of the eighteenth century. The tobacco trade created a wealthy leisure class of southern plantation owners who had both the time and the wealth to develop a flourishing program of leisure pursuits. Both their leisure and their wealth were enhanced by the arrival, beginning in 1619, of Africans, whose slave labor provided necessary manpower to work the fields, as well as to work as domestic servants.

Among aristocratic plantation owners, foxhunting, horse racing, golf, lawn bowling, and dancing were extremely popular activities. Economic conditions in the South also provided opportunity for wealthy landowners to engage in a variety of forms of wagering on sporting outcomes, particularly in horse racing. We might not expect to find much sporting activity among slaves, since they would not have had the time for sport nor the permission of their owners. Yet this was not the case. Slaves often participated in sporting activities, particularly as jockeys and boxers, thus providing both entertainment and gambling opportunities for the wealthy whites.

## Tavern Games and Amusements

As conditions in the New World stabilized and settlements became larger and more defined, the early settlers gradually broke away from their earlier restraints and began to find more time for leisure pursuits and amusements. Taverns rapidly became commonplace in every city and town as centers for meeting, socializing, entertainment, and diversion from work. In many instances, tavern patrons developed their own styles of games and sports or replicated activities found in their homelands. Such leisure diversions as animal baiting, cockfighting, billiards, darts, dice, cardplaying, and skittles (later to become bowling) were particularly popular. Tavern patrons frequently combined these amusements and games with wagering and drink, leading officials in many of the colonies to establish specific laws prohibiting these "inn" games. Despite the prohibitions, though, the tavern games and amusements continued unabated.

## Early Forms of Education

As early as 1647, a system of public schools was established in the New World. In the Massachusetts Bay Colony, every community with more than fifty families was required to hire a schoolteacher and to maintain some form of elementary school. The elementary schools were often held in simple one-room facilities or in the homes of women, in the so-called dame schools.

Early elementary education concentrated on the basic subjects of religious catechism, reading, writing, and simple arithmetic. Communities with over one hundred families were required also to maintain a secondary school, known as the Latin grammar school. The purpose of the grammar school was to prepare young men for ministerial studies or, in later years, for the study of medicine or law. Girls rarely attended either the elementary or the grammar schools. Instruction in physical activity was not to be found in any of the schools.

In 1636 Harvard College was established as the colonies' first institution of higher education. It was at Harvard, and at other colleges which followed, that graduates from the secondary schools completed their training for the ministry, or, in later years, for the practice of law and medicine. Students at Harvard studied such subjects as Latin, Greek, Hebrew, logic, rhetoric, ancient history, and mathematics. Under the influence of Puritanical beliefs, physical activity was frowned upon. However, much to the dismay and displeasure of local officials, the young men at Harvard managed to indulge in a variety of sporting forms and activities. This was especially so at the yearly commencement exercises, when horse racing, games, dancing, and general merrymaking were common festivities.

As the colonies grew and became more settled, attitudes gradually changed. Interest in school programs of physical activity began to grow, especially in the middle of the eighteenth century. The Latin grammar schools, whose primary purpose was to prepare men for admission to the university, were gradually replaced by a new school structure known as the academy.

The first academy in the colonies was founded by Benjamin Franklin in 1749 in Philadelphia. Unlike the Latin grammar school, the purpose of the academy was to train young men, primarily of the middle class, in lifelong practical skills as well as in academic subjects.

The development of the academy gradually led to a concern for the physical welfare of the students. Benjamin Franklin was an early advocate of including physical activities in the academy curriculum. In his *Proposals for the Education of Youth of Pennsylvania,* he recommended frequent exercise in the form of running, leaping, wrestling, and swimming to keep young men healthy.[3] Franklin was a strong proponent of swimming.

Although the first academy opened its doors in 1749, the idea of schools providing practical preparation for life did not become widely accepted until after the Revolutionary War. Further, although the seeds for school-based instruction in physical activity were planted in Franklin's Philadelphia Academy, it was not until the early 1800s that the concept began to take hold.

## ORGANIZED SPORT AND PHYSICAL EDUCATION IN THE NINETEENTH CENTURY

The roots of America's sporting heritage can be traced, as we have seen, to the amusements and sporting activities of the colonists. Modern forms of sport and physical education in the United States, however, did not develop until the middle of the nineteenth century.

The social, political, and economic expansion of the United States that occurred immediately after the Revolution continued well into the next century. In the 1700s many colonies had grown rapidly in both population and wealth, and the influence of Puritanism in New England and elsewhere had declined. In addition to the English, several non-English groups had migrated to the colonies in large numbers. The importation of African slaves also increased greatly just prior to the Revolution. The scene was thus set for economic expansion after the war.

Although farming remained a mainstay of the economy, urban life rapidly developed. Cities grew in both size and number. As trade and commerce flourished, the economy rapidly expanded. Settlements spread from the eastern coastal communities to the far West. Canals and railroads opened the interior of the country to the swift development of both settlement and trade. The movement to the West was matched in the Northeast by rapid economic growth. The factory system became firmly established in the East. A communications revolution occurred, centering on a system of inexpensive newspapers.

Thus, as America grew from a few scattered and disunited colonies along the East coast into a unified, modern, and highly industrialized nation, the old customs and practices of colonial days were replaced by new customs, beliefs, and practices. By the end of the nineteenth century, America had developed a strong national identity and a distinctive culture.

## Early Developments in Organized Sports

American sport as we know it today began in the early 1800s when sporting activities became highly organized and clearly different from the games and pastimes of earlier days. As the century went on, the United States experienced several major cultural shifts, and the physical activity patterns of Americans changed along with everything else. Sporting patterns shifted most notably from individual participation in games and amusements to involvement in highly organized sports and athletics by both participants and spectators.

Many factors were responsible for the direction that sport took in the nineteenth century. According to Betts (1969) some of the major reasons were (1) the continued expansion of America as a rural society; (2) the growth and development of major cities; (3) the development of an industrialized society contributing to the rise of a new working class; (4) the decline of Puritan orthodoxy; (5) the English amateur sport movement; and (6) and the contributions of significant individuals who had a profound effect on the sporting scene.[4] Although certainly a contributing factor, the spirit of nationalism was never a strong force, as was the case in many European countries.

Unlike the amusements and games of the colonial years, sport became highly organized and serious business in the 1800s. It was during this time that many of America's more popular sports developed into their present form. Such imported sports as horse racing, boxing, lacrosse, handball, cricket, baseball, archery, track and field athletics, soccer, golf, tennis, squash, football, bowling, and rowing all developed into highly organized activities. Other organized sports, notably basketball and volleyball, originated in the United States.

Most noticeably, sporting forms in the 1800s took on a pattern of standardization and organization that clearly distinguished them from the games and amusements of previous times. Sports in the 1800s evidenced several new characteristics, namely (1) formal patterns of organization; (2) formalized and standardized rules and regulations; (3) statistics and record keeping; (4) the emergence of various levels of competition; (5) the need for and the training of specialists (professionals); (6) the emergence of sports media; and (7) a real division between players and spectators[5] (see Table 3.1).

**TABLE 3.1  The Characteristics of Premodern and Modern Ideal Sporting Types**

| PREMODERN SPORT | MODERN SPORT |
|---|---|
| 1. **Organization**—either nonexistent or at best informal and sporadic; contests are arranged by individuals directly or indirectly (e.g., tavern owners, bettors) involved. | 1. **Organization**—formal; institutionally differentiated at the local, regional, and national level. |
| 2. **Rules**—simple, unwritten, and based on local customs and traditions; variations exist from one locale to another. | 2. **Rules**—formal, standardized, and written; rationally and pragmatically worked out and legitimated by organizational means. |
| 3. **Competition**—locally meaningful only; no chance for national reputation. | 3. **Competition**—national and international, superimposed on local contests; chance to establish national and international reputations. |
| 4. **Role differentiation**—low among participants; loose distinction between playing and spectating. | 4. **Role differentiation**—high; emergence of specialists (professionals) and strict distinctions between playing and spectating. |
| 5. **Public information**—limited, local, and oral. | 5. **Public information**—reported on a regular basis in local newspapers, as well as national sports journals; appearance of specialized magazines, guidebooks, etc. |
| 6. **Statistics and records**—nonexistent. | 6. **Statistics and records**—kept and published on a regular basis; considered important measures of achievement; records sanctioned by national associations. |

*Source:* From Melvin Adelman, *A Sporting Time: New York City and the Rise of Modern Athletics,* copyright 1986 by the Board of Trustees of the University of Illinois. Used with the permission of the University of Illinois Press.

## Sport Becomes Serious

Accompanying these changes in the sporting forms was an emphasis on the seriousness of sport from economic, social, and philosophical perspectives. Instead of being viewed as enjoyable but casual pastimes, sports in the 1800s began to be valued for their potential contributions to both economic and social well-being. Many people began to link participation in sports with economic productivity. Others believed that sport could contribute to positive societal values.

One of the earliest and most popular sports to develop during the nineteenth century was horse racing. Although popular in the early southern and Mid-Atlantic colonies, horse racing became much more highly organized during the nineteenth century. Following the Civil War, numerous race tracks were built throughout America. With the formation of the National Trotting Association in 1870, harness racing was transformed into a modern sport. By 1890 over 300 tracks were in operation across the country, gambling activity was common, racing schedules were well established, and purses paid to winners were quite large.

Harness racing and trotting became very popular forms of racing, particularly in the cities. The rapid growth of racing, accompanied by the lack of any governing authority and by gambling and corrupt activity, led to the formation of the American Jockey Club in 1894, which became the governing body of horse racing in the United States.[6]

Another popular amusement of the colonial era that became transformed into an organized sport in the nineteenth century was boxing, more commonly known as prizefighting. Although the roots of modern boxing can be traced to the Industrial Revolution in eighteenth-century Europe, Americans in the nineteenth century developed a fascination and love for the sport. Attracting both participants and spectators, bare-knuckled fighting became the major sport of the working class. Known for its brutality, prizefighting was associated with the manly virtues of brute strength, brawn, and the ability to withstand physical punishment. It was also associated with ethnic and religious divisions within the working class, often pitting Irish immigrants against native-born Americans, Protestants against Catholics, and blacks against whites. The boxing world also had a reputation for attracting an undesirable element of society, particularly gamblers, hustlers, and occasionally dishonest officials. Because of its violent nature and its identification with betting, prizefighting was illegal in most communities and matches were often hidden from the eyes of the law. The sport remained officially illegal until the early 1920s.

The mid- to late 1800s were marked by a series of championship fights that captured the attention of millions. John L. Sullivan dominated the ring from 1882 to 1892 and gained boxing immortality when he knocked out Jake Kilrain in a seventy-five-round free-for-all in 1889. The Sullivan-Kilrain fight was the last of the bare-knuckled championship fights. The first championship match fought with boxing gloves was between Sullivan and James J. Corbett in 1892. In that match, Corbett defeated Sullivan, thereby ending the career of America's first national sports hero.

During the nineteenth century, many other team and individual sports became modernized and very popular in the United States. One of these was rowing, which originated in England. Traditionally depicted as an amateur sport for the wealthy upper class, rowing first took hold in eastern cities of the United States. The first rowing clubs were formed in the 1830s and 1840s in Philadelphia, New York, and Boston. By 1870, there were over 200 rowing clubs, some consisting of professionally paid rowers. In the late 1850s, an estimated crowd of 10,000 watched the annual regatta of two professional racing clubs in New York City. Concerned that the sport might become entirely professional and thereby lose its amateur character, the National Association of Amateur Oarsmen (NAAO) was formed in 1872. The association, which was formed as the governing body of rowing, established uniform rules and regulations. One of its major rules was the exclusion of professionals from the sport, thereby preserving its amateur status. By the late 1800s, rowing was a thoroughly modern sport, but it was limited primarily to amateur clubs and elite universities.

Another English amateur sport that was modernized in nineteenth-century America was yacht racing. This sport became very popular in the mid-1800s, and numerous boating clubs were formed throughout the country. In 1844 the New York Yacht Club was formed and soon became the premier yachting club in

America. In 1851 the club's position in the yachting scene became firmly rooted when the yacht *America* won a major international race. The prize launched the historic America's Cup races, which were successfully defended by the New York Yacht Club for over a century. Most of the yachting enthusiasts were rich Americans who had the time and the resources to sail, and the sport became associated with people of great wealth.

Although the modern version of baseball was developed in the United States in the nineteenth century, the roots of the game can be traced to the sixteenth-century English games of cricket and rounders. Subsequent modifications of these games appeared in a game called town ball and in a version of baseball played in the New York area in the mid-1840s. The popular myth that Abner Doubleday invented baseball in Cooperstown, New York, in 1839 is totally without foundation. The myth was created by Albert Spalding in an attempt to promote baseball by claiming that it was a truly American invention. Although students at Harvard may have played a form of the game as early as 1734 (Smith, 1988), the modern version of baseball began in New York City in 1845 when Alexander Cartwright, a banker, organized a group of men into a social and fraternal club. The club was called the Knickerbocker Base Ball Club, after a volunteer fire company. On two afternoons each week, members of the club, all white-collar workers, met to play a game of baseball. The charter members of the club regarded the game as a purely amateur activity, to be played for its health and recreational benefits. The club adopted the first formal rules of baseball, designed a uniform, and enacted a strict code of behavior. Between 1845 and 1855, several other clubs formed in the New York area, a trend that led to competition among the various teams. In 1846 the first recorded game of baseball was played at the Elysian Fields in Hoboken, New Jersey, between the Knickerbockers and the New York Base Ball Club. The Knickerbockers lost the four-inning contest by a score of 23 to 1.[7]

As word spread, New York's version of baseball rapidly gained in popularity, and teams sprang up in cities and towns from coast to coast. By 1860 there were over 100 clubs in the New York area alone. Factors contributing to the rapid growth of the game were undoubtedly the nature of the game itself, its social potential, its capacity to foster neighborhood and urban rivalries, and the popularity that earlier forms of the game enjoyed with American boys and men. The game eventually became so appealing that it was regarded as America's "national" game and dominated the American sport scene for decades. As early as 1856, the New York *Mercury* referred to the game as "The National Pastime."

Although initially started as a social and fraternal club for amateur players, baseball soon took on a very serious element. As the number of teams proliferated and baseball craze swept the country, players began to deviate from the original social and fraternal aspects of the game. Emphasis shifted from purely amateur competition to winning and to economic benefit. Both players and officials engaged in shady practices. Gambling and wagering were common among the spectators. Charging admission to the games became common practice. Several players began accepting payments for playing. Concerned with the lack of standardized rules, questionable practices, and unacceptable conduct, the Knickerbockers and fifteen other clubs banded together in 1858 to form the National Association of Base Ball

Players (NABBP). Its purpose was to promote the interest of baseball playing and to "regulate various matters necessary to its good government and continued respectability."[8]

Despite such attempts to regulate the amateur aspects of the game, baseball continued to grow and develop into a commercial enterprise. In 1871 the National Association of Base Ball Players was replaced by the National Association of Professional Baseball Players (NAPBP), acknowledging baseball as a professionalized sport.

The development of track and field (or athletics, as it was called in many countries) as a modern sport started in England during the nineteenth century. Although track and field contests were held in the United States as early as 1839, the sport did not gain popularity in this country until the late 1860s. From the 1850s to the 1870s, Americans were influenced by the track and field activities conducted by Scottish immigrants, who organized games and competitions on an annual basis. Although the English had developed their own version of amateur track and field athletics, the Scottish Caledonian Games were perhaps the single most important influence on track and field in America. The Caledonian Games, first held in the United States in 1853, featured numerous running and throwing events. These games provided the opportunity for competition among the various Caledonian social clubs that had developed to perpetuate the manners, customs, and athletic games of Scotland. The highly organized games often provided cash prizes, and they attracted large crowds of spectators.

The period following the Civil War was characterized by growing debate over amateur and professional sport issues. Based on concern that track and field was being dominated by professional athletes and gamblers, the New York Athletic Club was formed in 1866. Its purpose was to promote amateur competition in track and field in the New York area, modeled after the English program. In 1868 the club sponsored its first amateur track and field meet. Soon thereafter, hundreds of other athletic clubs formed throughout the United States, and the sport of track and field became firmly established. By 1880 amateur track and field athletics was in the hands of the city athletic clubs. The various athletic clubs later expanded their mission to promote competition in a variety of other amateur sports.

In 1888 fifteen of the more prominent athletic clubs joined together to form the Amateur Athletic Union (AAU) of the United States. The AAU was originally formed to deal with problems of professionalization and gambling in track and field and to organize national amateur championships in that sport. Since its inception, the AAU has been the governing body for amateur track and field in the United States. Today it serves as the governing body for many other amateur sports as well.

## Sports of American Origin

Theories abound about the evolution of American football, but most historians believe the sport represents a modification of soccer and the English game of rugby. American football evolved slowly in the nineteenth century. It first made its appearance at the college level and then grew to become one of America's most popular team sports by the end of the century. On November 6, 1869, the first intercollegiate football game in the United States was played between Rutgers and

Princeton. That early version of the game hardly resembled the game of American football as we know it today. The contest was more of a soccer match than a football game. There were twenty-five players on each team. The scoring was decided by goals and not by touchdowns and field goals. Rutgers won the game. A week later, Princeton won a rematch of the game.

Within months other universities had developed football programs, and the development of American football was on its way. In 1874 a revised set of rules was adopted by students in a game between Harvard University and McGill University of Montreal, Canada. That contest, which introduced the rules of English rugby to the game, marked the beginning of a new era in football. Rugby football allowed running with the ball, tackling, and lateral passing. Shortly thereafter, many colleges adopted the game of rugby football. In 1876, in an effort to standardize the rules and conduct of the game, four universities (Princeton, Rutgers, Yale, and Columbia) founded the Intercollegiate Football Association (IFA). Delegates to the IFA convention also decided to establish a schedule of competition and to hold a championship game at the end of the season. Three years later, in 1879, under the leadership of Walter Camp, who was a student and later a coach at Yale, the game began to evolve into an American sport that was clearly distinct from English soccer and rugby. Under Camp's influence, American football adopted a set of organized rules and regulations, the size of a team was established at eleven players, the dimensions of the playing field were set, and a standardized scoring system was developed. Today Walter Camp is widely considered the father of American football.

Two distinctly American sports evolving in the latter part of the nineteenth century were basketball and volleyball. Basketball was invented in 1891 by Dr. James Naismith at the Young Men's Christian Association Training School (later known as Springfield College) in Springfield, Massachusetts. The Young Men's Christian Association (YMCA) was a worldwide organization that grew rapidly in the United States in the years before 1900. The YMCA strongly believed in the concept of "Muscular Christianity," which held that competitive, organized sport and physical activity are major contributors to the development of Christian values and morals. In 1892 there were approximately 150 YMCA gymnasiums throughout the country.

When he first introduced the game of basketball, Naismith hung two peach baskets at the ends of the gymnasium. The game was played with a soccer ball, and a team consisted of nine players. At first the game had a set of only thirteen rules, established by Naismith. Additional rules were later established by the YMCA and by the Amateur Athletic Union. In 1895 the YMCAs formed the Athletic League of North America, which for a short time served as the governing body of all YMCA sports. A few years later, the league joined the Amateur Athletic Union.

Although originally a sport played in YMCA gymnasiums, basketball soon became popular on the high school and college levels. The first intercollegiate contest was played in 1897, and the Eastern Intercollegiate League was formed in 1902.

An adapted version of basketball was introduced that became very popular with women. In 1892 Senda Berenson, an instructor of physical activity at Smith

College, introduced the modified version of basketball, which was less strenuous than the men's version.

Like basketball, the sport of volleyball had its origins in the YMCA. The game was developed in 1895 by William Morgan, the physical director of the YMCA in Holyoke, Massachusetts. His intent was to provide an activity that was more recreational and less demanding than basketball. Volleyball was widely played in YMCAs throughout the country, but it did not become popular in schools and universities until well into the twentieth century.

Several other early forms of sporting activity took modern shape during the latter part of the nineteenth century. Tennis was introduced in the United States soon after the Civil War, and in 1881 the United States Lawn Tennis Association was organized. Golf became popular in the late 1880s, and in 1894 the United States Golfing Association was founded. Bowling, a very popular activity during colonial times, achieved modern status with the establishment of the American Bowling Congress in 1895. By the end of the century, national championships were held in numerous activities including billiards, rifle shooting, croquet, archery, canoeing, bicycling, bowling, fencing, golf, handball, and horsemanship.

## Organized Athletics on the College Level

By the middle of the nineteenth century, Americans' love of organized sports found its way into colleges and universities. By the end of the century, intercollegiate programs were found on most college and university campuses. The first recorded intercollegiate athletic event took place in 1852, when students from Harvard and Yale competed in a rowing match. The second sport to find its way into intercollegiate competition was baseball. The first intercollegiate baseball game was held in 1859 between students from Amherst College and Williams College. Amherst won the game by a score of 73 to 32. Students from Princeton and Rutgers engaged in the first intercollegiate football game in 1869, though the game was more like soccer. The first intercollegiate track and field meet was held in 1874, and the first intercollegiate swimming contest was held in 1897. In 1897 students from Yale and Pennsylvania competed in the first modern intercollegiate basketball game.

There is little question that of all the sports appearing on the intercollegiate competitive scene in the nineteenth century, football was the most influential in establishing the role of organized sports in college and university life. There is also little disagreement that while baseball was perhaps the most widely played sport on college campuses throughout the 1800s, football dominated intercollegiate competition at the end of the century and well into the twentieth century.

From its inception, intercollegiate athletics developed in the United States largely through student initiative. Competitions were, for the most part, organized and administered under student control. The students themselves organized clubs, scheduled the contests, managed the finances of the games, and determined the rules. College administrators paid little attention to the program until late in the century. Several of the sports established formal associations in an attempt to standardize rules, organize competitions, and promote the sport. In 1870 the Rowing

Association of American Colleges was established and became the governing body of that sport. In 1873 and again in 1876, the Intercollegiate Football Association was established to oversee intercollegiate football. In 1875 the Intercollegiate Association of Amateur Athletes of America (ICAAAA) was organized to oversee and promote intercollegiate track and field.

As the intercollegiate program grew, so did concern among college officials about student control of the program, the lack of restrictions and eligibility standards in most sports, and the growing violence associated with several of the sports, particularly football. Since its inception, college football was noted for its violent nature. Because of the rough and physical way in which the games were played, there were many deaths and injuries. By the late 1890s, college football had also developed a commercial aspect. Financed by lucrative gate receipts, star players were often handsomely rewarded with free tuition and room and board. By the end of the century, football programs were hiring coaches and building stadiums.

Toward the end of the century, several institutions called for the control and management of intercollegiate athletics by college administrators. There is little doubt that the rise of football played a major role in this move. In 1884 an unsuccessful attempt was made to establish an agreement between students and college administrators from twenty-two institutions relating to rules and governance of intercollegiate competition. In 1885 Harvard briefly banned football on the premise that the game was demoralizing and extremely dangerous. But other college administrators were quick to realize the positive and tangible benefits of intercollegiate sports, especially football, to the colleges. In 1895 faculty representatives from seven schools in the Midwest formed the Intercollegiate Conference of Faculty Representatives, thereby establishing control over their collegiate programs. Also known as the Western Conference, the association later became known as the Big Ten Conference. However, it was not until early in the twentieth century that men's intercollegiate athletic programs came under the control of college and university officials.

Women at Vassar, Smith, and Wellesley participated in a variety of physical activities and sports. Although an increasing number of women engaged in sports during the later part of the nineteenth century, their participation was rarely seen as important or desirable. For the most part, the Victorian attitudes of the era discouraged females from participating in strenuous physical activity, as it was seen as less than "ladylike." The medical community also believed that highly competitive sports would harm a female's reproductive system. Aggressive and highly competitive forms of sports were therefore shunned.

However, despite these attitudes, women did participate in such sports as archery, croquet, golf, bicycling, and tennis by the late 1880s. These activities were often viewed as feminine; they did not require immodest clothing, and they were nonvigorous. A few of the more aggressive women, particularly those attending the women's colleges, engaged in more strenuous forms of activity. Nevertheless, although women rowed, hiked, rode horseback, and skated on several of these campuses before the end of the century, they rarely engaged in activities of a competitive nature.

## The Development of Professional Sports

Perhaps no issue was so pronounced on the nineteenth century sport scene than the clash that developed after the Civil War over questions of amateurism and professionalism. While amateur sports mushroomed, the commercialization of sport and the presence of athletes "playing for pay" also began to permeate the American sport scene, particularly in the popular spectator sports on the college and community levels. Debate raged throughout the country. Professionalism was seen by many as a major threat to the integrity of amateur sporting values. Nevertheless, professional sports were firmly established in the United States by the end of the century.

From the time of their original appearance on the American sport scene, horse racing and boxing were commonly associated with commercialism and professionalism. Wagering, charging admission fees, large crowds of spectators, and in many instances fat payments and prizes to jockeys and prizefighters were common in both these sports. Jockeys and owners of winning horses were often rewarded with lucrative purses. Prizefighters were also handsomely rewarded, as illustrated by the John L. Sullivan–Jake Kilrain fight in 1889. That match was fought not only for the championship title but also for a winning purse of $20,000 and a diamond belt.

Horse racing and prizefighting were not the only sports in which participants received payment. Even before 1871, athletes were known to play for pay in several sports. Payments were often made under the table and in secret. Or the players were offered well-paying jobs that required little effort. Of all of the modern sports emerging during the nineteenth century, baseball was the one that contributed the most to Americans' acceptance of professional sports.

Originally a purely amateur sport, baseball rapidly developed into a commercial business, and playing became a career for many players. By the late 1860s, baseball was so popular that many clubs began charging admission, and several athletes received secret payments for their services. In 1869 all that changed when the Cincinnati Red Stockings fielded for the first time an all-salaried team. Although this club was not the first to pay players, it was the first to have a truly all-salaried team in baseball. Salaries ranged from $500 to $1400 a season. The establishment of the Cincinnati Red Stockings as a professional team brought the amateur-professional controversy to a head. In 1871 the National Association of Professional Base Ball Players (NAPBBP) was formed as an official body to represent professional baseball. The NAPBBP broke away from the National Association of Baseball Ball Players (NABBP), which advocated preservation of the amateur nature of the game. This development marked the beginning of professional major league baseball in the United States.

As other teams were formed, baseball clubs became dominated by commercial and professional interests. Some clubs financed their operations by selling shares of stock, whereas others depended exclusively on gate receipts. As the popularity of the sport grew and the commercial aspect became more widespread, the first baseball league, the National League of Professional Base Ball clubs, was formed in 1876. The original league consisted of eight teams representative of large cities. In 1882 clubs from other big cities banded together to establish the American Base Ball

Association, later known as the American League. In 1903 the two professional leagues agreed to settle player and franchise disputes by playing a World Series.[9]

As professional baseball became firmly established, the professionalization of other sports soon followed. In 1892 William (Pudge) Heffelfinger became the first known professional football player when the Allegheny Athletic Association paid him $500 to play a single game against the Pittsburgh Athletic Club. Thirteen years later, the first game between professional football teams was played in Latrobe, Pennsylvania. By the time of World War I, professional sports were firmly established in the United States. Besides baseball and football, sports such as basketball, golf, tennis, and ice hockey gained professional status early in the twentieth century.

## Early Development of Physical Activity Programs in the Schools

As the United States entered the nineteenth century, the academies of the earlier decades continued to gain popularity and did so until well into the middle of the century. By 1850 at least 6,000 academies were known to exist. Some of them admitted women. However, compulsory education for both boys and girls gradually became a recognized necessity, as it was in Europe, and by the middle of the century the universal free public high school began to replace the colonial grammar school and private academy systems of education. Elementary, or so-called common schools, and secondary schools began to appear on a very limited basis. The purpose of the public schools was to provide an education for all that focused on meeting the needs of individual children. By 1856 public high schools existed in Boston, New York City, Portland (Maine), Philadelphia, Baltimore, and several other large cities. By the end of the century, the number of tax-supported public schools for children and adolescents had increased dramatically throughout the country; and the number of public high schools had risen to approximately 800.

While the concept of a free and compulsory education was growing, the enrollment of girls in public schools took a little longer to fully implement. Girls often received education in the free common schools, which later developed into the modern elementary school. Boston opened a high school for girls in 1826 but closed it two years later. Although the education of women was not considered a necessity, the early part of the nineteenth century did see the development of several private colleges for women. By the middle of the century, female seminaries such as Mount Holyoke, Vassar, and Elmira had been founded.

Before 1850, only a handful of schools incorporated programs of physical activity in their curricula. Benjamin Franklin's theories on the importance of physical activity, introduced at his Philadelphia Academy in the late 1700s, did not take hold elsewhere. It was not until a new wave of immigrants arrived in the United States in the early 1800s that the impetus for school programs of physical activity began to be taken seriously. German immigrants in the early 1800s, heavily influenced by the gymnastics system of physical training devised by Friederich Jahn and the German *Turnverein* movement, brought with them their love and fervor for gymnastics. Settling predominantly in Midwestern cities, the Turners were instrumental in developing exercise halls and playgrounds for practicing their system of gymnastics. The first Turnverein in the United States was established in Cincinnati in 1848. More than 150 Turner societies flourished in the United States by 1880.

Fleeing political persecution in Germany, three of Jahn's closest followers, Charles Follen, Charles Beck, and Francis Lieber, were instrumental in introducing the German system of gymnastics to America. Charles Follen (1796–1840) arrived in Philadelphia in 1824 and found employment as an instructor of German at Harvard. He established a program of German gymnastics there the next year and the first college gymnasium in the country. Follen established a similar program a year later at the Boston Gymnasium, which was the first public outdoor gymnasium to be built in the United States. Other colleges rapidly followed the lead of Harvard, and by 1830 gymnasiums could be found at Yale, Brown, Amherst, and Williams. Similarly, private gymnasiums were opened in several eastern cities.

In 1825 Charles Beck (1798–1866) was employed as an instructor of German gymnastics and Latin at the Round Hill School in Northampton, Massachusetts. The Round Hill School, a private preparatory school for boys, was established in 1823 by Joseph Cogswell and George Bancroft. Through the efforts of Cogswell, Bancroft, and Beck, the Round Hill School was the first school in the United States to require exercise and activity as an essential part of its total school curriculum. Beck's program of exercise included gymnastics, swimming, wrestling, dancing, boxing, and other games and sports such as baseball and archery.

Francis Lieber (1800–1872), immigrating to the United States in 1827, succeeded Follen at the Boston Gymnasium. While serving as an instructor of gymnastics there, Lieber also opened the first swimming pool in the United States.

These three men and other followers of the German Turnverein movement planted the seeds for the development of physical education in American schools. In 1825 New York City high schools were offering their students instruction in gymnastics. In 1853 Boston became the first U.S. city to require a program of daily physical activity for schoolchildren. Many others followed suit. German gymnastics were introduced in the schools in Cincinnati in 1860 and in many other cities in the Midwest during the next two decades. The Turners, who objected to the stress placed on games and sports in American society, strongly believed that the major purpose of German gymnastics in the public schools should be to provide for the physical, social, and moral training of children and youth.

To meet the need for trained instructors in the German system, the Normal School of the North American Gymnastic Union was established in New York City in 1866. Its graduates, trained in the German system, became instructors in various Turnvereins and public schools throughout the country. By the late 1880s, the German system of gymnastics had become firmly rooted in many of the nation's public schools and major Turner festivals were held in numerous cities throughout the country.

While the German system of gymnastics and other isolated forms of exercise programs were making their appearances in the schools for boys and young men, interest in exercise and physical activity was also developing in women's seminaries and academies. A handful of private schools for women, mostly in the Northeast, began to experiment with a variety of forms of light exercise. As early as 1823, Catherine Beecher (1800–1878) was expounding the value of exercise for women. In her *A Course of Calisthenics for Young Ladies,* published in 1831, Beecher was a strong advocate of exercise for women. Rejecting the German system as too strenuous for ladies, her program included lessons in physiology as well as a system of light exercises she called *calisthenics.*[10] Beecher founded the Hartford Female Seminary for women in 1823 and a similar school in the 1830s in Cincinnati, Ohio. At both these institutions, she promoted the need for programs of daily exercise for women. She later published a second book, *A Manual of Physiology and Calisthenics for Schools and Families* (1856).

Similarly, Mary Lyon, founder of the Mount Holyoke Female Seminary (1836), later known as Mt. Holyoke College, became a pioneer advocate of a program of daily exercise to promote the health and welfare of the women attending that institution.

## The Development of Physical Education in Education

In 1832 John Warren, a professor of anatomy at Harvard University, published a philosophical book entitled *The Importance of Physical Education.* Although his book never attracted much interest, several individuals by the middle of the nineteenth century began to experiment with a variety of forms of physical activity based on belief in the health and wellness benefits of systematic exercises. One such person was Dioclesian Lewis. Heavily influenced by the philosophy espoused by Catherine Beecher, Dio Lewis (1823–1888), developed a system of light gymnastics that he called the "new gymnastics." Unlike the German system of gymnastics, which stressed development of strength, Lewis's program stressed development of agility, grace of movement, flexibility, and general health and posture. His program, which was extremely popular from the 1850s through the 1870s, incorporated a variety of exercises using Indian clubs, handheld wands, rings, and light dumbbells. In 1861, Lewis founded the Normal Institute for Physical Education in Boston, which trained both men and women to teach his system. It was thus the first physical education teacher training institution in the United States. In 1862 he published a book entitled *The New Gymnastics for Men, Women, and Children.* The Normal Institute closed in 1868, but approximately 500 individuals had completed its ten-week training program.

In 1866 California became the first state to pass a law requiring a program of physical exercise in the public elementary and secondary schools. The law required that all students receive instruction in health, with due attention given to physical exercises that were conducive to the health and vigor of the body, as well as the mind. The law further specified that primary school children receive a minimum of five minutes twice each day for gymnastics and breathing exercises.[11]

Although the German system of gymnastics was firmly rooted in many public elementary and secondary schools, the Pehr Ling system of *Swedish gymnastics* began to find its way into schools in the later part of the century. Unlike the German system, which stressed heavy apparatus work and muscular strength training, the Swedish system focused on light, rhythmic exercise and the medicinal value of exercise. In the Swedish system, health was viewed as the harmonious relationship of the nervous, respiratory, and circulatory systems. In 1883 Hartvig Nissen introduced the Swedish system at the Swedish Health Institute in Washington, D.C. In 1889 Mary Hemenway founded the Boston Normal School of Gymnastics, which stressed Swedish gymnastics. Nils Posse (1862–1895) also led in the development of the Swedish system and was very instrumental in developing the Posse Normal School, which opened in 1890 to train teachers in Swedish gymnastics. In 1885 the Boston public schools began to experiment with the Swedish system of gymnastics, and by 1890 the system was formally adopted for all the public schools in that city. In 1890 Edward Hartwell (1850–1922), who had been the director of the gymnasium at Johns Hopkins University from 1885 to 1890, was hired as the city's director of physical training.

## Physical Training in Colleges and Universities

Just as programs of physical activity were being incorporated in the public school systems throughout the country, significant developments were also occurring on the college and university level. In 1861 Amherst College appointed Edward Hitchcock as professor of hygiene and physical education. Edward Hitchcock (1828–1911), a medical doctor, remained at Amherst for over fifty years. Students under his supervision were required to attend hygiene and exercise classes, which included both light and heavy gymnastics, marching, running, and a variety of sporting activities such as boxing and baseball. A strong believer in the health and physiological benefits of exercise, Hitchcock became a leader in the development of *anthropometrics*.[12] Throughout his career, Hitchcock maintained records of changes in height, weight, chest girth, arm girth, lung capacity, and strength in students participating in his program. In 1885 Hitchcock became the first president of the American Association for the Advancement of Physical Education (AAAPED), which was organized to promote the emerging field of physical education.

Similarly, in 1879, Harvard College appointed Dudley A. Sargent, a medical doctor, as director of its new Hemenway Gymnasium. Dudley Sargent (1849–1924) served as professor of physical training at Harvard until 1919. While serving in this capacity, he developed an extensive, health-related program that focused on gymnastics, anthropometric measurements, and *physical training*. Unlike other systems of physical training, Sargent's system prescribed individual programs of exercise based on physical examination and evaluation of each person. His measurement and evaluation system included anthropometric measurements, strength tests, lung capacity tests, and examination of the heart before and after exercise. While at Harvard, Sargent designed numerous pieces of developmental equipment and machines that were the forerunners of today's exercise machines. In 1881 he founded the Sargent Normal School, which provided both a practical and a theoretical curriculum for individuals interested in becoming teachers of physical training. Although coeducational, the school prepared women instructors almost exclusively.

Following the programs established at Amherst and Harvard, other institutions appointed medical doctors to direct their gymnasium programs. Such institutions as Yale, Oberlin, Johns Hopkins University, and Columbia soon developed physical training programs, and many established normal schools for the training of physical education teachers.

Meanwhile, in 1889, the Young Men's Christian Association Training School in Springfield, Massachusetts, appointed Luther H. Gulick (1865–1918) as its supervisor of physical training. Strongly influenced by the concept of muscular Christianity, Gulick was totally dedicated to the use of organized games and sports as a major educational focus. He was especially fond of team sports. Gulick later became the director of physical training in the public schools of New York City and was instrumental in establishing the Playground Association of America.

Following the earlier philosophies of Catherine Beecher and Mary Lyon, programs of physical activity also found their way into several women's colleges in the later part of the nineteenth century. In 1861 Vassar College established a special school of physical training based on the belief that good health was essential for the development of women's mental and moral powers. The Vassar program required students to participate in Swedish calisthenics, some modified after the works of Dio Lewis, and in simple feminine sports such as archery, croquet, boating, gardening, and walking. In 1866 first-year women at Vassar formed the Laurel and Abenakis baseball clubs, with the support of a female physician who thought exercise for women was essential to good health.[13] Other colleges followed suit. Women at Wellesley College were required to take exercises and sports, with rowing and winter sports being particularly popular.

## The Battle of the Systems

By the late 1800s, several well-known educators and scientists were emphasizing the value of physical education. At the same time, wide variations existed in the programs of exercise and physical training found in the nation's public schools and colleges. Vigorous discussion and debate developed as to which system of exercise was best for the physical training and welfare of American children and youth. Although numerous educators advocated the German system of heavy gymnastics, others strongly supported the Swedish system. Still others believed in a French system of exercise. In the 1890s Francois Delsarte introduced the Delsarte System of Physical Culture, which was based on the belief that certain physical exercises that stress poise, grace, and beauty are conducive to better acting and singing. Besides the followers of the German, Swedish, and French systems, other educators believed strongly in the programs of physical training and hygiene developed by Sargent and Hitchcock. Still others were committed to the value of sports and organized games, which had become an integral part of intercollegiate programs by the late 1800s.

In 1889 a major conference called A Conference in the Interest of Physical Training was held in Boston that addressed the benefits of the various systems of exercise. The Boston Conference considered the various systems of physical exercise and was instrumental in bringing them to the attention of both educational leaders and the general public. Although most of the widely held views were expressed and discussed, most notably missing from attendance at the conference were representatives of the organized sports movement. In addressing the conference, Dudley Sargent's remarks are most interesting:

> What America needs is the happy combination which the European nations are trying to effect; the strength-giving qualities of the German Gymnasium, the active and energetic properties of the English sports, the grace and suppleness acquired from French calisthenics, and the beautiful poise and mechanical precision of the Swedish free movements, all regulated, systematized, and adapted to our peculiar needs and institutions.[14]

Although heavily discussed and debated among the conference's 2000 participants, the question of which system was most appropriate for America would not be answered until early in the twentieth century.

## TRANSFORMATION TO AN AMERICAN SYSTEM OF SPORT AND PHYSICAL EDUCATION IN THE TWENTIETH CENTURY

As the United States entered the twentieth century, organized forms of sport and physical activity were firmly entrenched in American society. As reported in an article in *Harper's Weekly* in 1895:

> Ball matches, football games, tennis tournaments, bicycle races, [and] regattas, have become part of our national life, and are watched with eagerness and discussed with enthusiasm and understanding by all manner of people, from the day laborer to the millionaire.[15]

Just as societal events of the nineteenth century were instrumental in shaping the direction sport took during that century, so did events of the twentieth century influence the direction that sport and physical education took during the 1900s. The twentieth century in the United States was marked by several significant and profoundly influential foreign and domestic events. On the international level, wars and ethnic skirmishes occurred almost without interruption. From 1945 until well into the 1980s, the United States engaged the Soviet Union in a period of hostile diplomacy designed to contain the spread of communism. A major part of the Cold War was marked by the race for nuclear supremacy.

On the domestic level, numerous economic, technological, and sociological events brought sweeping changes to life in the United States. During the early years of the twentieth century, Americans continued to move from the country to the cities and then to the suburbs. The nation's economy had shifted from an emphasis on the production of goods to a focus on mass consumption and leisure.

The changing nature of work, the increase in personal income, a shorter work-week accompanied by an increase in leisure time, and the quest for the good life contributed enormously to economic prosperity in the early 1900s. Although the entire century is generally characterized as prosperous, the economy was nevertheless marked by a series of ups and downs in productivity and economic wealth. The economy entered a period of spectacular growth in the 1920s, only to be followed by the stock market crash of 1929 and the Great Depression of the 1930s. Following the depression, the economy experienced its greatest growth immediately following World War II.

The twentieth century was also marked by significant advances in science and technology. New forms of transportation developed with the advent of the automobile, the airplane, and rockets to outer space. Americans enjoyed new forms of communication and entertainment with the major expansion of the print media and the introduction of radio, television, and movies. Most recently, the introduction of computer technology has set the stage for the twenty-first century.

The twentieth century in the United States also saw dramatic and profound changes and advances in civil and human rights. The role of the American woman changed dramatically in the 1920s. The Nineteenth Amendment to the Constitution, enacted in 1920, gave all women the right to vote. This legislation was soon followed by new opportunities for education and careers for women. In *Brown v. Board of Education of Topeka*, decided in 1954, racial segregation became illegal in all public schools in the United States. The Civil Rights Act of 1964 banned discrimination in employment, voter registration, and in all public accommodations. During the later part of the century, the drive for equality that began initially with women and African Americans spread to other minority groups. Today, laws at various governmental levels prohibit discrimination based on race, color, sex, religion, age, and disability.

Without question, the social, cultural, and economic events and changes of the twentieth century greatly influenced developments in sports and physical education. Most of the sports that developed in the nineteenth century grew and continued to prosper during the twentieth century. In the early 1900s, the most heavily promoted sports were football, baseball, and basketball. By the 1920s both amateur and professional sports of all kinds flourished, and organized sports rapidly achieved prominence in American life equal to that of business, religion, education, and politics. The years between 1919 and 1930 have been called the golden age of sports. It was during this period that Americans developed an obsession with sports. The public's fascination with sports, coupled with a desire for economic profit, led to the creation and marketing of spectator sports on the amateur, intercollegiate, and professional levels. Beyond the commercial motives was the excitement of competition and winning. Americans in the twentieth century were ready to be entertained, and entertainment through sport became big business.

As the popularity of professional and amateur sports soared, Americans developed a strong admiration for individual accomplishment. Sports superstars won the adulation of the public. The stars of sports' golden age in the 1920s included Red Grange, Knute Rockne, and George Halas (football), Bobby Jones (golf), Jack Dempsey and Joe Louis (boxing), Bill Tilden (tennis), and the immortal Babe Ruth in baseball.

While organized sports flourished on both the amateur and professional levels, compulsory physical education and interscholastic athletics became integral to the public school curriculum. Outside the school program, community sports programs became commonplace as the various cities and towns developed a variety of sport activities for both youth and adults. Throughout the twentieth century, Americans continued to view sports and recreational activities as having beneficial value to both the individual and society.

During times of war and international crisis, concern for the fitness of young men undoubtably contributed to the emphasis placed on sport and exercise. World War I had a widespread effect when it became known that approximately one-third of the men called into military service could not meet the minimum physical standards. The same concerns arose during World War II and the Korean War. Frederick L. Paxson had offered a different view in 1917, when he suggested that America's fascination with and acceptance of sports was due to an increase in leisure time, an increase in the number and extent of professional and amateur sports organizations, an increase in affluence, advances in technology, a dramatic increase in publicity and promotion, and greater possibilities of fame and fortune.[16]

## Expansion of Professional Sports

Whereas the basic organizational patterns for professional sports had been established in the late 1800s, the twentieth century saw the proliferation of professional sports. Professional baseball was firmly established by 1900, and boxing and horse racing remained extremely popular, but numerous other sports became professionalized during the 1900s. As early as 1916, the Professional Golf Association (PGA) was established and was holding professional championships. The Ladies Professional Golf Association (LPGA) formed in 1949. The National Hockey League was founded in Canada in 1917, with franchises locating in Boston, New York, Detroit, and Chicago in 1926. In 1920 the American Professional Football Association, which changed its name to the National Football League (NFL) in 1922, was formed when eleven teams were granted charters. A well-known Native American by the name of Jim Thorpe became president of the newly formed association. In 1933 the NFL held its first championship play-off game. In 1936 it conducted its first draft of college players. By the 1970s professional football had overtaken professional baseball in popularity among American spectators.

The seeds of professional basketball were planted in 1925 with the formation of the American Basketball League, which was dominated by the Original Celtics. The Original Celtics had been formed as a semi-professional team in 1914. Along with two all-black teams, the New York Renaissance (Rens) and the Harlem Globetrotters, it led professional basketball during the late 1920s and 1930s. The National Basketball League, organized in 1938, developed into the National Basketball Association (NBA) in 1949. It was not until the late 1950s that professional basketball blossomed and became firmly established on the American sporting scene. In 1978 the Women's Professional Basketball League (WBL) was formed, only to disband for financial reasons in 1982. In 1997 professional basketball for women returned with the establishment of the Women's National Basketball Association (WNBA).

In 1943, when major league baseball was faced with a severe shortage of players due to the war efforts, a group of entrepreneurs created the first professional baseball league for women. Four teams formed in the initial year of operation, and in 1944 the All American Girls Professional Baseball League expanded to six teams. By 1946 eight teams were playing 110 to 120 games per season.

The elite amateur sport of tennis became professionalized as early as 1926, and by the early 1970s it had become heavily commercialized. By the later part of the century, most organized team and individual sports became professionalized, including wrestling, auto racing, bowling, soccer, skiing, figure skating, and track and field.

During the latter part of the twentieth century, many professional sports acquired a distinctly international flavor. Foreign athletes have been attracted to leagues in the United States in a variety of professional sports. Similarly, many Americans have been lured with lucrative contracts to professional sport leagues rapidly developing in other countries. During the last quarter of the century, professional sports in the United States have also been plagued with problems and issues revolving around franchising, expansion, player contracts, and free agency. By the late 1980s, salaries of professional athletes reached astronomical heights with individual player contracts often amounting to millions of dollars. Many of the professional issues resulted in player strikes. The first strike in professional baseball took place in 1971, and a major strike curtailed a large part of the 1995 season. Professional football players went on strike in 1974. The first player strike in the history of the National Hockey League occurred in 1991.

## Intercollegiate Athletics

Sport and athletic competitions became integral to college life in the twentieth century. A myriad of conferences and governing bodies were established out of necessity to regulate competition. In 1900 football was by far the most popular sport on American college campuses. The rugged nature of football, however, which had resulted in numerous injuries and deaths, prompted many institutions to discontinue the sport. Others urged that football be either reformed or abolished. Responding to the call for reform to make the sport safer, President Theodore Roosevelt convened a White House conference in 1905 that was attended by many college athletic officials. The conference led to development of a safer game of football as well as to the formation of the Intercollegiate Athletic Association of the United States (IAAUS). The IAAUS, officially constituted in 1906, was formed to oversee the governance of intercollegiate athletics. In forming this association, the founders transferred control of intercollegiate athletics from the students to the institutions. The original governing body of the IAAUS had a membership of thirty-eight institutions. In 1910 the IAAUS was replaced by the National Collegiate Athletic Association (NCAA). During the first few years of its existence, the NCAA was primarily a discussion group and rules-making body. However, in 1921 the association held its first national championship competition in track and field. Gradually, more championships were added. Today the NCAA is the primary governing body of all intercollegiate athletic programs in the country. Its activities range from establishing policies, rules, and regulations for both men's and women's programs and athletes to sponsoring national championships in all sports. Its membership consists of all sizes and types of institutions from large state universities to small private and church-affiliated colleges. Through the NCAA, the member institutions maintain the principle of institutional control of, and responsibility for, all intercollegiate sports in the United States.

The 1900s also brought a slowly changing philosophy regarding the value of sports and exercise for women. Gradually, the Victorian philosophy of the nineteenth century gave way to the view that exercise and physical activity made a woman healthier for housework and childbearing. In the early 1900s, numerous athletic clubs and associations for women emerged throughout the country, and organized competitions were staged in such recreational activities as tennis, golf, biking, archery, bowling, and fencing. Likewise, women's colleges began to offer instruction not only in the traditional "ladies" sports, but in team sports as well. In many colleges, such sports as basketball, volleyball, golf, field hockey, and track and field were taught under the auspices of physical education. However, despite the exposure to new forms of sport and games, competitive intercollegiate programs for women did not emerge until the early 1950s. Even then, competitions between women's teams consisted of play days, sports days, and telegraphic meets. This form of competition was very different from the approach of the men's program, which was characterized by national and regional championships, athletic scholarships, exposure to the mass media, and gate receipts. The primary purpose of the women's programs was to allow as many women to play as possible and to let them have fun.

Initially, the organizing body of women's athletics was the Women's Division of the National Amateur Athletic Federation (NAAF). For several years this organization strongly supported the view that women's programs should remain distinctly different from men's programs. However, the women's programs gradually drifted more toward the model adopted by their male counterparts. By the mid-1970s, women's programs had endorsed a model embracing highly organized intercollegiate athletics and national championships. In 1971 the Association for Intercollegiate Athletics for Women (AIAW) became the official governing body of all intercollegiate programs for women. In 1982 the AIAW merged with the National Collegiate Athletic Association (NCAA). Today the NCAA remains the official governing body for all intercollegiate athletic programs for women, as well as for men.

## Breaking the Racial Barriers

During the early part of the twentieth century, racial discrimination and segregation in sport were common practices in the United States. Participation by black athletes in professional sports, outside of boxing and horse racing, was virtually nonexistent during the first half of the twentieth century. Although a handful of black players were members of white baseball clubs in the late 1800s, blacks were excluded from professional baseball and other sports toward the end of the century. Several professional Negro leagues and teams were established for black athletes, most notably in baseball and basketball. Blacks formed their own baseball league in 1920 with the establishment of the National Association of Colored

Professional Baseball Clubs. The New York Rens and the Harlem Globetrotters were two very strong and well-known African American professional basketball teams in the mid-1920s and the 1930s.

The National Football League opened its doors to an African American in 1920 when the Akron Indians signed Frederick Douglas. Later, though, the National Football League barred black players from playing from 1934 to 1946. It was not until the late 1940s that the racial barrier in professional sports was firmly broken. In 1946 Branch Rickey, owner of the Brooklyn Dodgers, signed Jackie Robinson to a professional baseball contract, and in April 1947 Robinson became the first black to play in major league baseball. With the signing of Jackie Robinson, the doors to integrated professional sports finally swung open. Other players of color soon found their way into major league baseball. In 1950 the National Basketball Association became integrated with the signing of Nat "Sweetwater" Clifton and Chuck Cooper. Cooper was the first black player drafted into the league. Clifton was the first black to sign a professional contract. In 1948 Bill Spiller became the first black golfer to play in a major Professional Golf Association tournament. In 1957 the Boston Bruins hockey team signed Willie O'Ree. That same year Althea Gibson became the first black to win the United States women's tennis championship. She also became the first African American to win the championship at Wimbledon. In 1997 21-year-old multiracial Eldrick "Tiger" Woods won the prestigious Masters Tournament for professional golfers.

On the college and amateur level, segregation and racial discrimination against black athletes paralleled the professional situation. Although a small number of racially integrated colleges and universities provided the opportunity for individuals of color to participate with whites in organized sports, segregation of the black athlete was predominant. The emergence of black colleges in the United States provided the greatest opportunity for blacks to participate in organized sports. Popular sports among blacks on the college and amateur levels included football, baseball, and track and field. Black colleges encouraged black women to participate especially in track and field, whereas white women's colleges often stressed more "feminine" activities such as golf and tennis. Thus, while there were a handful of desegregated programs, integrated sports on the intercollegiate level were not available to most blacks until the late 1940s.

In 1967 Harry Edwards, a black sociology instructor at San Jose State College, organized a protest movement in an attempt to focus attention on the plight of African American athletes. Among other things, Edwards called for a boycott by black athletes of the 1968 Olympic Games and for the desegregation of the New York Athletic Club. Although the Olympic boycott failed, the New York Athletic Club opened its doors to blacks. The movement further mobilized the unrest and militancy among blacks and black athletes that surfaced in racial protests on the nation's college and university campuses in the late 1960s.

## Youth Sports Programs

Accompanying the proliferation of professional and college sports was a dramatic increase in community sports programs for youth, particularly during the later half of the twentieth century. In the early 1900s, many educators and religious leaders espoused the health and social values of play and physical activity for youth. Individuals such as Luther Gulick, G. Stanley Hall, John Dewey, and Edward Thorndike stressed the importance of play and exercise as important learning tools. Subsequently, cities and towns throughout the country developed an increasing number of parks and playgrounds. In 1906, Gulick founded the Playground Association of America. The Boys Club of America was formed soon after. Other organizations such as the YMCA, the Amateur Athletic Union, and the Catholic Youth Organization (CYO), as well as a number of sports-related agencies and municipal recreational associations, contributed significantly to the increasing development of youth programs.

Since the introduction of Little League baseball in 1939, organized youth sports programs and leagues have developed in a number of sports. Today, organized youth programs can be found in soccer, football, ice hockey, basketball, swimming, gymnastics, and tennis, as well as many other sports. Pop Warner football, Pee Wee hockey, Biddy basketball, and youth soccer are particularly popular. It has been estimated that in the mid-1980s, approximately 35 million boys and girls between the ages of six and sixteen participated in some kind of formalized sports program outside the school setting.[17]

In 1988 the Institute for the Study of Youth Sports at Michigan State University conducted a comprehensive survey of the activity patterns of American youth between the ages of ten and eighteen. (Ewing & Seefeldt, 1989). Over 8,000 youth participated in the study. Fifty-one percent of the survey participants were girls, and 49 percent were boys. The study examined the activity preferences and patterns of these young people both inside and outside of school settings. Table 3.2 shows the findings of the study regarding the percentage of children who participated in each sport, broken down by age. The survey included those who either joined or planned to join selected nonschool teams during the 1987–1988 school year. Clearly, baseball, basketball, swimming, volleyball, and soccer were high on the list of preferred sports.

## A Uniquely American System of Physical Education

As the United States entered the twentieth century, the schools offered a variety of programs stressing physical training, gymnastics, and/or games and sports. The Boston Conference of 1889 had explored the benefits of the various systems of gymnastics and physical training, but it had not reached consensus as to what type of school program was most appropriate for American children. While the issue was still being debated at the turn of the century, a new concept of physical education began to emerge.

During the early years of the twentieth century, education was being greatly influenced by a change in philosophy. This new philosophy focused primarily on the need to design educational experiences that would meet the needs and interests of each individual child, and on the development of desirable social and behavioral outcomes. This new approach viewed education as a "doing" process, based on the belief that the individual learns best by doing. It also believed that for

**TABLE 3.2   Sports Children Do in Their Free Time, by Chronological Age**

| | 10 | 11 | 12 | 13 | 14 | 15 | 16 | 17 | 18 | Mean Percentage |
|---|---|---|---|---|---|---|---|---|---|---|
| | | | | | CHRONOLOGICAL AGE | | | | | |
| Archery | 8.4 | 7.6 | 7.0 | 5.3 | 5.6 | 5.9 | 4.9 | 6.5 | 6.9 | 6.2 |
| Baseball | 28.6 | 27.5 | 26.0 | 25.0 | 20.4 | 18.9 | 20.3 | 18.0 | 16.4 | 22.2 |
| Basketball | 29.7 | 35.0 | 34.5 | 34.7 | 30.0 | 27.7 | 28.6 | 26.3 | 24.9 | 30.2 |
| Bowling | 19.6 | 28.2 | 20.9 | 18.0 | 16.3 | 17.8 | 20.7 | 21.8 | 23.0 | 20.7 |
| Cross Country | 8.6 | 6.9 | 9.0 | 5.5 | 5.4 | 5.6 | 5.0 | 3.8 | 5.8 | 6.1 |
| Field Hockey | 5.1 | 4.6 | 4.2 | 2.2 | 2.3 | 2.6 | 1.3 | 1.2 | 2.6 | 2.7 |
| Figure Skating | 11.0 | 13.4 | 7.9 | 5.8 | 6.8 | 5.5 | 5.6 | 6.4 | 3.3 | 7.5 |
| Flag Football | 10.6 | 11.5 | 11.0 | 9.6 | 8.8 | 7.7 | 11.4 | 10.2 | 10.8 | 9.9 |
| Tackle Football | 18.3 | 24.9 | 23.2 | 18.8 | 17.8 | 17.7 | 17.3 | 18.3 | 17.7 | 19.2 |
| Golf | 11.9 | 16.2 | 12.0 | 7.9 | 7.7 | 8.6 | 7.7 | 8.9 | 6.7 | 9.9 |
| Gymnastics | 16.1 | 18.8 | 13.4 | 11.2 | 9.6 | 7.5 | 8.2 | 5.1 | 5.2 | 10.5 |
| Ice Hockey | 3.5 | 3.6 | 2.7 | 2.7 | 1.9 | 2.7 | 3.0 | 2.5 | 3.0 | 2.8 |
| Lacrosse | 2.9 | 3.5 | 3.1 | 1.7 | 2.8 | 2.9 | 3.4 | 2.6 | 2.6 | 2.9 |
| Skiing | 12.3 | 16.0 | 11.2 | 10.3 | 11.2 | 11.6 | 12.1 | 16.3 | 10.6 | 12.4 |
| Soccer | 26.9 | 33.1 | 26.8 | 23.4 | 18.4 | 16.1 | 15.2 | 11.9 | 14.1 | 20.8 |
| Softball | 20.7 | 19.3 | 20.4 | 19.4 | 21.5 | 19.8 | 21.7 | 20.7 | 17.7 | 20.0 |
| Swimming | 33.3 | 38.2 | 33.0 | 26.7 | 28.4 | 24.2 | 30.8 | 26.3 | 24.2 | 29.4 |
| Tennis | 13.4 | 22.7 | 16.2 | 15.8 | 16.7 | 14.8 | 18.3 | 16.8 | 14.1 | 17.1 |
| Track & Field | 10.4 | 11.7 | 9.5 | 9.4 | 6.6 | 9.2 | 8.8 | 7.5 | 6.5 | 8.8 |
| Volleyball | 20.9 | 22.8 | 21.6 | 18.4 | 22.3 | 19.8 | 21.6 | 21.2 | 17.8 | 21.0 |
| Wrestling | 11.0 | 13.9 | 12.3 | 8.7 | 8.0 | 8.3 | 9.6 | 5.7 | 1.8 | 9.5 |
| Other | 17.8 | 19.7 | 14.1 | 10.4 | 9.4 | 11.2 | 12.6 | 11.8 | 10.4 | 11.5 |

*Source:* M.E. Ewing and V. Seefeldt. *Participation and Attrition Patterns in American Agency-Sponsored and Interscholastic Sports.* North Palm Beach, FL: Sporting Goods Manufacturers Association (SGMA), 1989.

schools to be effective centers of learning, they must be interesting. The new philosophy thus focused on educational activities that were meaningful and significant to the total development of each individual student. It also stressed the importance of programs that helped individuals learn democratic processes. Play was seen as integral to the total development of the child. John Dewey (1859–1952) was one of the major leaders of this twentieth-century philosophy, which is commonly referred to as *pragmatism.*

Leading proponents of this new educational ideology, such as Clark Hetherington, Thomas D. Wood, Jay B. Nash, Luther Gulick, and Jesse Feiring Williams, led the call for a *"new" physical education.* In stressing the need to develop the whole individual, physical education began to stress development of the whole individual from biological, psychological, and sociological perspectives. Prior to this, gymnastics and physical training programs had concentrated primarily on the development and training of a healthy body. Participation in the "new" physical education was seen as an effective way to develop not only physical benefits, but mental, social, and psychological benefits as well.

In focusing on the individual, and on the development of democratic values, the "new" physical education moved away from the formal gymnastic systems of the late 1800s and stressed the need to include exercise, games, sports, and free play in the program. However, while the "new" physical education included gymnastics, swimming, dance and other forms of physical activity, games and sports were clearly the central focus. According to Robert Knight Barney:

> If sport played a major role as a form of entertainment for adults in twentieth-century America, it served a different purpose for the thousands of American schoolchildren enrolled in public school physical education classes. Indeed, sport formed the core of the physical education expression which developed in even stronger tones as the century progressed.[18]

By the mid-1920s, the "new" physical education, with its focus on sports and play, had become firmly established in the elementary and secondary schools as America's system of physical education.

The "new" physical education also strongly endorsed the development and expansion of interscholastic athletics, particularly on the high school level. Although athletic competition between high schools was seen in several sports as early as 1890, interscholastic athletics skyrocketed after World War I. They were seen as an integral part of education and were administratively housed under the umbrella of the physical education program. In general, the high school programs that developed were imitations of college and university programs. In 1923 the National Federation of State High School Associations (NFSHSA) was established as the governing body of all interscholastic athletic programs. By 1925 state high school athletic associations existed in every state.[19] To this day, interscholastic athletics is overseen by NFSHSA.

Another significant outcome of adopting the "new" physical education was the proliferation of teacher training programs in colleges and universities. By 1930 thirty-nine states had enacted some form of legislation requiring instruction in physical education in the public schools. By the mid-1970s, every state in the country had legislated some form of physical education standards.[20] Consequently, the need for trained athletic coaches and teachers of physical education mushroomed. The professional preparation programs required prospective teachers to obtain a broad general education, a knowledge of educational theory and practice, including child growth and development, and specialized training in physical education. By the late 1990s, over 600 colleges and universities were providing professional preparation programs for students preparing for careers in physical education and related fields.

Accompanying the growth in teacher training programs was the advancement of research in the field of physical education, as well as the further development of professional organizations and associations. The largest of the professional associations devoted primarily to school physical education has been the American Alliance for Health, Physical Education, Recreation and Dance (AAHPERD).[21]

## Conflicting Goals in a Changing Society

Since the adoption of the American system of physical education in the 1920s, the direction of physical education has been significantly influenced by two major factors: (1) conflicting philosophies among educators as to the central purpose of physical education, and (2) a variety of societal changes and events. At least three broad purposes have contended for dominance of the physical education program since the 1920s. One view strongly holds that the major function and purpose of physical education is to train and develop the body. Proponents of this philosophy strongly believe in the value of organic fitness and the mastery of physical skills. A second philosophy stresses the importance of developing the whole individual (physically, mentally, socially, and emotionally) through the medium of physical activity. Supporters of this view believe that participation in a variety of games, sports, and other forms of physical activity is necessary for the total development of the individual. The third philosophy maintains that the primary purpose of physical education is to provide education for leisure activities and for the productive use of leisure time. Recreational and lifetime activities are viewed as essential elements of the program.

While the profession has consistently struggled with these questions of function and purpose throughout the century, many global and national events also have greatly influenced America's perception and acceptance of physical education. During the Great Depression of the 1930s, financial difficulties forced many schools to abandon athletics completely and to drop physical education from the school curriculum. However, while school programs suffered, community recreation programs flourished. Faced with unemployment and little money, people turned to recreational activities as an inexpensive and socially acceptable use of their idle time.

During times of international crisis, such as World War II and the Korean War, programs of physical education emphasized physical fitness and training, primarily to meet the needs of the military. Sports and athletics were valued in terms of their contribution in promoting physical fitness.

In times of peace and economic prosperity, the public has perceived the function and value of physical education primarily in terms of its importance and contributions to individual students. This view strongly supports student choice, a concept that allows students considerable freedom in deciding which physical activities, if any, are most appropriate and of individual interest to them. From the 1970s to the early 1990s, physical education emphasized the development of skills and interests in "lifetime sports." Such activities as aerobic dance, backpacking, orienteering, bowling, golf, and tennis became very popular in many physical education programs. Toward the end of the century, activities promoting individual wellness and health came to the fore.

On the other hand, the trend toward more flexibility and free choice within the curriculum led to a lower valuation of physical education. In some instances, the public's perception of the value of physical education has led to the elimination of required student participation in the program. In other instances, the entire physical education program has been threatened with elimination from the school curriculum.

Since the early 1970s, programs in physical education and sports in the United States have also been greatly influenced by legislation emphasizing human rights and equality of opportunity. Through numerous federal mandates, attempts have been made to radically reduce, if not eliminate, discriminatory practices and to provide sport and physical activity for all. Today, the *Sport for All* movement is firmly entrenched within American society. By the late 1990s, the scope of sport and physical education opportunities had broadened to include programs throughout the life span for both males and females, and for populations with special needs as well as for the able-bodied.

## Gender Equity in Sports and Physical Education

Although opportunities for women expanded in the earlier part of the twentieth century, participation by girls and women in sports have mushroomed since the mid-1970s. Changing attitudes toward women in general have undoubtedly contributed to the growth in opportunities for women, but the passage of Title IX of the Educational Amendments Act of 1972 has been a tremendous influence. Title IX, which extended the antidiscriminatory provisions of the Civil Rights Act of 1964, mandated that no person in the United States, on the basis of gender, could be excluded from participation in, be denied the benefits of, or be subjected to discrimination under any education program or activity receiving federal funds. Since its adoption in 1972, this single piece of legislation has had a profound effect on physical education and athletics programs in the United States. Girls' and women's programs have grown rapidly in only a few short years. According to a 1995 survey completed by the National Federation of State High School Associations, 3,666,917 males but only 294,015 females participated in interscholastic sports on the high school level in 1971. By 1995 the number of participants was 3,536,359 males and 2,240,461 females. Another 17,609 students were competing in 1995 in coeducational sports.[22] Similarly, a 1994 study completed by the National Collegiate Athletic Association reported that in 1984–85 there were 91,669 females and 201,063 males participating in intercollegiate sports. Ten years later the number of male participants had dropped to 189,084, but the number of females had increased to 110,524.[23] As shown in Figure 3.1, the number of males participating in intercollegiate athletics in 1995–96 had dropped to 188,399, while the number of female participants had grown to 116,272.

In addition to providing for equal opportunity in sports participation, Title IX contained other important provisions. Within school physical education, the law

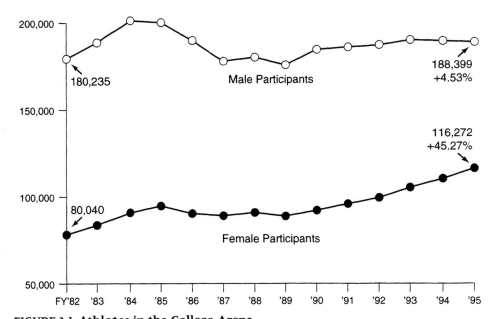

**FIGURE 3.1 Athletes in the College Arena.**
Overall number of intercollegiate athletes by gender.

*Source: The Providence Journal-Bulletin* (April 22, 1997, p. A9). Reprinted with permission.

stipulated that no discrimination by sex could occur in program offerings, quality of teachers, or availability and quality of facilities and equipment. Physical education classes were required to be coeducational, though classes could be separated by sex for instruction in certain contact sports. Within interscholastic and intercollegiate athletic programs, the law mandated that equal opportunities exist for all athletes regardless of sex. Separate teams for men and women or a coeducational team had to be provided in all federally assisted schools and colleges. Equal opportunity was also extended to include such factors as athletic scholarships, housing, travel allowances, medical training services, and compensation of coaches. If an institution failed to comply with the federal mandates, all federal funds earmarked for that institution would be withheld.

## Opportunities for Individuals with Disabilities

Since the mid-1970s, the federal government has enacted several laws in support of the right of all people with disabilities to have the same opportunities as the able-bodied. These mandates resulted in significant changes both in physical education programs in the public schools and in the nature and extent of sports opportunities for all individuals with disabilities. In 1975 the Education of All Handicapped Children Act, P.L. 94-142, mandated that physical education services are to be made available to every schoolchild regardless of disability. While stating that each child with a disability is to be provided an education in the least restrictive environment, the law further stipulates that each student is also to be provided with an individualized educational program (IEP).

In 1978 Congress passed the Amateur Sports Act, which authorized the United States Olympic Committee to develop programs and opportunities specifically designed for the disabled. Since passage of this law, the number of individuals with disabilities participating in competitive sports has increased dramatically. National and international competitions for Americans with disabilities include the Paralympics, the Special Olympics, the World Games for the Deaf, the Wheelchair Games, and others.

In 1990 the Americans with Disabilities Act (ADA) was passed, mandating an end to discrimination against individuals of all ages based on disabilities. The five specific areas addressed by the law included employment practices, public accommodations, public services, transportation, and telecommunications. In the area of sport and physical education, the ADA requires that all sport and recreational facilities must provide for equal access and equal services to individuals with disabilities.

## Physical Education and Sport at the End of the Century

Despite numerous advances, programs of American sport and physical education still face major issues and problems. As the United States enters the twenty-first century, both fields are at critical stages of development.

Physical education was once a required subject in schools in almost every state in the country, but considerable evidence suggests that inclusion of physical education in America's schools is on the decline. In a 1997 survey of 1,504 parents with children in grades 4 to 12, it was found that 34 percent of the children attended physical education classes on a daily basis, but 23 percent of them had no physical education at all. The study, which was conducted by the International Life Sciences Institute, also reported that only 22 percent of the children were physically active for thirty minutes every day.[24]

The discipline of physical education is still struggling for its identity and for an established place in American society. As the overtaxed and cost-conscious public continues to clamor for accountability and quality, the question of the relevancy and value of physical education continually arises. The lack of a single agreed-upon curriculum model has severely hampered progress in this area. While some programs stress fitness and wellness, others focus on competitive sports or on lifetime activities.

One of the major issues is the relationship between physical education and athletics. Although the general public in the United States views physical education and athletics essentially as one discipline, the two programs have in reality gone their separate ways. Physical education continues to stress its educational value to society, whereas athletic programs are driven by the need to win. Athletic success is measured in terms of economic profit, entertainment, and recognition.

Success in physical education is measured in terms of the physical, mental, social, and psychological development of the individual. The goals are very different.

Major problems also continue to plague competitive sports on both the professional and amateur levels. Professional sports are dominated by labor disputes between players and owners. Salaries of professional athletes have skyrocketed, and player strikes have become common. Belligerent owners think little of picking up and moving their franchises to greener pastures, regardless of expense to spectators and taxpayers. College and university athletic programs are faced with drug abuse among their athletes, recruiting violations, gambling, and an unusually high level of player violence. College players and coaches alike engage in ethically questionable practices, both on and off the playing field. The "win at all costs" philosophy has permeated almost all aspects of the organized sport scene, and has left America with a conflicting set of values.

Similarly, the place of interscholastic athletics in the educational process has been severely questioned. Many of the abuses found on the college and university level have found their way into the high schools. The use of drugs and the prevalence of violence in high school sports have become major problems in interscholastic athletic programs. The overemphasis on success at this level of competition has led to many ethically questionable practices by both coaches and players.

As we examine the current situation and seek solutions to problems in sport and physical education in the United States, it is important to keep in mind that these issues are a direct reflection of problems facing all of American society. No doubt, as the United States changes during the twenty-first century, so too will its programs of sport and physical education.

## SUMMARY

The development of sport and physical education in the United States has been influenced by a variety of social, political, religious, economic, and cultural factors. During colonial times, play and recreational patterns generally reflected the diverse cultural and religious traditions and beliefs of the European settlers. Gradually, these early forms of play and recreational patterns evolved into organized programs of sport and physical activity. During the nineteenth century, the seeds were planted for organized sport and physical education to become permanent fixtures in American society. A diversity of programs reflected the influence of German, Danish, and Swedish systems of gymnastics as well as the English system of sports and games. During the late 1800s, organized sport in the United States became modernized and ultimately serious business. Amateur sports were also extremely popular and rapidly spread throughout the country, particularly on the college and university level. The various programs of gymnastics found their way into the nation's schools, laying the foundation for what was to become physical education.

In the twentieth century, organized sport and physical education became an integral part of American society. As the United States developed its own unique system of sport and physical education, programs and opportunities mushroomed.

The adoption of the "new" physical education in the early 1920s led to compulsory school-based physical education. Accompanying that was the proliferation of amateur and professional sports, the rise of teacher training programs, and a significant and profound increase in opportunities for minorities, women, youth, and the disabled. Today, Americans have more opportunities to participate in a wider variety of sports and physical activities that at any other time in history. However, despite the abundance of opportunities, numerous philosophical, financial, and ethical problems plague present-day sport and physical education. Both areas are at critical stages of development.

## STUDY QUESTIONS

1. "The development of what was to become a uniquely American system of physical education can be traced precisely to the influence of the German and Swedish systems of gymnastics, the influence of the English sport and athletic movement, and the profound influence of theologians, educators, and physicians." Discuss this statement and indicate how each of the forces significantly influenced the development of the American system of physical education.

2. The value of physical education in the school curriculum has consistently been a subject of considerable controversy and debate. Discuss what you consider to be the central purpose of physical education in American society.

3. Today, organized forms of competitive sport have become focused primarily on the outcome rather than the process. In particular, the need to win seems to have become the driving force behind current practices and activities. Should more emphasis be placed on the educational values of sport? If so, how can organized sports, particularly on the competitive athletic level, focus more on educational values?

4. What can be done to curb the increasing abuses and unethical practices found in competitive sports, particularly the increasing levels of drug use and violence?

5. Discuss and analyze the relationship between physical education and athletics. Should they be considered totally separate entities or should they be considered a single discipline?

6. Where should youth sport be organized? Should it be part of the school curriculum or organized by sports clubs and community leagues?

7. Discuss the influence of Title IX on the development of physical education and sport for women in the United States.

## RECOMMENDED READINGS

Betts, John R. *America's Sporting Heritage: 1850–1950*. Reading, MA: Addison-Wesley, 1974.
Edwards, Harry. *The Revolt of the Black Athlete*. New York: Free Press, 1969.

Ewing, M. E., and V. Seefeldt. *Participation and Attrition Patterns in American Agency-Sponsored and Interscholastic Sports: An Executive Summary.* North Palm Beach, FL: Sporting Goods Manufacturers Assn., 1989.

Gerber, Ellen W. *Innovators and Institutions in Physical Education.* Philadelphia: Lea and Febiger, 1971.

Lapchick, Richard E., and John B. Slaughter. *The Rules of the Game: Ethics in College Sport.* New York: Macmillan, 1989.

Lockhart, Ailene S., and Betty Spears. *Chronicle of American Physical Education: 1855–1930.* Dubuque, IA: Wm. C. Brown, 1972.

Lucas, John A., and Ronald A. Smith. *Saga of American Sport.* Philadelphia: Lea and Febiger, 1978.

Michener, James A. *Sports in America.* New York: Random House, 1976.

Mrozek, Donald J. *Sport and American Mentality, 1890–1910.* Knoxville: University of Tennessee Press, 1983.

Polidoro, J. Richard. "Survey Examines Coaches' Concerns about Ethics." *NCAA News* 26, no. 41 (November 20, 1989): 4–6.

Rader, Benjamin G. *American Sports: From the Age of Folk Games to the Age of Televised Sports.* Englewood Cliffs, NJ: Prentice-Hall, 1990.

Redmond, Gerald. *The Caledonian Games in Nineteenth-Century America.* Rutherford, NJ: Fairleigh Dickinson University Press, 1971.

Riess, Steven A. *City Games: The Evolution of American Urban Society and the Rise of Sports.* Urbana: University of Illinois Press, 1989.

Sage, George H. *Sport and American Society.* Reading, MA: Addison-Wesley, 1970.

Smith, Ronald A. *Sport and Freedom: The Rise of Big Time College Athletics.* New York: Oxford University Press, 1988.

Struna, Nancy L. "Sports and Colonial Education: A Cultural Perspective." *Research Quarterly for Exercise and Sport* 52, no. 1 (March 1981): 117–135.

Swanson, Richard A., and Betty Spears. *History of Sport and Physical Education in the United States,* 4th ed. Dubuque, IA: Brown and Benchmark, 1995.

Welch, Paula D., and Harold A. Lerch. *History of American Physical Education and Sport.* Springfield, IL: Charles C. Thomas, 1981.

Weston, Arthur. *The Making of American Physical Education.* New York: Appleton-Century-Crofts, 1962.

# NOTES

1. Richard A. Swanson and Betty Spears, *History of Sport and Physical Education in the United States,* 4th ed. (Dubuque, IA: Brown and Benchmark, 1995), 10–13.

2. Thomas Davis, "Puritanism and Physical Education: The Shroud of Gloom Lifted," *Canadian Journal of History of Sport and Physical Education,* 3, no. 1 (May 1972).

3. Benjamin Franklin (1749), *Proposals for the Education of Youth of Pennsylvania* (Ann Arbor: William L. Clements Library, 1927), 10.

4. John R. Betts, "The Technological Revolution and the Rise of Sport, 1850–1900," in John W. Loy and Gerald S. Kenyon, *Sport, Culture and Society* (Toronto: Macmillan, 1969), 145–146.

5. Melvin Aldelman, *A Sporting Time: New York City and the Rise of Modern Athletics, 1820–1870* (Urbana, IL: University of Illinois Press, 1986), 6.

6. In the early 1900s, horse racing was almost eliminated as most states passed antigambling laws that banned bookmaking. By 1908 only a handful of tracks were still operating in the United States. It was not until state legislatures agreed to legalize parimutuel betting in exchange for a share of the money wagered that racing reappeared. By the end of World War I, horse racing prospered.

7. Geoffrey C. Ward and Ken Burns, *Baseball: An Illustrated History* (New York: Alfred A. Knopf, 1994), 5.

8. Ibid, 6.

9. Paul Hoch, *Rip Off: The Big Game* (Garden City, NY: Anchor Books, 1972).

10. The word *calisthenics* is derived from the two Greek words: "kalos," which signifies beautiful, and "sthenos," which signifies strength. Beecher's system of calisthenics was therefore designed to develop a beautiful and strong body.

11. Dudley S. DeGroot, "A History of Physical Education in California (1848–1939)" (Ph.D. dissertation, Stanford University, 1940), 23.

12. Anthropometrics is the study of physical measurements of body segments, both girths and lengths. It was an extremely popular method of research in many disciplines in the late 1800s.

13. Ward and Burns, *Baseball,* 18.

14. Dudley A. Sargent, "The System of Physical Training at the Hemenway Gymnasium," *Physical Training: A Full Report of the Papers and Discussion of the Conference Held in Boston in November, 1889* (Boston: Press of George H. Ellis, 1890), 62–76.

15. Henry Smith Williams, "The Educational Value and Health-Giving Value of Athletics," *Harper's Weekly* 39 (February 16, 1895): 165.

16. Frederick L. Paxson, "The Rise of Sports," *The Mississippi Valley Historical Review* 4 (1917): 33.

17. Rainer Martens, "Youth Sports in the USA," in M. Weiss and D. Gould, *Sport for Children and Youth* (Champaign, IL: Human Kinetics, 1986).

18. Robert Knight Barney, "Physical Education and Sport in the United States," in Earle F. Zeigler, *History of Physical Education and Sport* (Champaign, IL: Stipes, 1988), 211.

19. Deobold Van Dalen and Bruce L. Bennett, *A World History of Physical Education* (Englewood Cliffs, NJ: Prentice-Hall, 1971), 448.

20. Barney, "Physical Education and Sport," 213–214.

21. The American Alliance for Health, Physical Education, Recreation and Dance was first formed as the Association for the Advancement of Physical Education (AAPE) in 1885. Subsequent name changes in the twentieth century include the American Physical Education Association and the American Association for Health, Physical Education and Recreation.

22. Amy Lewis, "National Federation of State High School Associations Sports Participation Survey," *www.arcade.uiowa.edu/proj/ge/up_to_date.html#230*

23. Amy Lewis, "The National Collegiate Athletic Association Participation Report" (February 16, 1994), *www.arcade.uiowa.edu/proj/ge/up_to_date.html#230*

24. Nanci Hellmich, "Few Kids Get Daily Exercise," *USA Today* (July 1, 1997): D1.

CHAPTER FOUR

■ ■ ■ ■ ■

# THE GENESIS OF
# INTERNATIONAL SPORTS

## URIEL SIMRI

Although a small and insignificant number of international sport events took place prior to the middle of the nineteenth century, the second half of that century saw the true genesis of international competitive sports. Yet, despite the growing number of international events, international sports were conducted on a haphazard and sporadic basis until well into the twentieth century.

In 1851 the American schooner *America* defeated fourteen English yachts in a race around the Isle of Wight in Great Britain. Nineteen years later, the winners of that race donated the cup they had received as a prize for future races. The first yacht race for the America's Cup took place in New York in 1870, and it was followed by nine more races before the turn of the century. The cup, which is the world's oldest sporting trophy, remained in American hands until 1983.

In 1858 an English cricket team toured the United States, and a year later golf players from the two countries met for the first time. In 1869 a rowing eight from Harvard University went to England, only to be defeated by a student crew from Oxford University.[1] Also of significance in the 1860s was the formulation of the Marquis of Queensbury rules in modern boxing (1865). The rules required the use of gloves, limited rounds to three minutes, prohibited wrestling holds, and provided for ten-second knockout counts. The use of these rules was common practice by the 1890s; they form the basis of today's boxing rules.

Whereas cricket did not become popular in North America, the same does not hold true for Australia, a country that was toured by an English team in 1861. A periodic exchange of visits between English and Australian cricket teams soon developed. When the visiting Australians succeeded in defeating their English hosts for the first time in 1882, England was in a state of shock and mourning. The *Sporting Times* wrote that "the body (of English cricket) will be cremated and its ashes taken to Australia." Thereafter, each cricket competition between the two countries was referred to as competing for "the Ashes." In 1888 an English team also visited South Africa to open a regular series of international games.

The 1870s witnessed the emergence of international soccer, which was based, to a large extent, on earlier versions of Eton and Cambridge football. The

English Football Association was created in 1863. Although soccer was played in Argentina as early as the late 1860s, the game's invasion of the European continent in the 1870s was the significant development. Soccer was destined to become the world's number one sport in the twentieth century. By 1873 regular annual matches were being held among the national teams of England, Scotland, Wales, and Ireland. Even today, these four components of the United Kingdom are recognized as independent territories by the International Soccer Federation (FIFA).[2] Each fields its own team in international competitions.

The modern game of lawn tennis was introduced in England in 1874 by Walter C. Wingfield, who initially named the sport after an ancient Greek game called *sphairistike*. Three years later, the first All-England tennis championship was played at Wimbledon. That championship, however, did not open its doors to participants from abroad until the twentieth century. Likewise, the United States Open Championship, which took place for the first time in 1881 in New York, was open only to U.S. players. Yet in 1883 the first international tournament was held with participants from the United States and Great Britain. The game of tennis had been imported to the United States in 1874 via Bermuda.

The first international federation of a sport that was to be included in the future Olympic Games was created in 1881. However, that federation, namely the one for gymnastics, was not created for the sake of international competitions. Its aim was to further the spread of the German Turnen system, which at the time was fighting a battle with the Swedish system of gymnastics. It was not until almost fifteen years after its founding that it became involved in organizing international competitions. It would therefore be more accurate to look upon the federations that were established for skating (1892), rowing (1892), and cycling (1893) as the first truly international sport federations.

In the 1880s, the first international competitions were held in lacrosse (1883), polo (1886), and weight lifting. In weight lifting, a one-time world championship was held in 1888, but regular international competitions in that sport started only with the European championship of 1896.

Data about the beginning of modern boxing on the international scene are contradictory. Various dates and events are named for the first universally recognized world championship, with most sources citing 1881 or 1882. Even the date of the first championship fight under the Marquis of Queensbury rules is still under discussion. Although 1892 is the most widely cited year for the first championship fight with gloves, some claim that such a fight took place as early as 1885. Weight limits for featherweight, welterweight, and middleweight fights are known to have been used in the 1880s.

## THE FIRST MODERN OLYMPIC GAMES

In June 1894, on the initiative of the French baron Pierre de Coubertin, a conference at the Sorbonne University in Paris decided to create an International Olympic Committee. It was decided to hold the first Olympic Games of modern times in 1896. Although Coubertin is officially credited with providing the impetus for the renewal of the Olympics, others before him had attempted to renew the

ancient tradition of quadrennial games. The Zappas family of Athens had organized and financed the so-called Panhellenic Games (all-Greece games) five times
as of 1859, with the declared goal of renewing the Olympic tradition. In the 1859
games, the opening ceremony included religious rites, the playing of an Olympic
anthem, and the swearing of an Olympic oath. As in the ancient games, the athletes were required to train together for a prolonged period prior to the start of
competition. The 1875 Panhellenic Games included athletic competitions, gymnastic exercises, and shooting. Only after the fifth failure in 1888 did the Zappas
family forsake the idea.

According to original ideology, Coubertin's modern Olympic Games were to
be held solely for the benefit of the players, and only amateur athletes could compete. The games were to be free from both political and professional influences.
Coubertin was of the opinion that the games would provide a forum where the
young men of the world could unite in peaceful and friendly competition. He
believed the games would expose athletes to different cultures and values, thus
broadening their horizons and contributing to the development of positive international relations and goodwill. From their inception, however, the modern
Olympic Games have been the center of controversy and debate.

Contrary to the present belief, political influences have permeated the
Olympic movement from the very beginning. For example, in planning for the
Sorbonne conference in 1894, the French government successfully persuaded
Coubertin not to invite a German delegate. This occurred a full twenty-three years
after France's defeat by Germany in the 1871 war. Another major political problem erupted in regard to the location of the games. The Greeks wanted them to be
held permanently on Greek soil. Coubertin wanted them to be held in a different
country each time they were held. As we all know, Coubertin and the International Olympic Committee held the upper hand in this bitter discussion.

In addition to political overtones and influences, another basic concern that
was to haunt the Olympic movement throughout most of its history was the issue
of amateurism. As early as the games of 1896, concern was voiced over what
defined an amateur. Persons who wish to protect the reputation of the founders
of the modern Olympic movement claim that the founders simply misinterpreted
developments at the ancient Olympic Games. Their opponents claim that the
Olympic founders had in mind the creation of socially elitist games that would be
open only to wealthy gentlemen of the upper social classes. This view is confirmed
by the fact that the International Olympic Committee has never been a democratic organization. From its inception the IOC has consisted of a self-elected body of
members who belonged to nobility and to the upper social and socioeconomic
classes. In any case, the amateur envisioned by Coubertin and his associates never
existed in ancient Greece and was much closer to the leisure-class gentleman of
nineteenth-century England. As originally conceived, athletes in the modern
Olympic Games were supposed to participate solely for the love of sport, without
receiving any kind of gain from their participation in the games or from their
preparation for the games. The result of this ruling was the breeding of hypocrisy
and deceit that grew from one game to another up through the 1990s.

The first modern games did not bear much resemblance to today's Olympic Games. They opened in Athens on April 6, 1896, and lasted for ten days. The number of participants was less than 300, and only 80 of the participants were from countries other than Greece.[3] Altogether, athletes from only thirteen countries participated in the games, and these participants did not attend within a framework of national delegations. The United States, for example, was represented by five "delegations."

In the games of 1896, only nine sports were included in the program. Only four of these—track and field, swimming, gymnastics and fencing—have been included in the program of every subsequent Olympics. In 1896 the total number of events reached thirty-nine, much less than the number of events in track and field alone today. One event, the marathon race, was an innovation on the international sports scene. Held in 1896 at the suggestion of Michel Breal of France, it immediately became very popular.[4]

As in the ancient games, no game or team activity was included in the first Olympic Games of modern times. These sports developed outside the Olympic movement. Nor were women invited to participate in the first games, following the example of the games of antiquity. In spite of the limited program and the rather small number of athletes, the games at Athens were considered a tremendous success. Much of the success can be attributed to the enthusiasm of their Greek hosts.

## EXPANSION OF THE INTERNATIONAL SPORTS PROGRAM

The world witnessed a major expansion of the international sports program in the 1890s. Two of the three most popular sports worldwide, basketball and volleyball, were invented at American YMCAs in 1891 and 1895, respectively. Basketball rapidly became very popular on the international scene. Within its first decade, the game spread to both the Far East and to Europe.

Baseball and badminton were of minor importance to the initial development of international sports. Baseball was an American adaptation of the English game of rounders, or townball, and badminton was an English adaptation of an Indian game known as poonah. Field hockey, however, was a game that did enter the international scene in the 1890s. The introduction of annual games between England and Ireland, commencing in 1895, played a pioneering role. In the same year, what might be considered the first international track and field meet of modern times took place when the New York Athletic Club invited the London Athletic Club to a meet in New York. In 1899, the game of *gossima*, the forerunner of modern table tennis, was invented, but introduction of the celluloid ball soon changed its nature.

Earlier introductions of new sports came primarily from England. In 1823 the public school at Rugby began to play its own kind of football. American football is an offspring of the game of Rugby football, which was first introduced to

North America by way of Canada. Most sources agree that American football, though very different from rugby, had its origin in a Rugby football match between McGill University of Montreal and Harvard University in 1875.

England has been called the motherland of modern sports. Insofar as England deserves this title, it is not so much for the invention of new sports but rather for the creation of organizational frames within which sports could be practiced on a regular basis. According to the noted historian H. A. Harris (1975:210), a "sport explosion" occurred in England between 1860 and 1885. Accompanying the increase in the number of modern sports was the development of numerous national sport associations whose authority and rules were recognized throughout Great Britain. By 1885 national associations existed for a variety of sports including cricket, rugby, soccer, track and field, swimming, rowing, golf, cycling, and tennis. These associations were organized primarily by members of the new leisure class that was a product of the industrial revolution, as opposed to earlier, less-organized sports in which participation was limited primarily to the nobility. It was these highly organized sports that the English successfully exported. Because of its great international influence during the second half of the nineteenth century, England could easily spread its cultural values and practices, including sports, to its vast empire—which included Australia, India, and Canada—and to the United States.

## THE FIRST WORLD AND EUROPEAN CHAMPIONSHIPS

The 1890s were marked by a series of official world and European championships. These championships were an important step in the development and organization of international sports.

Ice-skating held its first championship on the eve of the decade when it organized the first unofficial world championship in speed skating in 1889. This championship was followed by an unofficial world championship in figure skating, held in 1890 in St. Petersburg, Russia. That particular event was won by Louis Rubinstein, a representative of Canada. The first official world championships were organized in 1893 for speed skating and in 1896 for figure skating. In figure skating, the first European championship was staged in 1891; in 1895 the first North American championship was held. The first North American championship in speed skating took place in 1897 in Montreal. Once organized, all these championships became regular annual events.

In 1893 the first world championship in cycling was organized. This was soon followed by a North American championship the same year. The sport of rowing held its first European championship in 1893, an event that because of its open character served de facto as a world championship until the beginning of World War II. As already mentioned, annual European championships in weight lifting have been held since 1896. In 1893 competition for the Stanley Cup in ice hockey was organized with the participation of American and Canadian amateur teams. Stanley Cup competitions have been held regularly ever since. In the 1870s, competitions in international soccer were held in the United Kingdom, thus paving the way for soccer to emerge as the world's major sport in later years.

Thus, as the nineteenth century drew to a close, international sporting events were becoming exceedingly popular and well organized. Although still at an early stage of development, the seeds were firmly planted for major expansion in the twentieth century.

## SUMMARY

Modern developments in international sport competition began primarily during the second half of the 1800s. Although the events were sporadic and not always well organized, international competitions were held in several sports.

Equally significant was the development of several international sport federations and associations. The sport federations were established to govern international competition as much as to hold world and continental championships. By the end of the century, several federations had in fact staged world or continental championships. Much of the credit for the spread of international competition during the late 1800s should be given to England, which successfully used sports to disseminate its cultural values and practices throughout its vast empire and to the United States.

After the establishment of the International Olympic Committee in 1894, the first Olympic Games of modern times were held in 1896. Although of minor interest at that time, the modern Olympic Games became the major international sport event of the twentieth century. The modern Olympic Games have attempted to foster positive international relations and goodwill, but political influences have in fact permeated the Olympic movement since its inception.

## STUDY QUESTIONS

1. England has been called the motherland of modern sports. Discuss this label and whether it is justified.
2. Identify and discuss America's contribution to the world of modern sports in the nineteenth century.
3. Compare the first modern Olympic Games to the present games.

## RECOMMENDED READINGS

Bennett, Bruce L., Maxwell L. Howell, and Uriel Simri. *Comparative Physical Education and Sport.* 2nd ed. Philadelphia: Lea and Febiger, 1983.
Golesworthy, M. *The Encyclopedia of Association Football.* 3rd ed. London: Robert Hale, 1959.
Harris, Harold A. *Sport in Britain—Its Origins and Development.* London: Stanley Paul, 1975.
Lucas, John A., and Ronald A. Smith. *Saga of American Sports.* Philadelphia: Lea and Febiger, 1978.

Mandell, Richard D. *The First Modern Olympics.* Berkeley: University of California, 1976.

Menke, Frank. G. *The All-Sports Record Book.* New York: A. S. Barnes, 1950.

Menke, Frank G. *The Encyclopedia of Sports.* 6th ed. New York: Doubleday, 1977.

Naismith, James. *Basketball—Its Origin and Development.* New York: Associated Press, 1941.

Odd, G. *The Hamlyn Encyclopedia of Boxing.* London: Hamlyn, 1983.

## NOTES

1. Oxford and Cambridge have been holding their annual rowing competition on the Thames River ever since 1829, making this athletic event the one with the longest tradition in international sports.

2. Today FIFA recognizes only Northern Ireland as part of the United Kingdom, not of course the independent republic of Eire.

3. In recent years, the data on participation in the Olympic Games have been revised frequently by the International Olympic Committee. Earlier publications mentioned a total of 311 participants in the 1896 Olympics.

4. The first Boston Marathon race was organized in 1897.

# CHAPTER FIVE

# INTERNATIONAL SPORTS IN THE TWENTIETH CENTURY

## URIEL SIMRI

The young international sports movement, which was born in the second half of the nineteenth century, could barely stand on its feet at the turn of the century. The early years of the twentieth century should therefore be considered the movement's years of infancy.

The Olympic movement started the twentieth century on the left foot. Both the second games in Paris (1900) and the third ones held in St. Louis (1904) were virtually fiascos. There is not even agreement as to how long these games lasted. Both were part of important international exhibitions and were scheduled so as to amuse visitors to those exhibitions. The Paris games lasted over five months. The games held in St. Louis were staged over a period somewhere between 121 and 146 days! Coubertin had no say at all at the Paris games. He was relegated to serve only as secretary of the track and field events. He avoided the games in St. Louis completely. Whereas over 1,000 athletes participated for the first time in the Paris games, the number of participants was almost halved at St. Louis. The games there were further marred by the inclusion of so-called anthropometrical competitions, whose sole purpose seems to have been to prove the supremacy of the white race. One of the few positive aspects of those unfortunate games was participation by women in the Paris games. This was possible only because Coubertin, who was far from being a supporter of women's sports, was pushed aside, thus enabling the organizers to invite female tennis players and golfers to compete. Coubertin had once gone so far as to claim that women's sports were "against the laws of nature."

The fledgling Olympic movement was saved by the staging of well-organized interim games, which were organized in 1906 in Athens to celebrate the tenth anniversary of the first modern games. However, the Olympics ran into trouble again during the 1908 competitions held in London. The problems confronting those games were primarily political. The Finns and the Irish insisted on appearing under their own flags even though Finland and Ireland were at that time part of the Russian and British empires, respectively. Further, it was customary at the time to run the games by the rules prevailing in the host country. The British rules were not accepted by one and all, causing further upheavals—so much so that the games were considered to be in serious danger of being terminated. The main disagreement in this respect occurred between the hosts and the Americans, as the Americans were not willing to submit to British rules. One result of the disagreement was that the Olympic movement decided to allow, in the future, only sports that were organized in an international federation and only those which had a universally accepted set of rules.

The Olympic movement was saved by the well-organized games held in Stockholm in 1912. The London games and the Stockholm games each attracted over 2,000 participants. Both games clearly indicated a growing interest in the Olympics and in international sports.

Interesting innovations at the 1908 London games were the inclusion of figure skating in the summer games and determination of the distance of the marathon race. Figure skating was to return to the games only in 1920, as the organizers of the Stockholm games refused to include a typical winter sport in the program of the summer games. (Up to that time, the organizers of the games had much say about the content of the games.) As for the marathon race, the agreed-on distance was not the distance from Marathon to Athens (which is less than 25 miles), but the distance from the Olympic stadium to the royal palace at Windsor. The increase in distance came about because King Edward VII wanted to watch the race from the palace and did not see fit to attend a sporting event in a public stadium. The resulting distance of 26 miles and 385 yards (42.195 kilometers) was to become the standard distance for the race thereafter.

The most interesting innovation at the 1912 games was introduction of the modern pentathlon. This new sport was an invention of Coubertin, who got the idea from a story of the hardships a French messenger had to undergo during the Napoleonic war in Russia (1812). The pentathlon consists of cross-country riding, fencing, pistol shooting, 300 meters' swimming, and a cross-country race to the distance of four kilometers. Initially the pentathlon was carried out over five days. Today the event is completed in one day.

The success of the Stockholm Games definitely helped the Olympic movement survive the cancellation of the games in 1916. They had been scheduled for Berlin, but World War I intervened. Despite the successes of 1912, the Stockholm Olympics were blemished by an affair that had nothing to do with the organizers. Jim Thorpe, a Native American, had excelled at the games, winning both the pentathlon and the decathlon. Thorpe, an All-American football player who had earned letters in eleven sports, had been called "the greatest athlete in the world" by the king of Sweden. At the awards ceremony, the king insisted on handing the medals to Thorpe personally. Upon returning to the United States, Thorpe was given a hero's welcome, marked by a ticker-tape parade in New York City. Sometime after the games, it was uncovered that Thorpe had received a payment of $25 a week as a minor league baseball player in 1909 and 1910. According to the then existing rules, Thorpe was thereby declared a professional by the Amateur Athletic Union of the USA and asked to return his medals, which he did. When the medals were returned to the International Olympic Committee (IOC), the Swedish athletes who had placed behind Thorpe refused to accept them. A movement to reinstate Thorpe started years later, claiming that he had been dealt with harshly because of his racial origin. Avery Brundage, American president of the International Olympic Committee from 1952 until 1972, refused to assist in the reinstatement. This deed was left for IOC president Juan Antonio Samaranch to complete. In 1982 the medals were returned to Jim Thorpe's children.

The IOC decision regarding the terms for including a sport in the Olympic Games gave another push to the creation of international federations for various sports. In the nineteenth century, the only federations were for gymnastics, rowing, cycling, and skating. Prior to the 1908 decision of the International Olympic Committee, federations for soccer (1904), shooting (1907), sailing (1907), ice hockey (1908), and swimming (1908) were created. Soon after 1908, federations for fencing (1913), tennis (1912), track and field (1912)[1] and wrestling (1912) were formed. Although the International Federation for Weightlifting listed its founding year as 1920 in the 1986 Olympic Directory, it reported its date of founding as 1905 in the 1991 directory.

During the first two decades of the twentieth century, the number of world championships increased. Weight lifting started annual championships in 1903 (prior to the creation of an official international federation). Tennis followed in 1913, with international championships that were held until 1924. Championships in ice hockey, on the other hand, started in 1910 with annual European championships. In the years prior to World War I, the first attempts were made to organize regional multisport events. Stemming from the initiative of the International YMCA, the first Far Eastern Games were held in 1913. Other major sport events that began in the first decades of the twentieth century included tennis games for the Davis Cup, and the Tour de France cycling race. The games for the Davis Cup were held for the first time in 1900, with the United States winning the cup in the first two competitions (1900 and 1902). The next winners were Great Britain (1903–1906) and Australasia (a combination of Australia and New Zealand), which won from 1907 until 1911. Those three countries each won the Davis Cup one more time before World War I. The first Tour de France was raced in 1903 and became a regular annual event. This race is still considered the major international event in road cycling.

While the Northern Hemisphere was engaged in World War I, international sports continued to develop in the Southern Hemisphere. The countries of South America convened their first continental championship in soccer in 1916. This was followed by the second championship one year later. These games were held in Buenos Aires and Montevideo, with the national team of Uruguay winning on both occasions.

## INTERNATIONAL SPORTS BETWEEN THE WORLD WARS

The guns of World War I had scarcely stopped roaring in November 1918 when the international sports movement again became active in Europe. Within six months, 1,500 athletes from eighteen countries assembled in Paris to participate in an event called the Inter-Allied Games. These international games, which included competitions in twenty-four sports, grew out of an American-French military initiative. It was a major success.

The Olympic Games of 1920 were held in summer that year in Antwerp, Belgium. Following the custom of the ancient games, Germany and its allies were denied participation in the games for one Olympiad. The games in Antwerp were carried out in rather primitive conditions, as the city had suffered severe destruction during the war, but the participants knew to appreciate the efforts made by their hosts. Ice hockey and figure skating made an appearance at the 1920 games. Although part of the program, archery was expelled from the Olympic program following the Antwerp games because the officials of that sport could not agree on an international set of rules.

Two innovations that were to play an important role in future Olympic protocol were introduced at the Antwerp Olympics. The Olympic flag, with its five entwined rings, was flown for the first time at the 1920 games. The design, a suggestion of Coubertin, had been approved for the official Olympic flag in 1914. The second innovation was the oath taken by a representative of the participating athletes at the opening ceremony. The oath included a pledge to abide by the rules of the games. In all probability, it was the Jim Thorpe affair of 1912 that led to this innovation.

At the personal request of Coubertin, who was about to retire from the presidency of the IOC, the 1924 games were assigned to Paris for a second time. The games attracted for the first time more than 3,000 athletes. The major innovation of these games was the introduction of a week of winter sports. Originally, the conservative International Olympic Committee refused to recognize those sports as part of the 1924 Olympic Games but was forced to do so retroactively in 1926. At that time, it was decided that each organizer of the summer Olympic Games should also organize the Winter Games, as long as geographical and topographical conditions permitted. The games of Chamonix, France, held in 1924, thus became the first Winter Olympics.

Two additional events—or nonevents—marked the 1924 Olympic Games. No athletes from Germany participated in the games. Prior to the opening of the games, the French hosts hinted very strongly that they could not guarantee the safety of German athletes on French soil. The second noteworthy event was the expulsion of tennis from the Olympic program following the completion of the games. This occurred after the international tennis federation refused to abide by the strict amateur rulings established by the IOC. Whereas it took archery fifty-two years to return to the Olympic program after its expulsion, tennis stayed out of the Olympics for sixty-four years, returning only after professional players were allowed to participate in the 1988 games.

The third Olympic Games of the 1920s were held in Amsterdam in 1928. The Winter Games were held in St. Moritz, Switzerland. The major event of the Summer Games was the participation of female athletes in five track and field events. This development was the result of lengthy arguments between the International Federation of Women's Sports (FSFI), which was founded in 1919, the International Olympic Committee, and the International Federation for Track and Field (IAAF). The arguments continued until 1936, when a nine-event program for women in track and field was promised. At the same time the International Federation of Women's Sports organized its own World Games. The last of these quadrennial games took place in London in 1934. It is interesting to note that the first FSFI World Games were called the Women's Olympics. The FSFI was forced to change the name when the IOC threatened to sue the women's federation for breach of copyright.

Other serious competition to the Olympic Games arose with the formation of the Workers' Olympics. These games, which were first held in Frankfurt, Germany, in 1925 and for the last time in 1937 in Antwerp, Belgium, were created by the International Organization of Socialist Sports (SASI). The SASI movement, together with the German Turnen (gymnastics) movement, played a major role in bringing to an end one of Coubertin's dreams. Coubertin had always hoped that the Olympic Games would become a movement of the masses. The declared policy of the SASI was to thwart the record-seeking goals of "bourgeois" sports by deemphasizing individual competitions and individual sport "stars." The activities of this organization clearly favored team efforts such as relays and team sports. The socialist sports movement came to an end, for all practical purposes, in 1938 after the Nazis dissolved the movement's associations in Germany, Austria, and Czechoslovakia. These three countries had been the strongholds of the SASI.

The 1932 Olympics were held in Los Angeles with only 1,331 athletes participating. This figure suggests that, at the time, Europe was the center of international sports. Innovations at the 1932 games included the photo-finish camera and automatic timing devices. Despite the small number of participants in the Los Angeles games, the IOC decided to stick to its resolution to hold the games alternately in sites located in Europe and outside Europe.

The 1936 Olympic Games were awarded to Berlin, following a decision made in 1931. When the Nazi party came to power in Germany early in 1933, the German government decided to use the games to demonstrate the supremacy of its political system and especially the supremacy of the "Aryan master race." The International Olympic Committee made no comment on the fact that the games were being used for political purposes. A movement to boycott the so-called Nazi Olympics was started in various countries, but it failed. The motion to boycott the games was defeated in the United States by a very slim margin.

The Berlin games undoubtedly were the most grandiose in the history of the modern Olympics. Germany employed all available means to assure their success. Although a great deal of pageantry was added to the Olympic protocol, only the torch relay from the ancient site of Olympia (Greece) to the venue of the games was to remain in future years. Much to the sorrow of the Nazis, the outstanding athlete of the games turned out to be a black American by the name of Jesse Owens, who won four gold medals (for the 100- and 200-meter sprints, the long jump, and the 400-meter relay). Owens's prowess prompted the Nazis to attack the United States for "having to use black auxiliary forces because of the weakness of the white race." After the Winter Games, the German minister for propaganda,

Josef Goebbels, claimed that "the Olympic games were worth more than thirty army divisions to Hitler," as could be seen when the German army occupied, unopposed, the demilitarized Rhine Valley soon after the games ended. When World War II broke out three years later, the world was to pay an enormous price for not realizing the Nazi danger in time.

Several accusations were made that many members of the IOC had clear pro-fascist tendencies. Not only did they look at the Berlin Olympics as a tremendous success, they awarded the 1940 games to Japan. Japan was an ally of Nazi Germany. The IOC was also considering holding the 1944 games in Rome, the capital of then fascist Italy. The American IOC member, Emil Jahncke, had the distinction of being expelled from the supreme body of the Olympic movement for resisting the organization of the Nazi Olympics. When Japan gave up the 1940 games because of its war against China, the games were moved to Finland. When Finland gave up the games because of World War II, the IOC offered the organization of the 1940 Winter Games to Nazi Germany, the country that had started the war.

Jesse Owens was not the only black athlete to hurt the feelings of the "superior race" of "Aryan" Germans. In 1937 the "Brown Bomber" Joe Louis became the world champion in boxing. A year later, Louis defeated Max Schmeling, the pride of Nazi Germany, in only 124 seconds while defending the title. Louis held the title for a total of eleven years, defending it successfully twenty-five times. He retired undefeated.

The second most important international sports event began to take shape in the 1930s. The Soccer World Cup was organized for the first time in 1930 and thereafter on a quadrennial basis. Although the beginning was quite modest, as only thirteen national teams showed up for the final stages in Uruguay, the interest in the games grew rapidly. In 1934, when the games were held for the second time, twenty-nine teams participated in the preliminary matches and sixteen reported to the final stage in Italy. The third time the Soccer World Cup games were held, a major political dispute broke out. Austria, after qualifying for the final stage to be held in France, was annexed to the German Reich in March 1938. The Germans refused to let the Austrians appear in the games as an independent national team, and they also included a number of Austrian players on their own national team. Thus the same athletes played for one country in the preliminary matches and for another country in the final stage. This was clearly against the rules, but the International Soccer Federation gave in to a German ultimatum. As this action shows, the appeasement of Germany occurred not only in politics but also in sports. None of the acts of appeasement were successful in preventing Germany from starting World War II a year later.

Soccer was not the only sport to start a world championship in the years between the two world wars. In the 1920s, ice hockey (1920), table tennis (1927), shooting (1929), and skiing (1929) held world championships. They were followed in the 1930s by championships in bobsledding (1931), fencing (1936), and canoeing (1938). Leaders of track and field and swimming decided at that time to have their world championships decided in the quadrennial Olympic Games. This move contributed immensely to their status in the Olympic Games. These sports also began a periodical European championship, swimming already in 1926, and track and field in 1934. Additional firsts for European championships can also be found in boxing (1924) and basketball (1935 for men and 1938 for women). The world championships in fencing and canoeing were preceded by a continental championship in Europe. Fencing initiated its championship in 1930 and canoeing in 1933.

New attempts at organizing regional games were also made during the years between the two world wars. In 1926 the first Central-American Games were held in Mexico. In 1934 the Western-Asian Games were organized (for a single time only) in India. In 1930 the British Empire Games were held for the first time in Hamilton, Ontario (Canada). The British Empire Games were held quadrennially up to World War II and then renewed as the British Commonwealth Games in 1950. The Maccabiah Games, the so-called Jewish Olympics, were organized on a religious basis and held for the first time in 1932 in Tel Aviv (then in Palestine).

## INTERNATIONAL SPORTS AT THE BEGINNING OF THE COLD WAR

Even before the end of World War II, the Soviet Union had sent out clear signals that it was interested in becoming part of the international sports scene. The clearest sign of this interest came when the champion Soviet soccer club, Dynamo Moscow, was sent on a competitive tour to Great Britain. In 1946 the Soviets accepted an invitation to participate as "guests" in the European track and field championship in Oslo, Norway. However, despite their interest in international competition, the Soviet Union did not join the Olympic movement until 1951. Even then, they decided not to participate in the 1952 Winter Games. The reason for this delay is generally thought to be Soviet desire to link its participation to political gain. One major Soviet demand was the expulsion of Franco's Spain from the Olympic movement. Only when the IOC showed no inclination whatsoever to give in to this and other Soviet demands did the USSR decide to participate in the Olympic Games without conditions.

The 1948 Olympics, held in London, were thus held without the participation of the USSR, in spite of very serious efforts to convince the Soviets to take part. The games were much like the Antwerp games of 1920. Like Antwerp, London was partially destroyed during the war, and building facilities for the 1948 games was seen as part of its reconstruction. The size of the 1948 games reached new records when fifty-eight countries sent over 4,000 athletes to compete. Competitions were held in 138 events in seventeen sports.[2]

As in 1920, Germany and its allies were barred from the 1948 games. On the other hand, Italy was allowed to participate, because it had switched sides shortly before the end of the war. The ending of the era of colonialism could also be sensed at the London games, as countries like Lebanon and Iraq participated for the first time. African countries were gradually to follow, making their first appearance in 1952. Table 5.1 summarizes these and other highlights of the modern Olympic Games from 1896 to the present.

**TABLE 5.1 The Modern Olympics**

| YEAR | GAMES | LOCATION | NOTES |
|---|---|---|---|
| 1896 | Olympic Games | Athens | First modern Olympic games. Limited international participation. An all-male event. |
| 1900 | Olympic Games | Paris | A fiasco. Drags on for more than 5 months as part of a world's fair. About 1,000 participants, including 11 women (in tennis and golf). |
| 1904 | Olympic Games | St. Louis | Exact content and participation still under discussion. Women participate only in the unofficial activity of archery. |
| 1908 | Olympic Games | London | Dispute over rules. Figure skating in the summer. Definition of marathon distance. A breakthrough for women, with 43 officially competing. |
| 1912 | Olympic Games | Stockholm | Well-organized games. Over 2,000 participants. Dishonor of the Jim Thorpe affair. Women compete in swimming for the first time. |
| 1916 | — | — | Games cancelled because of World War I. Originally scheduled to be held in Berlin. |
| 1920 | Olympic Games | Antwerp | Germany and its allies not allowed to participate. Ice hockey and figure skating at summer games. Adoption of Olympic flag and oath. Archery expelled after a rules dispute. |
| 1924 | Winter Olympics | Chamonix, France | For the first time, a separate week of winter sports. |
| | Summer Olympics | Paris | Germany not welcomed by the French hosts. Over 3,000 participants. |
| 1928 | Winter Olympics | St. Moritz, Switzerland | Sonja Henie wins first (of three) gold medals in figure skating. |
| | Summer Olympics | Amsterdam | Women compete in 5 track and field events and gymnastics. Tennis dropped from the Olympic program, not to return till 1988. |
| 1932 | Winter Olympics | Lake Placid, New York | Decrease in participation from overseas. |
| | Summer Olympics | Los Angeles | First time IOC decision to hold games alternately in Europe and outside Europe is implemented. Photo finish and automatic timing devices introduced. |
| 1936 | Winter Olympics | Garmish, Germany | A popular success, drawing half a million spectators. |
| | Summer Olympics | Berlin | An attempt to organize an international boycott of the games fails. Dominated by the politics of Nazi Germany. |
| 1940 | — | — | No games. Summer games were awarded first to Japan, then to Finland; winter games to Japan and later to Switzerland and to Germany. Finally cancelled because of World War II. |

*continued*

**TABLE 5.1** continued

| YEAR | GAMES | LOCATION | NOTES |
|---|---|---|---|
| 1944 | — | — | No games because of World War II. |
| 1948 | Winter Olympic | St. Moritz, Switzerland | The first post-war winter games. |
| | Summer Olympics | London | Record participation with over 4,000 athletes from 58 countries. Germany and Japan barred from the games. |
| 1952 | Winter Olympics | Oslo | USSR does not participate in spite of joining the Olympic movement in 1951. Subsequent winter and summer games are to be held in different countries. |
| | Summer Olympics | Helsinki | First games in which African countries and the USSR participate. Avery Brundage becomes IOC chair. Emil Zatopek becomes the first and only athlete to win the 3 distance races. |
| 1956 | Winter Olympics | Cortina d'Ampezzo, Italy | First appearance of the USSR in the winter games. |
| | Summer Olympics | Melbourne | First games in the Southern Hemisphere. Boycott by 6 countries for political reasons. |
| 1960 | Winter Olympics | Squaw Valley | The American ice hockey team wins the gold medal over heavily favored Soviet and Canadian teams. |
| | Summer Olympics | Rome | Marathoner Abebe Bikila is first black African to win Olympic gold medal. Taiwan forced to call itself Formosa. |
| 1964 | Winter Olympics | Innsbruck, Austria | Lack of snow threatens the games. |
| | Summer Olympics | Tokyo | South Africa expelled for apartheid policies. People's Republic of China, Indonesia and North Korea boycott the games as an aftermath of the GANEFO affair. |
| 1968 | Winter Olympics | Grenoble, France | French skier Jean-Claude Killy wins 3 gold medals in Alpine skiing. |
| | Summer Olympics | Mexico City | Police kill an unknown number of students demonstrating against the Olympics. Black athletes demonstrate for racial equality; two of them are expelled from the games. Sex chromatin tests for female athletes required for the first time. |
| 1972 | Winter Olympics | Sapporo, Japan | Dispute over amateurism vs. professionalism comes to a head. |
| | Summer Olympics | Munich | Rhodesia expelled upon demand of other African countries. Eleven Israeli athletes and coaches killed by Arab terrorists. Mark Spitz wins 7 gold medals in swimming. Lord Killanin becomes IOC chair. |

*continued*

**TABLE 5.1** continued

| YEAR | GAMES | LOCATION | NOTES |
|---|---|---|---|
| 1976 | Winter Olympics | Innsbruck, Austria | Games first awarded to Denver, which declined. |
| | Summer Olympics | Montreal | Games incur a deficit of $1 billion! Communist countries win 44 out of 49 gold medals in women's competitions. |
| 1980 | Winter Olympics | Lake Placid, New York | First participation by People's Republic of China. Eric Heiden becomes the only athlete to win 5 races in speed skating. First games to declare bankruptcy. |
| | Summer Olympics | Moscow | Only 80 nations participate as a result of a U.S.-led boycott protesting the Soviet invasion of Afghanistan. Good athletic achievements, especially by Soviet and East German participants. Samaranch becomes IOC chair. |
| 1984 | Winter Olympics | Sarajevo, Yugoslavia | Poor weather conditions make competitions difficult. |
| | Summer Olympics | Los Angeles | Counter-boycott by the USSR fails, although it influences achievements in a number of sports. Close to 7,000 participants from 140 countries. |
| 1988 | Winter Olympics | Calgary | Doping begins to appear as the central issue of the games. |
| | Summer Olympics | Seoul | A mini-boycott instigated by North Korea and Cuba. The "Breakfast Games" scheduled to satisfy U.S. television. Professionals admitted. Tennis is back. |
| 1992 | Winter Olympics | Albertville, France | Games are spread out throughout the region. Only 18 of 57 events are held in Albertville. |
| | Summer Olympics | Barcelona | No boycotts. American "Dream Team" in basketball. Baseball for the first time. |
| 1994 | Winter Olympics | Lillehammer, Norway | "Very successful." For the first time winter games are held in a separate year. |
| 1996 | Summer Olympics | Atlanta | The centennial of the modern Olympics. More than 30% of competitors are women. |
| 1998 | Winter Olympics | Nagano, Japan | Weather problems. American and Canadian dream teams in ice hockey fall below expectations. |
| 2000 | Summer Olympics | Sydney | Tae kwan do and the triathlon included for the first time. |
| 2002 | Winter Olympics | Salt Lake City | Bribery scandal. |
| 2004 | Summer Olympics | Athens, Greece | Games of the XXVIII Olympiad |
| 2006 | Winter Olympics | Turin, Italy | |

In 1952 the Olympic movement paid another debt when it allocated the Summer Games to Helsinki, Finland. Thus the tradition of holding the games alternately in Europe and elsewhere was broken. In the same year, the IOC awarded the Winter Games to Oslo, Norway. Following the 1952 games, the Summer and Winter Games were never again held in the same region.

The biggest attraction at the Helsinki games was the appearance of athletes from the Soviet Union for the first time. The Korean War was being fought then, so the presence of Soviets brought Cold War tensions into the Olympic arena. The Soviets viewed the games as a way in which their regime could prove its superiority. When soundly defeated by the Americans, the Soviets took their loss very hard.[3]

The outstanding athlete of the 1952 games was a runner named Emil Zatopek from the small country of Czechoslovakia. Zatopek became the only runner in the history of the modern Olympics to win three individual long-distance races at the same games—the 5,000-meter, the 10,000-meter, and the marathon race.

The Finns used the games of 1952 to get even with the IOC in a very delicate way. Before the 1932 games, the IOC had disqualified the famous Finnish runner Paavo Nurmi for breaking the then-strict amateur rules. Nurmi had previously won a total of nine gold medals in individual as well as team events in the 1920, 1924, and 1928 games. The Finns' appeal of his disqualification was turned down, and Nurmi was not allowed to participate in the marathon race at the Los Angeles games. Now, at the Helsinki Olympics of 1952, the Finns bestowed on Nurmi the greatest possible honor, that of carrying the Olympic torch into the stadium during the opening ceremony.

## THE ERA OF AVERY BRUNDAGE (1952–1972)

In 1952 Avery Brundage, an American, was elected the fifth president of the International Olympic Committee. He strongly believed in the maintenance of strict amateur rules. He also supposedly held an idealistic view that emphasized total and complete separation of sports and politics. Yet, during his twenty years as president, the IOC was heavily involved in numerous political controversies.

Many historians believe that Brundage's main interest may not have been Olympic freedom from politics. Rather, he may have been more interested in using the Olympic movement to endorse his own personal political ideas. This view gains credence when we examine the differing ways in which the Olympic movement handled divided Germany and divided China. Brundage insisted that East Germany and West Germany must enter a single unified team at the Olympic Games. Yet he called for two separate Chinese teams, one from mainland China and the other from Taiwan. Political ideology—desire for noncommunists to be well represented at the Olympics—appears to be the only logical explanation for this policy. In the case of Germany, the pro-Western side seemed to have the upper hand and would dominate a unified team. In China, however, the communists were clearly in a superior position, and the noncommunist Taiwanese would be represented at the Olympics only if they had their own team. Further, the moment the German Democratic Republic of East Germany gained superiority in German sports, it was granted status as an independent team. Thus the Mexico Olympics of 1968 included two independent German teams, one from East Germany and one from West Germany. Had the athletes from West Germany not been recognized as an independent entity, they would have been only an insignificant minority on the unified team.

The 1956 Olympics in Melbourne, Australia, were marred by two political problems. The Netherlands, Spain, and Switzerland boycotted the games as a protest against participation by the Soviet Union. Just weeks before the games, the Soviet Union had crushed the Hungarians who had revolted against Hungary's communist government. Additionally, the only three Arab states that were members of the Olympic movement at the time (Egypt, Iraq, and Lebanon) stayed away from the games after their demand to expel Great Britain, France, and Israel was rejected. Great Britain, France, and Israel had opened the Sinai and Suez Canal campaign in October of that year. The International Olympic Committee did not even consider the demands for disqualification in either of these situations.

One of the strangest political decisions ever made by the IOC occurred prior to the 1960 games in Rome. To conciliate the communist People's Republic of China, the IOC required representatives of Taiwan to appear at the games under the name of Formosa, which was the Japanese name for their island. In order not to leave the Olympic scene entirely in the hands of Red China, the Taiwanese representatives agreed to the demand, but they marched into the stadium during the opening ceremony bearing a placard that read "Under Protest." To compound the irony, the People's Republic of China stayed home and did not appear at the Olympics until the Winter Games of 1980.

In the Olympiad preceding the Tokyo Olympics of 1964, the world witnessed the creation of a serious anti-Olympic movement. The IOC had expelled Indonesia from the Olympic movement after that country failed to invite Israel and Taiwan to participate in the Fourth Asian Games, which were held under the auspices of the Olympic movement. In reaction, Indonesia, with the support of the People's Republic of China, organized the Games of the Newly Emerging Forces (GANEFO). A significant number of Third World countries became members. Many Western countries also cooperated with the movement, primarily for economic reasons. It was fortunate, therefore, for the Olympic movement when GANEFO disbanded. The failure of the GANEFO movement can be attributed to three factors, all external to the organization. The major factor was the removal from power of President Sukarno of Indonesia. A second contributing factor was the defeat of Egypt in the Six-Day War with Israel. The Cultural Revolution in China in 1966, which called for the seclusion of China from the rest of the world, can be seen as a third contributing factor.

In 1964, to prevent African countries from joining the GANEFO movement, the IOC did not allow South Africa, a country notorious for its discrimination against blacks, to participate in the Tokyo Olympics. Global opposition to South Africa's policies of apartheid kept that country out of the Olympic movement until 1992, when the political situation in South Africa had changed.

The 1968 Olympics, held in Mexico City, are best remembered for two political demonstrations. A few days before the games opened, the Mexican police fired on unarmed students who were demonstrating against the games. The students were protesting the government's wasting of limited national funds on a spectacle like the Olympic Games. An unknown number of students were killed. Some sources estimate that the number may have reached into the hundreds. Despite the severity of this police action, the IOC declared that the demonstrations were an "internal Mexican affair that had nothing to do with the games." They simply ignored the situation.

On the other hand, Brundage saw to it that two black athletes who were members of the Black Power movement were immediately expelled from the games. Prior to the games, a number of black athletes had decided to boycott the games to heighten public awareness of the problems confronting black athletes. Many black athletes stayed away from Mexico City. During the games, several black athletes demonstrated for racial equality. Two demonstrating black American athletes, Tommie Smith and John Carlos, were immediately suspended by the IOC and sent home.

Before the 1972 Olympics in Munich, Brundage and the IOC gave in to threats from African countries to boycott those games if the Rhodesian team was allowed to participate. Rhodesia was expelled from the games and the boycott never materialized. The reason for the original demand is unclear. There never existed any apartheid in Rhodesian sports, and blacks were in fact a majority of the Rhodesian delegation.

During the Munich games of 1972, Arab terrorists occupied Israeli quarters inside the Olympic village and killed eleven Israeli athletes and coaches. The world was stunned, and there was an immediate call to cancel the games, but Brundage succeeded in convincing the IOC that "the games must go on." Indeed, following a day of mourning, the games did resume. In retrospect, most political analysts support the decision to continue the games, but for a different reason than the one stated by the IOC. They feel that the games should have continued because their disruption would have meant an important victory for international terrorism, not because the Olympic Games carried some kind of supreme value.

The political events during Brundage's regime as president overshadowed his efforts to protect amateurism in the Olympic Games. Still, the battle to protect the concept of amateurism in the Olympics continued despite growing hypocrisy in the matter. With the entrance of the Soviet Union into the Olympics in 1952, a new status of athletes emerged, "state amateurs." These athletes were clearly supported by their governments and were considered government employees. Brundage did not succeed in taking steps against the state amateurs, just as he could not touch student athletes who had received scholarships on the basis of their athletic ability, even though both forms of financial support were in direct violation of IOC rules. The fight against "creeping professionalism" reached its climax at the Sapporo (Japan) Winter Olympics in 1972, when Brundage caused the disqualification of Austrian superstar Karl Schranz. He even threatened to cancel the Winter Games altogether. Schranz was later reinstated by the IOC, but not until 1988. He was also given a medal of participation for the 1972 games. The concept of amateurism received yet another blow when the major international tennis tournaments decided in 1968 to become open competitions, allowing professionals to compete against amateurs.

The international sport scene in mid-century extended far beyond the Olympic movement. In 1948 the first Stoke-Mandeville Games for paraplegics were organized by Sir Ludwig Guttmann. These games were the pioneer international sporting event for athletes with disabilities. In 1949 the first world championship in men's volleyball took place. This was followed three years later by a parallel event for women. These championships paved the way for the entrance of both men's and women's volleyball into the Olympic program in 1964. When this occurred, Avery Brundage declared that "the Olympic program for women had been completed." World championships in basketball soon followed those in volleyball. Championships were staged in men's basketball in 1950 and in women's basketball in 1953.

In 1949, the international workers' sport organizations gathered in Ghent, Belgium, and decided not to revive the International Organization of Socialist Sports (SASI). Their resolution followed upon the German decision not to organize a separatist sport movement, as well as the wishes of other countries to compete within the frame of national sport associations. Austria and Israel were two countries expressing this preference.

In 1951, the first two continental games, the Pan-American Games and the Asian Games, were established. These were followed in 1965 by formation of the African Games. Since their inception, the Pan-American Games and the Asian Games have been held regularly on a quadrennial basis. The African Games established a regular schedule only in the late 1980s.

In 1950 soccer held its fourth World Cup games. At that time the International Soccer Federation (FIFA) had participants from more countries, seventy-three, than did the Helsinki Olympics or the Melbourne Olympics. In Helsinki, sixty-nine countries were represented, and in Melbourne the number dropped to sixty-seven. Soccer was on its way to becoming the number one sport in the world. Brazil began to establish itself as a superpower in international soccer when its national team won the World Cup three times in twelve years (1958, 1962, and 1970). Brazil's greatest soccer star, Pele, became his country's minister of sports in the mid-1990s. In 1994 Brazil gained the world title for the fourth time.

Other great athletes in international sport during this era include Mark Spitz, an American swimmer who won seven gold medals at the Munich Olympics. He established four individual world records and helped three American relay teams to do the same. Spitz's achievement was considered a kind of comeback, as four years earlier he had failed to live up to expectations. At the Mexico City Olympics in 1968, he had won "only" two gold medals in the relays, and a silver and a bronze in the individual events. A second great athlete of the period was the Ethiopian marathon runner Abebe Bikila. In 1960 Bikila became the first black African to gain an Olympic gold medal. He successfully defended his title four years later.

# THE EIGHT STORMY YEARS OF
# LORD MICHAEL (1972–1980)

In 1972 Lord Michael Killanin of Northern Ireland replaced Avery Brundage as president of the International Olympic Committee. His eight years in office were marked by one controversy after another.

The first problem during Killanin's regime arose with the Winter Games of 1976. Although the games were awarded to the city of Denver, the citizens of the state of Colorado voted in a referendum against holding the games there. Out of necessity, the IOC turned elsewhere and asked Innsbruck, Austria, to organize the games for a second time in twelve years. Colorado's refusal to allow Denver to host the games did not discourage the IOC from granting the Winter Games of 1980 to another city in the United States, Lake Placid, New York. These games made Olympic history by becoming the only ones ever to declare bankruptcy.

The Summer Games of 1976, which took place in Montreal, faced both political and economic problems. On the political scene, African countries, led by Tanzania, demanded the expulsion of New Zealand from the games because New Zealand had sent a rugby team to South Africa. At the time, the Olympic movement had declared a boycott against South Africa because of its apartheid policy. New Zealand responded that since rugby was not an Olympic sport, the Olympic movement had no control over it. When the IOC agreed with New Zealand, twenty-seven African states, plus Iraq and Guyana, decided to boycott the Montreal games. Killanin, however, unlike his predecessor, did not give in to political threats. Within a short time, all the boycotting countries had returned to the Olympic fold.

The African countries learned a lesson from the Montreal boycott and did not attempt any Olympic boycotts in the future. But they continued to exert political power in the field of sports, primarily in the British Commonwealth Games, where they had a much greater influence.

The economic problems afflicting the 1976 games turned out to be much more severe than the political controversy. When the final financial picture of the 1976 Olympic Games was determined, the city of Montreal discovered that it had suffered a deficit of one billion dollars. As Montreal had showcased the Olympics as the games of Quebec and not as the games of Canada, the federal government did not rush to the assistance of the city. To this day, the city of Montreal is struggling with repayment of its debt. As a direct result of this fiscal debacle, the Olympic movement faced difficulties until 1992 in finding cities willing to host the games.

Unlike Brundage, Killanin was a strong supporter of women's athletics, and female athletes benefited significantly during his tenure. Under his regime, four more sports opened their doors to female athletes within the frame of the Olympics. In the 1976 games, basketball, field handball, and rowing were added to the women's program. Four years later, field hockey followed as the eleventh sport in the Olympic program for women.

Whereas West Germany had succeeded in performing an "economic miracle" in the 1950s, East Germany began to show its "athletic miracle" at the

Montreal Olympics. East Germany, with a population of only 17 million people, outperformed the United States by winning a greater number of Olympic gold medals (40 to 34). The same outcome occurred the next time the two countries met in the Olympic arena. At the 1988 Olympic Games, the German Democratic Republic won 102 medals overall, 37 of which were gold medals. The United States won 36 gold medals and 94 medals overall. It was only in the 1990s that one of the major reasons for East German success was revealed: the systematic use of doping materials.

An indication of what was to come could be seen already at the first world championship in swimming, which was held in 1973 in Belgrade, Yugoslavia. The German Democratic Republic, which had not won a single gold medal in the Munich Olympics a year earlier, suddenly scored at the very top of the medal count by winning thirteen gold medals. The East German women especially excelled at this world championship, gaining eleven gold medals.

By organizing a separate world championship, the sport of swimming left track and field as the only sport still viewing the Olympic Games as the venue for its world championship. This situation did not last long. In 1977 the first World Cup competition in track and field took place. It included both continental teams and the best national teams. This first World Cup competition in track and field was later replaced by a regular world championship in 1983.

The 1980 Olympics were scheduled to take place in Moscow. When the Soviet Union invaded Afghanistan in December 1979, however, U.S. president Jimmy Carter threatened a worldwide boycott of the games unless the Soviets withdrew their troops. During the Winter Games at Lake Placid, declaration of the boycott became final and a prestigious battle over international influence began. The Soviet Union seems to have set a goal of attracting a greater number of athletes to the Moscow games than participated in the games held in Montreal. The Soviets believed that this would demonstrate to the world that the United States had less influence than the African states. As a result of all this, even though the number of member countries in the Olympic movement had grown in the preceding four years, only eighty-one countries participated in the Moscow games. The Montreal Olympics had attracted eighty-nine countries. Although the boycott had an effect, the Americans had reason to be unhappy with certain aspects of it, especially that Germany and Norway were the only significant European countries to participate.

Opinions about the effect of the Moscow boycott are still divided. Many believe it was a failure, because it did not drive a single Soviet soldier out of Afghanistan. Others insist that it laid the cornerstone for the downfall of the Soviet Union. As in most cases, the truth seems to lie somewhere in the middle. The international prestige of the Soviet Union definitely suffered as a result of the boycott. This occurred in spite of the high standards of the games. During the games, athletes from the USSR and East Germany won a collective total of 321 medals. At the 1980 Winter Games in Lake Placid, the American speed skater Eric Heiden was probably the most outstanding athlete. He won all five races in his sport.

## THE FIRST DECADE OF THE
## SAMARANCH ERA (1980–1990)

In 1980 Juan Antonio Samaranch, a Spanish member of the IOC, was elected president to replace Lord Killanin, who had resigned for health reasons. Samaranch had been a member of the IOC since 1966. He had also been a ranking government official during the Fascist Franco regime in his country up to the dictator's death in 1975. In 1977 Samaranch had been appointed Spain's ambassador to the Soviet Union.

The first years of Samaranch's presidency were far from being free of controversy. At the Olympic Congress in 1981, Seoul, the capital of South Korea, was allocated the 1988 Olympics. The only other candidate under consideration was Nagoya, Japan. That city, however, was eliminated from consideration when a delegation of Nagoya citizens demonstrated against the Olympic Games. The fear of holding the Olympics in Seoul was also great, however, because of the delicate political situation between the two Koreas. Many felt that another Olympic boycott was looming on the horizon.

The first years of Samaranch's presidency were also marked by concern over the Olympic Games of 1984. The city of Los Angeles had been awarded these games but had not secured the financial support of the federal, state, or city governments. The selection of Los Angeles to host the games had been very peculiar, inasmuch as no other candidates had even been considered. Other venues simply were not interested in hosting the games following the financial debacle of the Montreal Olympics.

A positive aspect of the 1981 Olympic Congress was the election of the first two women, Pirjo Haggman and Flor Isava-Fonseca, for membership in the International Olympic Committee. Previous to this, it was often claimed that the IOC was nothing but an "old men's order." In the coming years Samaranch became a great benefactor of women's sports.

Some people see another positive aspect of the early years of Samaranch's presidency. He became the first full-time president of the IOC. While not drawing a salary, he did maintain a significant expense account. In later years, Samaranch approved a decision that made the IOC presidency a salaried position, effective with his successor.

The 1984 Olympics in Los Angeles turned out to be an unqualified success, so much so that Samaranch declared the games to have been the greatest and the best ever, a phrase that became standard in his closing remarks at all subsequent games up to the Atlanta games in 1996. A counter-boycott in 1984, organized by the Soviet Union, led to the absence of nineteen countries from the games in Los Angeles. This hurt the quality of the games because of the absence of the Soviet Union and East Germany, the two top nations in the previous games. Despite the boycott by the USSR, a record number of 140 countries appeared in Los Angeles, including the People's Republic of China, Rumania, and Yugoslavia. Over 7,000 athletes competed in the games. Only the earlier games in Munich (1972) had a slightly greater number of participating athletes. The Soviet Union attempted to explain the limited effect of its boycott by saying that it did not wish to harm the Olympic movement. However, most observers thought that American diplomacy had celebrated a great victory over its Cold War opponents.

The greatest success of the Los Angeles Games was economic. Whereas only eight years earlier the Montreal games had shown a billion dollar deficit, the Los Angeles games ended up with a surplus of over $200 million. The Los Angeles games were run by a group of outstanding businessmen who succeeded in organizing the games with minimal costs and maximal income. University dormitories were used to house the athletes, a minimal number of new facilities were constructed, and those that were built were paid for by private sponsors. In addition, a record number of volunteers helped to assure the financial success of the games. The Los Angeles games thus demonstrated to the world that profits could be generated through proper organization. Gone were the days when a city could be awarded the games by default, as had happened for the 1984 and 1988 games. After the Los Angeles games, so many cities lined up for the games that an elimination procedure had to be established in the mid-1990s.

Income from the mass media was to become a major source of funding both during and after the Los Angeles games. During those games, American and foreign television media paid nearly $300 million for broadcast rights. The American Broadcasting Corporation (ABC) alone paid $225 million. This was clearly an indication of things to come in the relationships between the mass media and the Olympic movement.

The economic success of the Los Angeles games motivated the IOC to start "The Olympic Program" (TOP). The idea behind TOP was that sponsors should be asked to assist the Olympic movement on a permanent basis and not only through the sponsorship of particular games. Soon after its inception, TOP had attracted ten major sponsors, primarily in the United States, for the period of one Olympiad.

The athletic hero of the 1984 Olympic Games was Carl Lewis, who succeeded in repeating Jesse Owens's record of winning four gold medals in track and field. He continued his athletic career up to the 1996 Atlanta games, where he gained his ninth gold medal.

For the Winter Games of 1988, held in Calgary, ABC bid $309 million for the television broadcast rights. ABC's contract with the IOC and the Calgary Organizing Committee gave the media people extensive rights, leading to the nickname "the ABC games." The games were scheduled during the "chinook" season, which brought hot winds and sandstorms that caused postponement of several competitions. These events could not be rescheduled without the agreement of ABC, which of course was interested in rescheduling them at economically advantageous times. When confronted with a disagreement between ABC officials and local meteorologists, Samaranch was forced to intercede. Otherwise the games might not have been completed within their sixteen-day schedule.

The 1988 Olympic Games of Seoul could not have been held at a more suitable time. Mikhail Gorbachev had just assumed power in the Soviet Union and had declared a period of *glasnost* and *perestroika*.[4] This major political change, aided by the fact that South Korea had just held its first democratic elections, helped overcome the reservations that many countries had with regard to the games being held in a country that was in a state of permanent hostility with its northern neighbor. Only North Korea resented the games being held in Seoul, and it reacted by calling for an international boycott of the games. The response to this call was minimal; it was answered by only six other countries, led by Cuba.

Major changes took place at the games in Seoul. Not only was tennis readmitted to the Olympic program after a hiatus of sixty-four years, but top professionals were allowed to participate in the Olympic tournament. Steffi Graf of Germany, who already enjoyed top ranking in the tennis world, became the Olympic champion. All this was a far cry from 1924, when tennis was expelled for allowing large payments as expense money.

One reason for these changes in tennis was that the IOC, for the first time, left it to the various international federations to decide whether to permit professionals to compete in the various Olympic sports. All but three of the international federations opted in favor of allowing professionals to compete. The three federations that rejected the participation of professionals were those of baseball, boxing, and soccer. However, soccer permitted all players up to the age of twenty-three to participate, together with a limited number of older players (even if those players were professionals). The objective of the soccer federation (FIFA) was to protect its own World Cup Games and to prevent the Olympics from becoming a second world cup. The IOC was forced to give in to the position taken by the soccer federation, lest the Olympic Games should be left without a tournament of the number one sport in the world. In 1996 the International Baseball Association decided to allow professional players to compete in its Olympic competitions.

Another noticeable change at the 1988 Seoul Olympics was the scheduling of events. At the request of the U.S. television broadcaster, the finals in certain events were scheduled for the morning hours in order to show them during live prime-time hours in the United States. Some international federations resisted the pressure from the television officials, arguing that human biorhythm specialists were of the opinion that top performances could be achieved primarily in late afternoon or early evening hours. The plea of the federations fell on deaf ears, and the Seoul Olympics were nicknamed "the Breakfast Games."

Outside the Olympic movement, a series of international competitions developed in 1986. Ted Turner, an American entrepreneur, initiated the "Goodwill Games." These games were developed with hopes of demonstrating to the world that athletes from both the East and the West could again be brought together in the sports arena. This was something that the Olympic movement had failed to do in the Olympic Games of 1980 and 1984. The Goodwill Games were organized on a quadrennial basis and held on an alternating basis in the Soviet Union (later Russia) and in the United States. Despite incurring a $70 million deficit, the Goodwill Games were held for a fourth time in 1998 in New York. The games have in fact succeeded in bringing athletes from the East and West together, but they have failed to leave a deep impression on international sports.

## INTERNATIONAL SPORTS IN THE 1990S

Although any account of recent events in international sports necessarily lacks historical perspective, we cannot ignore several important developments occurring during the 1990s. After twenty-four years of boycotts and threats of boycotts, the Olympics of 1992 took place in Barcelona with unlimited participation. The city of Albertville, in France, hosted the Winter Games. This was considered a kind of compensation for Paris not being awarded the Summer Games. The most memorable event of the Barcelona games was the premiere of the American "Dream Team" in basketball. The Dream Team was made up of professional players from the National Basketball Association.

During the 1990s, the International Olympic Committee decided to stagger the Summer Games and Winter Games in future, so that both events would not be held in the same year. Lillehammer, in Norway, organized the very successful Winter Games in 1994. The city of Nagano (Japan) hosted the Winter Games of 1998, Salt Lake City will host the Winter Games of 2002, and the Winter Games of 2006 will be held in Turin, Italy.

The 1998 Nagano games, which were organized extremely well, suffered greatly from weather conditions. Many specialists claimed that weather mishaps were to be expected because of the climate, a fact that caused many to declare at the end of the games, "Never again in Japan." An outstanding feature of the 1998 Winter Games was the appearance of the American and Canadian "dream teams" of ice hockey professionals, an appearance that ended in major disappointments when both teams failed to reach the final.

As the modern Olympics reached their hundredth birthday, Atlanta outbid Athens for the right to organize the Centennial Games of 1996. The Summer Games of 1996 established a new record for participation, attracting 197 countries. A record number of spectators also attended the games. Despite these record figures, the Atlanta Olympics were affected by serious organizational problems, particularly in the areas of communication and transportation. In the eyes of many IOC members, the atmosphere of the games had become overly commercial, leading to a decision to allow a city to organize future games only if there was full cooperation between the organizing committee and the city and country governments. The Atlanta games were also marred by a bombing in a nearby park that killed one person and injured 111 others. Despite the logistical problems and the isolated act of violence, the Atlanta Games were a total success in terms of athletic achievement. Furthermore, for the first time, women accounted for more than 30 percent of all the athletes participating in the games. Immediately following the Atlanta games, the Paralympics were staged in the same venue. These games for athletes with disabilities attracted 3,400 participants from throughout the world. There were 517 events held in seventeen different sports.

In 1997 the International Olympic Committee allocated the 2004 Summer Games to the city of Athens, in Greece. The awarding of these games to Athens was generally viewed as compensation to the city for not having been awarded the 1996 games.

In the mid-1990s, the International Olympic Committee decided to extend the maximum age limit of its regular members to eighty years. Excluded from the ruling were "life members" and members of the executive committee. These decisions created a renewed image of the "old men's club," despite a limited number of female members.

Amid continual claims that the games were getting too large, new sports were added to the Olympic program. Baseball was added in 1992, softball in 1996, and tae kwan do and the triathlon in the year 2000. Not a single sport was deleted from the program regardless of various plans and suggestions to do so. The addition of new sports has forced the IOC to raise the number of participants allowed from 10,000 athletes to 10,500 or even higher.

The National Broadcasting Company (NBC) purchased North American broadcasting rights for the Summer and Winter Olympic Games from the year 2000 to 2008. This period encompassed three Summer and two Winter Games. The amount paid for the broadcast rights was a staggering $3.5 billion dollars.

The wealth of the International Olympic Committee is not exactly known. The governing body has its official residence in Lausanne, Switzerland, and Swiss laws do not require the publication of holdings. Without question, though, the IOC owes much of its dominating position in the world of sports to its financial status.[5]

Outside the Olympic movement, the major sports news of the 1990s came from the International Federation for Track and Field (IAAF). In 1991 the IAAF decided to turn its quadrennial world championships into a biennial event. These world championships became the major attraction in European sports because they were scheduled four consecutive times on that continent. World championships were held in Stuttgart, Germany (1993), Göteborg, Sweden (1995), Athens, Greece (1997), and Seville, Spain (1999). Additionally, the IAAF began to pay bonuses for victories in the world championship, as well as for world records. This action stemmed from the belief that it was the athletes who produced income for the federations. The IAAF even called on the IOC to follow in its footsteps. To date the IOC has not responded.

In the 1995 African Games, two major stars of African sports refused to represent their respective countries. Moses Kiptanoui of Kenya and Haile Gebresellasie of Ethiopia both held world records as long-distance runners. The reason for their refusal is unknown, but some observers claimed that the reason may have been that they were not offered money to participate.

The 1998 World Cup in soccer, which was held in France, turned out to be a tremendous success despite efforts by English and neo-Nazi German hooligans to disturb the games. Many labeled the games as the greatest sport event in the world. For the first time in the history of World Cup soccer competition, thirty-two nations were represented at the final stages. Interest in the games was enormous, even in nonparticipating countries. In many countries, the final match between France and Brazil received a television rating of nearly 50 percent. After France defeated Brazil in the finals, more people turned out to celebrate in the Champs Elysees than for Charles DeGaulle's entry into Paris toward the end of World War II.

Many of the international federations adopted new rules and events during the late 1990s. In response to outcries of various organizations against exploiting children in sport, a number of international federations raised the minimum age for participation in their international events. A number of international federations also began to sponsor world championships for women. For many this was a necessity, since they feared expulsion from the Olympic Games unless they did so. Among the federations adding championships for women were those for wrestling, weight lifting, and the modern pentathlon. The International Federation for Boxing started a European championship as preparation for future world championships. The International Soccer Federation (FIFA) organized the first world championship for women in 1991. This federation also established an interesting precedent when it allocated the 2002 World Cup games to two countries, Japan and the Republic of Korea.

## DOPING—THE CURSE OF MODERN SPORTS

Doping[6] was the central issue of the 1988 Seoul Olympics. One day after winning the gold medal in the 100-meter race and establishing a fantastic world record, the Canadian sprinter Ben Johnson was disqualified for using doping materials. The results of a drug test taken soon after his winning performance revealed the presence of stanazol, an anabolic steroid. Inasmuch as there was little doubt that Johnson had been using performance-enhancing substances, questions arose as to the nature and extent of doping activities among other athletes as well. Was the Johnson affair an isolated incident, or was the use of doping substances a widely common practice? A review of the history of doping cases in the Olympic Games provides some clues to the answer.

The IOC first tested for drugs at the 1968 Winter Olympics. The first disqualification of an Olympic athlete for a doping offense occurred at Mexico City in the same year when a Swedish pentathlete was caught with too much alcohol in his body. In the 1972 Olympics, seven athletes were disqualified. These included the American gold medalist in swimming, Rick DuMont, who, as an asthmatic, had used a medication containing ephedrine. In the 1976 games, the disqualifications for reported substance use rose to eleven.

The Olympic Games held in Moscow in 1980 had no reported instances of doping among the athletes. Journalists, however, reported that the doping tests conducted at Moscow were not taken seriously, and the Medical Commission of the IOC apparently looked the other way. In 1984 a record number of twelve cases were reported, but the true number may never be known because some of the positive tests were shredded by mistake. The Olympic movement apparently feared the loss of sponsors at a time when the commercialization of the movement was in its infancy.

In the games of 1988, an American Olympic medical authority reported that a member of an American team "in a very popular sport " tested positive. The test was ignored in order to avoid having to disqualify the entire team. The IOC may have feared admitting the extent of doping, as it had already disqualified Ben Johnson as well as two Bulgarian gold medalists in weight lifting. It has also been claimed that the International Olympic Committee wanted to avoid getting into trouble with one of the superpowers.

In 1991 and 1992, Brigitte Berendonk, a long-time German investigator of doping, successfully showed to the world the worth of the Olympic medical examinations. Berendonk was an East German champion in track and field in the 1960s. She escaped to the West and started an investigation of the doping of athletes in the German Democratic Republic. In examining the files of the East German secret police (the Stasi), she established that most of the top athletes from East Germany were doped. This was done by an organization run by the East German government. The IOC ignored Berendonk's findings. She was sued for libel on numerous occasions and successfully defended her position in each case. Yet, no East German athlete has ever been disqualified for using doping materials at the Olympic Games. Now that the secret of the East German "athletic miracle" has been uncovered and proved, it is obvious that the Medical Commission of the IOC was either incapable of detecting doping cases or chose to ignore them.

Although the various international federations have been successful in detecting a growing number of doped athletes, the number detected at Olympic Games has amazingly diminished. In the 1992 Barcelona Olympics, the number of reported doping cases was down to five. At the Atlanta Games of 1996, there were two disqualifications. Five former Soviet Union athletes were initially disqualified from the games for using a substance not on the official list of banned materials, but they were subsequently reinstated.

Prior to the Centennial Games in Atlanta, the IOC Medical Commission announced that it would use the new high-resolution mass spectrometer for testing athletes. This instrument was capable of detecting both low levels of doping materials and the remnants of such substances. However, when the instrument supplied an unknown number of positive tests, the Medical Commission was no longer convinced that the tests were accurate and reliable. Outside observers, of course, wondered whether the tests were indeed unreliable or whether the commission was frightened by its findings.

The question still remains whether the 1988 disqualification of Ben Johnson was a deliberate attempt by the IOC to introduce a "fear psychology" to show top athletes that no one was immune from disqualification. But experts on doping claim that, since its inception, the drug testing program at the Olympic Games has been nothing but a fiasco. Certainly the limited number of cases and disqualifications have assisted the Olympic movement in selling the Olympics to sponsors as well as to the public.

Cases involving disqualification of athletes often end up in civil courts, since a disqualified athlete is likely to face a significant loss of income. During the early 1990s, two such cases drew attention. The first involved the disqualification of Harry (Butch) Reynolds, an American who held the world record in the 400 meters. In 1990 Reynolds tested positive for a prohibited chemical substance and was disqualified from competition for a period of four years. A year after his disqualification, he was exonerated by the American Athletic Congress (TAC) but not by the International Federation for Track and Field. Reynolds successfully sued the federation for millions of dollars but could not collect the indemnities awarded by the court. In 1993 he received an official pardon and placed second in the world championship.

The second case attracting attention involved the disqualification of Katrin Krabbe, the 1991 German world champion in the women's 100- and 200-meter races. After being caught a second time with doping materials in her body, Krabbe was disqualified from competition for life. Despite a ruling by a German court in her favor, she has not, as of this writing, been allowed to return to track and field competition.

The pardon granted to Harry Reynolds in 1993 was not an isolated event. The world of international sports has experienced a number of peculiar pardons for top athletes. When the German weight lifter Karl-Heinz Radschinsky was caught with a commercial quantity of doping materials in 1984, his case was not brought before the courts until 1985. Meanwhile, Radschinsky won a gold medal at the Olympic Games in Los Angeles. His medal performance seems to have influenced the nominal punishment he eventually received. In his defense, Radschinsky claimed that it had become virtually impossible to reach the top in weight lifting without using doping materials. The courts accepted this statement at face value.

In December 1984 the Soviet weight lifter Alexander Kurlowitsch was caught in Montreal attempting to smuggle a commercial quantity of anabolic steroids into Canada. He was sentenced to pay only a low fine but was disqualified for life by his national federation. Two years later, he received a pardon approved by the International Weightlifting Federation. He won the world championship in 1987 and won two Olympic gold medals in the games of 1988 and 1992. Similarly, the Russian weight lifter Alexei Petrow, who had been disqualified for life, was pardoned in time to win a gold medal at the 1996 Atlanta Olympics.

The 1998 Tour de France, the most prestigious cycling race in the world, turned into the biggest doping scandal ever. Cynics nicknamed the race the "Tour de EPO," a reference to the performance-enhancing drug erythropoietin. Before the race started, authorities arrested a man not officially connected with the tour when they found enormous commercial quantities of doping materials in his possession. Soon after the race started, a team was suspended from the tour because doping materials were found in the possession of team officials. French police then raided the living quarters of several cyclists and held a number of racers for interrogation. In protest, six teams left the tour (including all the Spanish teams), and all the participants took part in two strikes in protest against "inhumane treatment." The 1998 tour thus set a negative record when, for the first time since 1903, fewer than 50 percent of the cyclists reached the finish line. In the aftermath of the twenty-one–day tour, a number of arrests were made, bringing the total to twelve.

During the Tour de France scandal, Juan Antonio Samaranch, president of the International Olympic Committee, surprised the world of sport by declaring that the IOC should reduce the list of prohibited doping materials for future competitions. Many saw this declaration as a clear admission that the IOC was fighting a losing battle against the dopers.

It is no coincidence that the examples mentioned here involve weight lifting and cycling. They were known to be the two sports most afflicted with doping, yet relatively little was done by their international federations. The International Cycling Federation tried in 1997 to overcome that image by pioneering the introduction of blood tests in addition to the urine tests of the past.

Disqualification from future competition is not the only danger to athletes from the use of doping materials. Several athletes under the influence of performance-enhancing substances have died during performance. Their cases are well documented. The first known death from doping occurred in 1886, when an English cyclist died during a race in France. For all practical purposes, though, this incident went unnoticed by the sporting world. When Knut Jensen, a Danish cyclist, died during a race at the 1960 Rome Olympics, the Olympic movement did become aware of the problem. He was found to have taken a combination of amphetamines and a nicotine substance. Seven years later, a British cyclist named Tom Simpson died during the Tour de France. In the late 1980s, there were short-lived furors when the world learned of the death of the young West German heptathlete, Birgit Dressel, and the death of close to twenty Western European cyclists who had used the hormone erythropoietin.

Attention to the dangers of doping developed in the United States in 1993 with the death of football star Lyle Alzado. Alzado, who died at the age of 43, claimed that his brain cancer had been caused by frequent use of steroids during his playing career. In his last years, he became a major spokesperson against the use of steroids.

Also in the 1990s, the doping cases of Diego Armando Maradona, the Argentinean soccer star, as well as a case involving eleven Chinese athletes at the Asian Games in Japan, drew international attention to the problem. Of the eleven athletes cited for doping violations at the Asian Games, seven were swimmers. At the world championship in 1994, Chinese female swimmers won an amazing fourteen gold medals. Two years later, at the Atlanta Olympics, Chinese women were able to win only three gold medals, two of which were in diving. It is difficult to avoid drawing parallels between the achievements of the (doped) East German female swimmers in the 1970s and 1980s and those of their Chinese counterparts in the 1990s. This parallel is especially intriguing since many of the coaches and sports medicine specialists from the fallen state of East Germany became active in China.

The current state of affairs in the world of doping and sports presents at least two issues that may make spectators and sponsors feel uneasy. Because of the extremely light punishments and the number of pardons granted to doped athletes, certain athletic events may be dominated by lawbreakers. Since other athletes do not use doping materials, the "playing field" is decidedly uneven. Social commentators wonder what has happened to the value of "fair play."[7]

The second concern relates to the tendency of some professional sport associations, particularly in the United States, either to completely oppose systematic drug testing or to perform tests in a very limited, insignificant manner. Further, some of the professional sport associations that have adopted a systematic program of testing will not publish the results. The fact that professional athletes today are free to enter practically all major sport events in the world again raises questions of fair play.

## THE END OF THE SAMARANCH ERA?

In December 1998, serious allegations of corruption were raised against a significant number of International Olympic Committee members. This time, the IOC could not ignore the claims, as it had in the past when such allegations were raised primarily by the mass media. In this instance, charges of corruption and bribery were made by Marc Hodler, a highly respected veteran IOC member from Switzerland. Hodler accused the Organizing Committee of the Salt Lake City Winter Games of 2002 of being involved in the large-scale bribery of more than a dozen IOC members. The accusations led to investigations by U.S. federal and state authorities, by the International Olympic Committee, and by the United States Olympic Committee. Two leading officials of the Salt Lake City Organizing Committee resigned.[8]

The developing scandal was soon considered "the darkest days in modern Olympic history," but the IOC acted with unprecedented speed. It established an inquiry panel that completed its investigations and handed in its report by the fourth week of January 1999. Before the report was issued, three members of the IOC resigned; a fourth suspect died shortly before the panel began its deliberations.

The inquiry panel suggested—and the IOC Executive Board approved—the expulsion of six more IOC members, subject to final approval by the IOC General Assembly. One of the six members resigned within days. In addition to the recommended expulsions, three other members, all of whom had served in the past as members of the executive board, were to remain under further investigation. African membership in the IOC was decapitated, as over one-third of the African nation members either resigned or were recommended for expulsion. Six of the total of thirteen accused had served in the IOC for over twenty years.[9]

The IOC also decided to change its site selection procedures and to establish an ethics committee, but the question remained whether such steps could help cure a cancerous situation and restore confidence in the committee. This was especially so as new allegations pertaining to the past continue to appear and will be investigated. (This account reflects the status of the ongoing scandal only up to February 1, 1999.) Time will tell whether the IOC will be strong enough to clean its house completely. Cities that failed in recent bids to host the games have threatened the IOC with civil litigation for compensation.

For the first time in close to two decades, calls for the resignation of IOC President Juan Antonio Samarach were loud and numerous. He was unwilling, however, to leave the IOC in what may be considered disgrace. Samaranch asked the IOC membership for a vote of confidence in the meeting of the IOC General Assembly, scheduled for March 1999. The IOC's image and reputation were hurt significantly, as the media referred to the Salt Lake City bribery scandal as "the rise and fall of the Samaranch empire." For the first time in well over a dozen years, international polls did not name Samaranch as the most influential leader in international sports. That recognition went to the newly elected FIFA president, Joseph (Sepp) Blatter of Switzerland.

The slogan "the games must go on" prevailed again when the IOC decided that the 2002 Winter Games would after all be held in Salt Lake City. The same spirit supported the decision to keep the Summer Games of 2000 in Sydney, Australia. The Sydney games are, however, supposedly scheduled for investigation in the near future, along with all Olympic bids since 1990.

## SUMMARY

Although international competitions were held in several sports at the beginning of the twentieth century, the international sports movement was still in its infancy. The international Olympic movement, with seeds planted in the 1890s, began on very unstable ground, only to evolve into a strong and viable establishment. By the end of the twentieth century, the Olympic Games had become the the premier event in international sports, but evidence in 1998 of immoral conduct and bribery involving a number of IOC members damaged the movement. Not that the road up to that time had been without obstacles. In fact, conflicts and controversies abound throughout the history of the modern Olympics. Since their inception they have been plagued with a variety of political, economic, social, medical, and philosophical issues. Historically used as a political tool by many nations of the world, the Olympic Games today must deal with commercialization, unwieldy size, and the use of performance-enhancing drugs by athletes.

Besides the Olympic movement, the twentieth century also saw a proliferation of other international events and developments. Dozens of sports created international federations to govern and oversee international competition. By the end of the century, most of the sport federations were staging world and continental championships. Multisport events on a continental and regional basis, such as the Pan-American, the Asian, and the African Games, came into being.

As the world enters the twenty-first century, the Olympic Games and the World Cup in soccer vie for the top position in international sports. Further, in spite of all the difficulties and controversies, the international sports movement continues to increase in scope, size, complexity, and popularity.

## STUDY QUESTIONS

1. Should the structure of the International Olympic Committee be changed to resemble that of the United Nations, which adheres to the principle of "one country–one vote"?
2. As we have reached an era in which nearly all competitions in international sports are open to both professional and amateur athletes, are separate competitions for "true" amateurs needed?

**3.** Analyze and discuss the positive and negative aspects of the influence of mass media on international sports.

**4.** Since 1976, except in 1992, either the Summer or Winter Olympic Games have been held in North America. Are the Olympic Games therefore becoming essentially "North American Games" as many Europeans claim? If so, should this be considered a positive or negative phenomenon?

**5.** Could and should sports be free of politics?

**6.** A claim has been made that the Olympic Games are over-commercialized. Defenders of the system claim that without the commercialization, there would be no Olympics. Is the commercialization of sport justified, and if so, to what extent?

## RECOMMENDED READINGS

Ashe, Arthur R., Jr. *A Hard Road to Glory*. New York: Warner Books, 1988.

Bennett, Bruce L., Maxwell L. Howell, and Uriel Simri. *Comparative Physical Education and Sport*. 2nd ed. Philadelphia: Lea and Febiger, 1983.

Greenspan, Bud. *100 Greatest Moments in Olympic History*. Los Angeles: General Publishing Group, 1995.

Hoberman, John. *Mortal Engines*. New York: Free Press, 1992.

Kruger, Arnd, and Jim Riordan. *The Story of Worker Sport*. Champaign, IL: Human Kinetics, 1996.

Lucas, John A., and Ronald A. Smith. *Saga of American Sports*. Philadelphia: Lea and Febiger, 1978.

Mandell, Richard D. *The Nazi Olympics*. New York: Macmillan, 1971.

Mbaye, Kebu. *The International Olympic Committee and South Africa*. Lausanne: The International Olympic Committee, 1995.

Riordan, Jim. *Soviet Sport*. London: Blackwell, 1980.

Rollin, Jack. *The World Cup, 1930–1990*. New York: Facts on File, 1994.

Seagrave, John, and Donald Chu. *Olympism*. Champaign, IL: Human Kinetics, 1981.

Simri, Uriel, and Sarah Lieberman, eds. *Sport and Politics*. Netanya, Israel: Wingate Institute, 1984.

Simson, Vyv, and Andrew Jennings. *Dishonored Games: Corruption, Money and Greed at the Olympics*. New York: Sure Sellers, 1992.

Voy, Robert O. *Drugs, Sports and Politics*. Champaign, IL: Human Kinetics, 1991.

Wallechinsky, David. *The Complete Book of the Summer Olympics*. Boston: Little, Brown, 1996.

Wallechinsky, David. *The Complete Book of the Winter Olympics*. Boston: Little, Brown, 1993.

Wilcox, Ralph, ed. *Sport in the Global Village*. Morgantown, WV: Fitness Information Technology, 1994.

## NOTES

1. Although the International Federation for Track and Field was founded in 1912, it was formally created in 1913.

2. For comparison, the 1996 Olympic Games in Atlanta attracted a total of 197 countries and over 10,000 athletes. There were 271 competitive events in twenty-six different sports.

3. In future Olympics, the Soviets asserted their strength in international sports. Following the Olympics of 1952, the USSR maintained supremacy in six out of seven confrontations

with the United States. Only in the 1968 Olympics, held in Mexico City, did the Americans win more medals than the Soviets.

4. The era of glasnost and perestroika led to the end of the decades-long Cold War and hastened the downfall of the Soviet Union. Glasnost was Gorbachev's program of liberalizing the strict censorship policy of the Soviet Union and allowing greater freedom of speech. Perestroika was Gorbachev's program of economic and political reform.

5. One international federation that is richer than the International Olympic Committee is the International Soccer Federation (FIFI). Although the exact wealth of neither organization is known, FIFA appears to be significantly wealthier than the IOC.

6. Doping is the term used to refer to the illegal use of drugs to enhance performance in sport. The IOC rules against doping are found in Rule 48 of the Olympic Charter. This rule provides for the establishment of a medical code and the formation of a Medical Commission.

7. Some individuals are suggesting that free doping should be allowed in international competition. For such a view, see Norman C. Fost, "Steroids Should Not Be Banned from Sports," in *Sports in America*: *Opposing Viewpoints* (San Diego: Greenhaven Press, 1994), pp. 225–233.

8. Robert Sullivan, "How the Olympics Were Bought," *Time* 153, no. 3 (January 25, 1999): 38–42.

9. Ray Moseley, "IOC Leaders Move to Expel Six Members, *The Providence Journal* (January 25, 1999): D1, D4.

# CHAPTER SIX

# THE DEVELOPMENT OF OPPORTUNITIES AND PROGRAMS FOR WOMEN

## JOANNA DAVENPORT

Until recently, opportunities and programs for women in sport were far different from those for men. Prior to the nineteenth century, women's involvement in sport was sporadic and, for the most part, limited to nonstrenuous or noncompetitive activities. Since ancient times, however, women have participated in many forms of physical activity. In Egypt, ancient tomb drawings depict women engaging in dancing, acrobatics, swimming, and ball playing. In ancient Greece and Rome, women ran footraces. In ancient Greece, a quadrennial footrace for women was held in honor of the goddess Hera. These races were generally held one month after the conclusion of the ancient Olympic Games, which was an all-male event. During the Middle Ages and the Renaissance, women engaged in horseback riding, archery, dance, and various ball games. Footraces run by women were popular in various countries of Europe, especially during the seventeenth and eighteenth centuries.[1] Women's opportunities for sport, however, were more limited than those for men until well into the twentieth century.

Despite widespread differences between men and women in the realm of sport, many scholars and experts in sport history claim that there is no longer any reason for a book on sport history to have a separate chapter devoted exclusively to women. They contend that women have made such progress in the past few decades that the issues affecting sport for women should be encompassed within the body of information about sports in general. Someday this reasoning may be valid, but until full gender equity is a reality, a book such as this one should, in the opinion of its authors, include a special section devoted specifically to a review of sport for women. Coakley (1994) reinforces the need for a separate analysis of women's sports with the following view:

> Throughout history, sport participation has been greater for men than for women. Not only have fewer women than men participated, but they generally participate less often and in fewer sport activities. These differences raise special questions

deserving special attention. . . . When the differences disappear, there will no longer be a need for a special chapter on women.[2]

This chapter traces the development of opportunities and programs of modern sport for women with particular emphasis on important events of the nineteenth and twentieth centuries. This review will demonstrate how changes in attitudes and social mores have influenced, and continue to influence, women's sports throughout the world. Particular attention is paid to the historical involvement of women in the modern Olympic Games, because the Olympics serve as illustrations of changing philosophies toward the participation of women in sport. The Olympics also showcase the increasing scope of opportunities for women, as well as demonstrating improvements in the quality of their performance.

## THE EARLY YEARS: NINETEENTH-CENTURY DEVELOPMENTS

The origins of women's participation in modern sports can be traced to developments occurring primarily in England during the nineteenth century. The Victorian Age (1837–1901) was a time in which the vast British Empire was heavily influenced by a philosophy espousing puritanical sexual morality. Society believed that a woman's place was in the home. The Victorian woman was admired for her delicacy and paleness. A pale and weak woman was the ideal. Since fitness and vigor were not regarded as important womanly values, participation by women in vigorous forms of physical activity was usually thought to be outside the realm of decency. In addition, many physicians believed that strenuous and aggressive physical activity was inadvisable for women as it might hinder their homemaking and childbearing capacities. Thus, until late in the century, there were relatively few physical activities deemed acceptable for women.

In *The Revolt of American Women*, Jensen (1952) indicates how the social life of women in the United States had a definite bearing on their recreational activity.

> Before the Civil War, nice women exercised very infrequently; they wore skirts when they ran and to be utterly proper, they didn't run at all. Sometimes a few bold spirits would go ice skating, although a contemporary book of etiquette urged them to hang onto the coattails of their male partners, thus enjoying all the pleasures without incurring any of the fatigue of the exercise.[3]

Until the 1870s, most of the activities in which women participated were recreational rather than competitive. They tended to be informal, often coeducational, and they had either limited or no rules. The more popular early sports included croquet, archery, bowling, bicycling, tennis, and golf. These activities provided opportunities for women to participate in socially approved, ladylike recreational activities, and they permitted men and women of the middle and upper classes to be together in a less formal setting than was customary. The purpose of the activities generally was to encourage respectable social encounters, not to promote the physical benefits of exercise or fitness. Men often dressed meticulously for these activities in what we would call formal attire today, and the women wore full-length dresses with long sleeves and high collars. Naturally, this clothing was restrictive and cumbersome to any type of play that required vigorous movement and an all-out effort.

It is important to note that the women who participated in these early forms of recreational sports represented a very small proportion of the population. For the most part, they were members of the upper class who had both the wealth and the time to participate in leisure activity. Thus, although an increasing number of women participated in sporting activities toward the end of the century, their participation was still limited primarily to a select few and was not seen as having major societal importance.

Within this social class, then, and within the context of this prevailing philosophy, the seeds of modern sports for women were planted. As early as 1810, Scottish women were competing in golf, and women in the Netherlands were engaged in speed skating. In 1811 a few English women competed in a cricket match. By 1845 England was staging a British championship in archery for women. In 1867 the so-called mother country of modern sports (England) sponsored the first English open croquet championship. In this particular event, women were allowed to compete against men as well. The first English golf championship for women was held in 1873. In 1893 the British Ladies Golf Union was created; it was the first independent national sport organization for women. Between 1879 and 1897, national championships for women in tennis were held in several European countries as well as the United States, New Zealand, and South Africa. In 1884 Wimbledon opened its games to women tennis players. Tennis was the most highly developed of all women's sports in the nineteenth century.

By the late 1800s, the sport of cycling became very popular among women. Women's cycling races were very prevalent in Europe and in the United States during the 1890s. Many believe that cycling provided a major impetus for the growth of women's sports. This view is based on the belief that cycling represented a major social change for women. Many believe that cycling was more instrumental than other sports in changing societal attitudes toward the physiological benefits of exercise for women. Cycling showed that strenuous physical activity was beneficial to women and made them better suited for housework and childbearing. In addition, cycling enabled women to get out of the home, thereby providing them with more freedom of expression. Cycling also required the adoption of a more moderate style of dress. Long skirts and sleeves were considered too dangerous for the lady cyclists, so they began to wear middy blouses and bloomers.

In the United States, increased interest and participation in recreational sport brought a desire for regulations and formal competition. The first organized contest in the United States to include women was the National Archery Association Tournament held in Chicago in 1876. Twenty women entered this coeducational event. Archery flourished in the United States until the 1880s, when it declined in popularity because of growing interest in tennis. It was Mary Outerbridge from Staten Island, New York, who brought tennis to the United States. In 1874 she was vacationing in Bermuda when she saw British soldiers playing a new game they called lawn tennis. She brought back some racquets, balls, and a net and persuaded the Staten Island Cricket and Baseball Club to lay out a court on its lawn. Although initially a leisurely game, tennis soon became vigorous and competitive. In 1881 the United States Tennis Association was formed, and the first National Women's Singles Championship was held six years later.

In addition to archery and tennis, bowling, fencing, and ice-skating were popular among American women. In 1889 women started playing golf. By 1895, when the first national women's tournament was held, it was estimated that there were 100 women golfers in the United States.

## Programs at the Women's Colleges in the United States

A major thrust in the development of women's programs in the United States came from the all-female colleges, such as Vassar, Mt. Holyoke, Wellesley, and Smith. The coeducational colleges lagged far behind in opportunities for women to play sport. From its very first year, Mount Holyoke, the oldest women's college in the United States, required students to perform domestic duties that insured physical activity as part of their daily lives. Eventually, all the women's colleges incorporated programs of calisthenics and gymnastics as part of the curriculum. The exercise classes were designed to maintain or improve the students' health. By the end of the century, women students engaged not only in formal physical training programs but also in a variety of informal recreational activities and ball games.

Critics of the day, however, were shocked by these new sporting activities—opposed, in fact, to all higher education for women. As late as 1870, the renowned President Charles Eliot of Harvard University, quoting scientific and medical authorities, stated that "women cannot bear the stress put upon men in college." In 1896 the president of Michigan State University echoed the feelings of many college presidents when he stated that "although the addition of women improved the social side of college life, nothing in connection with the college brings up more perplexing problems than the presence of women."[4]

## Team Sports: Field Hockey and Basketball

The sporting activities popular among women during most of the nineteenth century tended to be individual and recreational. Even in American colleges, the sports program was rather leisurely, and intercollegiate competition was virtually nonexistent. Although women did compete with each other to some extent on an intramural level, participation for the most part remained recreational.

In the late 1880s, things began to change with the emergence of team sports for women. In 1887 the first women's field hockey club was established in England. Soon after, the sport was introduced throughout much of the British Empire and Europe. In the twentieth century, field hockey became a major team sport for women throughout the world.

In 1891 James Naismith invented the game of basketball in the United States. Within a year the game was adopted by women's schools and colleges, and it spread like wildfire across the country. Soon women's basketball teams were playing other schools on both the high school and college level. According to Naismith, writing fifty years later, the first girl's basketball game was played in 1892 between grade-school teams in Springfield, Massachusetts.[5] By 1895 the game had reached the southern states as well as the West Coast. In 1896 the first women's intercollegiate sports event was a basketball game between the University of California (Berkeley) and Stanford University.

However, despite basketball's initial popularity, it was obvious to some women leaders that many women did not have the strength or stamina to play the game as Naismith had designed it. These women thus modified the game and established different sets of rules.

At Smith College, which is credited with being the first women's college to play basketball, the rules were changed shortly after its introduction by the college's director of physical education, Senda Berenson. In an 1894 article, Berenson wrote that in order to control roughness and encourage teamwork she made these modifications: (1) the court was divided into three zones and players had to stay in their respective zones; (2) no snatching of the ball was allowed; (3) only a three-bounce dribble was allowed; and (4) the ball could be held only three seconds. She also stated that she felt basketball fostered physical courage, self-reliance, quickness, self-control, and gentle manners.[6]

Many colleges used the rules developed at Smith, while other institutions made entirely different changes or continued to use the men's rules. Regardless of which rules were used, the sport of basketball provided impetus for interscholastic and intercollegiate competition for girls and women.

In 1893 women's basketball was introduced in England, and that country soon adopted its own version of the game. In 1898 the English version became known as netball, a sport that is still played today.

## The Olympic Games of 1896

When the Olympic Games were revived in 1896, the entry of women was not even considered. The founder of the modern Olympic Games, Pierre de Coubertin, wanted the modern games to be similar to the ancient Olympic Games, and the exclusion of women was taken for granted. Thus no women competed in the first modern Olympic Games, held in Athens, Greece. Interestingly, there is evidence indicating that a woman's entry was denied for the marathon race. According to some reports, although denied entry, the woman may actually have run the race alongside the male runners.

Throughout his entire life, Coubertin remained adamantly opposed to women participating in the modern Olympics. Besides believing that the modern Olympics should be like the ancient games, Coubertin expressed the view that women's sports were against the laws of nature.[7] By his death in 1937, he had not softened his position on the participation of women in the Olympic Games, but he had expressed the view that it was permissible for women to participate in sport—but not in public.

## THE ADOLESCENT YEARS: 1900–1940

In 1900 marriage, homemaking, and motherhood were still considered prime societal values, and the woman who engaged in sport and physical activity did not represent society's notion of the ideal female. The consensus was that if a woman exercised at all, the exercise should be moderate and not strenuous so as to avoid physical harm and the possibility of becoming "masculinized." Thus, except for the traditional recreational sports for "ladies," the newly emerging women's team sports were virtually unknown to the general public. Women's involvement in sport at the female colleges in the United States was thought to be of marginal value at best. However, despite these perceptions, women were beginning to break new ground in the area of sports and physical activity.

On the global level, the Olympic movement of the twentieth century provided the major catalyst for women's participation in more competitive forms of sport and physical activity. With each succeeding quadrennial Olympics, more women gained entrance into Olympic events, and more events were added to the women's program. However, women paid a price for their increased involvement in organized competition by attracting criticism and even contempt.

In 1900 the second modern Olympic Games, held in Paris, saw the entry of eleven women into Olympic competition. Coubertin was adamantly opposed to their participation, but he was not in control of the program. The games were organized by the officials of the world's fair held in Paris that year, and the games were just one of the fair's attractions. As was the case four years earlier, Coubertin saw the Olympic Games as an exaltation of male athleticism, and he abhorred the thought of women making fools of themselves by sweating in public.[8]

In the 1900 Olympics, the eleven women competed in tennis and golf, which were socially accepted activities for women. Charlotte Cooper of Great Britain became the first female Olympic champion, winning two gold medals in tennis. America's Margaret Abbott won the gold medal in the nine-hole golf event. The Olympics of 1900 marked the only time golf was open to women. In the 1904 Olympics, when golf appeared for the last time as an Olympic event, it was open only to men. Tennis for women was not included in the games of 1904, but it reappeared in the 1908 Olympics.

In the 1904 games in St. Louis, eight women competed in the "unofficial" activity of archery. All eight were from the United States. Lydia Howell won three gold medals in these archery contests.

In 1906 the first official world championship for women in any sport took place when figure-skating enthusiasts organized a championship event. The International Skating Union (ISU) had organized a similar championship for men as early as 1896. The ladies' world championship event in 1906 actually preceded national championship competitions, which were staged in several countries shortly thereafter. The United States organized its national figure-skating championship in 1914.

The 1908 London Olympics marked the first major breakthrough for women's sports in the Olympic Games. Forty-three female athletes from Germany, Great Britain, Hungary, and Sweden participated. The program consisted of competitions in tennis, figure skating, and archery. Additionally, a group of females provided exhibitions in swimming, diving, and gymnastics, thus paving the way for the later inclusion of these sports in the Olympic program. Competitive swimming for women had begun to appear at the turn of the century. As early as 1900, female swimmers participated in the German national championships in the 100-meter freestyle. Other national championships soon followed. The International Swimming Federation (FINA) was founded in 1908 and, from its inception, took a very positive attitude toward women's swimming. In 1916 the United States Amateur Athletic Union (AAU) organized the first United States national swimming championship for women. Two years earlier, the AAU had begun to register female swimmers. Thus, swimming became the first sport in the United States in which the AAU registered female athletes.

Margaret Abbot's golf victory in the 1900 Olympic Games and the female archery contest in St. Louis in 1904 probably went unnoticed by most of the American public. But the London Olympics of 1908 may have changed public awareness of women competing at the Olympics. In the United States, a mild protest prior to the London games led the American Olympic Committee to bar all American women from the games. The *New York Times* described the attitude of the American Olympic Committee toward female athletes (an opposition that lasted until 1914) in the following way.

> The American Olympic Committee . . . went on record against women competing in the Olympic Games excepting in class work of gymnastic exhibitions. In other words, the committee was opposed to women taking part in any event in which they could not wear long skirts.[9]

The Stockholm Games of 1912 had two competitive events for women, tennis and, for the first time, swimming. The addition of swimming to the program was adamantly opposed by Coubertin, who issued the following statement:

> Can women be given access to all the Olympic events? No. . . . Then why permit them [women] some and bar them from others? And especially, on what basis does one establish the line between events permitted and events prohibited? There are not just tennis players and swimmers. . . . There are also fencers, horsewomen, and in America there have also been rowers. Tomorrow, perhaps, there will be women runners or even soccer players. Would such sports practiced by women constitute an edifying sight before crowds assembled for an Olympiad? We do not think such a claim can be made.[10]

The number of women competing in the Stockholm games increased to fifty-five, most of them in swimming. Eleven countries were represented including Austria, Australia, Belgium, Bohemia, Denmark, Finland, France, Germany, Great Britain, Norway, and Sweden. The Stockholm Games also included exhibitions by Scandinavian female gymnasts.

Prior to World War I, tennis was the major women's sport on the international level. Numerous international tournaments were staged not only at Wimbledon, but on a smaller scale in Monte Carlo (1901), Nice (1901), and Cannes (1907) as well. Perhaps the greatest female tennis player of this era was Dorothea Douglas Lamber Chambers of Great Britain. Chambers won the women's title at Wimbledon seven times between 1903 and 1914. She also won the gold medal in the London Olympics in 1908 and won five other international tournaments between 1908 and 1914.

## Decade of Controversy: 1920–1930

The 1920 Olympic Games in Antwerp saw no remarkable changes in the women's program. Seventy-six women from twelve countries competed in three sports: tennis, swimming, and figure skating. Altogether, there were ten events for women in the three sports. The 1920 Olympics were the last time that figure skating was included as part of the Olympic Summer Games. After 1920, it moved to the newly formed Winter Games, which were first held in 1924.

The most consistent and successful advocate for women's rights in sport following World War I was Alice Milliat of France. In 1919 she founded the Federation des Societes Feminines Sportive de France and immediately embarked on a program of demanding equal rights in sports, both nationally and internationally. Initially, Milliat attempted unsuccessfully to have track and field competitions for women introduced into the Antwerp Olympics of 1920. Track and field for women had made its appearance in the United States as early as the turn of the century, and a 1905 publication carried fourteen women's athletic records.[11] Introduction of this sport soon followed in several European countries, with France staging a national championship for women in 1917. When rejected by Olympic officials, Milliat proceeded to create in 1921 the Federation Sportive Feminine Internationale (FSFI). In 1922 the first important step taken by Milliat and the FSFI was organization of the first World Games for women. The games, held in Paris, were initially called the Women's Olympic Games. Under pressure from the International Olympic Committee (IOC), the name of the games was subsequently changed to the Women's World Games. They became a quadrennial event, with games held in 1926 (Göteborg), in 1930 (Prague), and in 1934 (London).

Through the efforts of Milliat and the FSFI, both track and field and gymnastics were introduced into the Olympic program for women in the 1928 Olympic Games, but on a limited scale. Despite this acceptance, the FSFI-sponsored Women's World Games continued to hold successful meets through 1934. It was only when an agreement was reached with the IOC in 1936 that provided for a nine-event program in women's track and field that the FSFI agreed to stop its world games and cease to function for all practical purposes. The Olympic Games in 1928 included only five track and field events for women; the games of 1932 and 1936 grew to six events.

Although women's track and field was barred from the 1924 Olympic program, the Paris Games had more than twice the female contestants as did the 1920 Antwerp games. Women athletes from twenty countries competed in Paris, a majority of them swimmers. Competitions were also held in tennis and, for the first time, in fencing. The number of events for women grew to eleven. At the first officially scheduled Olympic Winter Games, staged in Chamonix, France, in 1924, thirteen women competed in only one sport, figure skating (single and mixed pairs).

In 1928 the Winter Olympic Games were held in St. Moritz, Switzerland. Twenty-seven women competed in two events in figure skating. These games marked the successful appearance of Sonja Henie of Norway, who was to become the most successful figure skater of all time. She had gained her first national championship in 1922 at the age of ten. She became the world champion in figure skating in 1927 at the age of fifteen. Beginning in 1928, she won a total of three gold medals in Olympic competition, first in the 1928 games, and then again in 1932 and 1936. During her years at the peak of world figure skating, she won ten consecutive world championships until 1936. After leaving formal competition, Sonja Henie became a popular movie star, and many feel that it was her popularity that contributed to the rise of ice shows and skating exhibitions.

In the Summer Olympics of 1928, in Amsterdam, 290 women representing twenty-four countries participated. The increase in the number of participants was due largely to the introduction of five events in women's track and field (100 meters, 800 meters, 400-meter relay, high jump, and discus throw). These five events attracted over 100 competitors. Additional competitions were staged in swimming, fencing, and also, for the first time, gymnastics. Tennis had been dropped from the program after the 1924 Olympics when a conflict developed between the International Tennis Federation and the International Olympic Committee over the issue of who would control the events. It did not reappear as an Olympic event until 1988.

One significant aspect of the Amsterdam Olympics occurred after the women's 800-meter race. All the runners collapsed upon crossing the finish line. The male medical experts of the day declared that the collapse of the runners showed that "women were not capable of running a half mile or more." This view held back the development of female long-distance running for several years. It took the International Federation for Track and Field (IAAF) thirty-two years, until 1960, to reintroduce the 800-meter race for women into the Olympic program. Today women regularly compete in marathon races, which cover a distance of 26 miles, 385 yards.

Coubertin was not the only voice speaking against women's participation in the Olympics and against track and field as an Olympic sport for women. Many female leaders of physical education in the United States, particularly those associated with college and university programs, remained strongly committed to the health, play, and recreational benefits of physical activity. They vigorously opposed the trend toward serious competitive sports for women and were outraged when they heard that the Amsterdam games would include women's track and field events. They issued a variety of protests and resolutions against the addition of track and field—indeed against all events that fostered high levels of competition.[12] The prevailing American philosophy in physical education sought "a game for every girl and every girl in the game." In reiterating this philosophy, the Committee on Women's Athletics (CWA) of the American Physical Education Association (APEA) issued the following resolution:

[We] . . . go on record as being opposed to girls and women entering the Olympic Games . . . And opposed to the entry of girls and women in such formal spectator athletics contests.[13]

Similar resolutions were adopted in the United States by the National Association of Physical Education for College Women, the Midwest Association of Physical Education for College Women, and the Young Women's Christian Association (YWCA).

The Committee on Women's Athletics (CWA) had been established in 1917 to help develop rules and practices in the variety of sports which had begun to emerge for women. The need for such a committee was apparent to the American Physical Education Association because of the "insistent and increasing demands coming in from all parts of the country for assistance in solving problems in connection with the athletic activities for girls and women, which demonstrated the need for a set of standards which should be based on the limitations, abilities, and needs of the sex."[14] In 1932 the CWA was replaced by the National Section on Women's Athletics, which in turn is now known as the National Association for Girls and Women in Sport (NAGWS), and is housed within the American Alliance for Health, Physical Education, Recreation and Dance (AAHPERD).

The unity and power of the women leaders of physical education were so great that by 1923 most women's programs in the United States had dropped serious competition to focus on less formal "play days." A 1931 survey indicated that 93 percent of the colleges and universities polled were opposed to any form of intercollegiate competition for women.[15] This switch to play days and the deemphasis of high levels of competition stemmed primarily from the growth of women's basketball. During the beginning years, many coaches in women's basketball were men, and they naturally wanted to use men's rules. Additionally, many abuses developed that caused great consternation to school authorities, such as playing for gate receipts, rough play, a philosophy of winning at all costs, officiating by men, poor chaperonage, and the absence of standards regarding player welfare. These abuses were viewed by many as major negative factors of all competition. The diminishing of competitive opportunities for women came paradoxically at the same time that men's sports were dramatically expanding.

## Expansion of Women's Sports: 1930–1940

The 1930s were marked by major developments in women's sports. Women's sports expanded on all levels, despite major hurdles and battles along the way.

Although their protest against women's track and field at the 1928 Olympic Games was unsuccessful, the American leaders of physical education gathered their forces and tried to stem the tide for the 1932 Olympic Games to be held in Los Angeles. The Women's Division of the National Amateur Athletics Federation (NAAF) sent a resolution not only to the IOC but to all sixty-seven national Olympic committees asking that track and field events for women at the 1932 games be omitted. Indirectly, the group voiced its opposition to all Olympic events for women. The rationale for this position was that the Olympics (1) entailed the specialized training of the few; (2) offered opportunity for exploitation of girls and women; and (3) might cause "over strain" in preparation for and during the games themselves.[16] Other parts of the resolution included a promise to entertain women who came to participate in the 1932 games, as well as a proposal for alternative events to be held in Los Angeles in place of the Olympic events, such as "a festival which might include singing, dancing, music, mass sports and games, luncheons, conferences, banquets, demonstrations, exhibitions."[17] The resolution ended with a commitment by the Women's Division of the NAAF to continue its work in sports, but with the emphasis on participation rather than on winning.

The IOC rejected the petition, and women's track and field remained on the program in Los Angeles. The Women's Division of the NAAF did not submit a formal plea again but showed its steadfast opposition for years by promoting informal competition.

The Los Angeles games of 1932 was marked by a significant drop in participation by both male and female athletes. Only 127 women participated in the three women's sports (fencing, swimming, and track and field). The women were representative of seventeen countries, with women from Central American and South American countries participating for the first time. Gymnastics was dropped from the program, but it reappeared in the 1936 Olympics. The most popular athlete in the women's events was an American by the name of Mildred "Babe" Didrikson, who won two gold medals and one silver medal in track and field. In the high jump competition, she was awarded the silver medal in place of a third gold medal when she went over the bar head first. The officials, having never seen that technique and not sure what to do, awarded her the second-place medal. In later years, Didrikson became famous as a professional golfer. Also at the Los Angeles games, a Dutch swimming coach by the name of "Mama" Braun became the first female coach to appear at the Olympic Games.

In 1936 the Berlin Olympics attracted 328 women participants, almost twice as many as four years earlier in Los Angeles. This established a new record for female participation in the Olympics. In the Berlin games, competitions were held in women's swimming, fencing, track and field, and gymnastics.

The Berlin Olympics are also remembered for the expulsion of an American swimmer named Eleanor Holm by Avery Brundage, who was at the time the president of the United States Olympic Committee. While en route to Berlin via ship, Brundage expelled Holm from the U.S. swimming team for having a glass of champagne at a party on board ship, an action Brundage considered "undisciplined behavior." Holm had won a gold medal in the backstroke at the 1932 games and was a favorite to win another medal in Berlin. The incident was the culmination of a long-standing conflict between Holm and Brundage.

Like Coubertin, Brundage was adamantly opposed to women's sports in Olympic competition. After the Berlin games, he stated:

> I am fed up to the ears with women as track and field competitors. . . . her charms sink to something less than zero. As swimmers and divers, girls are beautiful and adroit, as they are ineffective and unpleasing on the track.[18]

Brundage's position on women's sports had a strong influence on future Olympic activity. During his twenty years as president of the IOC (1952–1972), the game of volleyball and the reintroduction of archery became the only additions to the women's program in the Olympic Games. When volleyball was introduced in 1964 as the sixth Olympic sport for women, Brundage declared that he considered the women's program to be completed.

During the 1920s and 1930s, outside of Olympic competition, world championships were instituted for women in a variety of sports. In 1927 table tennis staged its first world championship for women, to be followed two years later by a world championship in women's fencing. These were followed by world championships in Alpine skiing (1931), archery (1931), speed skating (1936) and canoeing (1938).

## A NEW ERA OF COMPETITION: 1940–1970

During World War II (1939–1945), women's sports, particularly on the international level, naturally diminished. However, despite the curtailment of international activity, programs continued to develop within several countries. This was particularly the case in the United States, where women's sports programs continued to function more than in any other country.

After the war, women's sport programs underwent dramatic reconstruction and an increase in both programs and opportunities. This increase occurred almost every year. With the advent of the Soviet Union on the sport scene, women's sports acquired a new dimension, particularly on the international level.

### Post-War Events and the Emergence of the Soviet Union

Because of World War II, no Olympic Games were staged in 1940 or 1944. The 1948 games were held in war-ravaged London. A record 385 women athletes from thirty-three countries participated in nineteen events. This last figure compares to the fifteen events held in the 1936 Berlin games. Three additional track and field events were added to the program as well as the sport of canoeing. The addition of canoeing to the program thus provided women with five Olympic sports. There were two historic achievements by women during these games. The Dutch runner Fanny Blankers-Koen won four gold medals in track and field events (100 meters, 80-meter hurdles, 200 meters, and the 400-meter relay). United States high jumper Alice Coachman became the first black woman to win an Olympic gold medal.

The Winter Games of 1948 were held in St. Moritz, Switzerland. A total of seventy-seven females participated. Although no new sports were added to the women's program, two skiing events were added (downhill race and slalom).

In 1952 the Olympics were held in Helsinki, Finland. The Helsinki games attracted a total of 518 female athletes from forty-one countries. For the first time, over 10 percent of the athletes participating in the Olympic Games were female.

Although no new sports were added to the women's program, six gymnastics events were added, including individual competitions for the first time. The 1952 Winter Games, held earlier in the year at Oslo, included for the first time a Nordic skiing event for women. The giant slalom was also added as an Alpine skiing event. The Oslo games attracted 109 women who competed in a total of six events.

The major news at the Helsinki games was Olympic participation by the Soviet Union for the first time. The Soviet entrance into the Olympics was to become a critical factor in the further development of international sports for women. It also signaled the arrival of the Cold War in global sports. The Soviets' success in women's competitions at Helsinki (eleven medals in track and field and ten in gymnastics) led them to argue for the expansion of the Olympic women's program. Almost naturally, the new IOC president, Avery Brundage, opposed expansion of the program.

The results of the pressure exerted by the Soviet Union and its communist allies and the investment made by the Soviet Union in women's sports were clearly evident in future Olympic endeavors. Although the immediate impact of female Soviet athletes was felt in only a limited number of sports, it rapidly became clear that Soviet sport leaders believed their best chance for international success was to be found in women's sports. Indeed, in the 1976 games in Montreal, representatives of communist countries won a total of forty-four gold, thirty-two silver, and thirty-one bronze medals in the forty-nine events held for women. Four years earlier in Munich (1972), the communist countries had gained but a little over 50 percent of the Olympic medals awarded to women.

The first Olympic Games held in the Southern Hemisphere were staged in 1956 in Melbourne, Australia. In those games, 384 women representing thirty-seven countries competed in a total of twenty-six events. No new sports were added to the program. The outstanding female athlete in the 1956 Olympics was the Australian sprinter Betty Cuthbert. She won the gold medal in the 100-meter race, 200-meter race, and the 400-meter relay. The American diver Pat McCormick repeated as the winner in both springboard and platform diving. She was later recognized in the United States as the Associated Press Athlete of the Year. At the 1956 Winter Games, held in Cortina d'Ampezzo, Italy, Tenley Albright became the first American woman to win a gold medal in figure skating.

In 1960 the Olympic Games returned to Europe and were held in Rome. Female participation reached a new record, with 610 female athletes from forty-five countries competing. Although no new sports were added to the women's program, the number of events rose to twenty-nine. The 800-meter race for women returned to the program after a thirty-two-year absence, and new events in swimming, fencing, and canoeing were added. The star of the 1960 Olympics was Wilma Rudolph of the United States. She won three gold medals in track and field (the 100 meters, the 200 meters, and the 400-meter relay).

The Winter Games of 1960, held at Squaw Valley, California, attracted 144 female competitors. Although no new sports were added to the program, four new events were added to speed skating.

Immediately following the 1960 Olympics, officials from the Soviet Union suggested that future Olympics should be greatly expanded to include women's sports that were active in international federations. The IOC not only rejected this proposal but declared that no new sports would be added to the program with the exception of volleyball, which had already been approved for inclusion in the 1964 games. The IOC eventually was to revise this policy.

The Tokyo Olympics of 1964 attracted a record number of 683 female participants from fifty-four countries. Japanese women dominated the competition in volleyball. With the addition of volleyball, as well as the addition of new events in track and field and swimming, women competed in a total of thirty-three events. American sprinter Wyomia Tyus won the gold medal in the 100-meter race.

In the 1964 Winter Games, held earlier in the year at Innsbruck, Austria, 200 female athletes competed in thirteen events. Luge was added to the program and included a singles races for women.

In 1966 a controversial new ruling revolutionized women's track and field. This was the mandatory *femininity test* (sex chromatin test) for women athletes, which is still in effect. In the mid-1960s, serious questions had arisen as to whether some of the top performers in women's track and field were indeed biologically female. The influence of the testing program was dramatic. When it was implemented, a number of top female athletes, most notably those from the Soviet Union, suddenly disappeared from the scene of women's track and field. In the European championships in track and field in 1954, Soviet women had won eight out of eleven gold medals, in 1958 seven out of twelve, and in 1962 six out of twelve. After introduction of the sex chromatin test in 1966, Soviet women managed to win only three gold medals. At the time, and continuing to this day, women's organizations have expressed rejection of this test.

In 1968 the Olympic Games were held in Mexico City. These games attracted a record number of 781 female athletes representing fifty-three countries. Although no new sports were added to the program, six swimming events were added, thus giving women the opportunity to compete in a total of thirty-nine events. The leading woman at the Mexico City games was Vera Caslavska from Czechoslovakia. She won four gold medals in gymnastics, adding to the three that she had gained four years earlier in Tokyo. Wyomia Tyus repeated her 1964 winning performance in the 100-meter race, thereby becoming the first Olympic athlete to win consecutive gold medals in this event. Athletes from East Germany appeared for the first time as a separate nation but won only one gold medal in women's track and field. The Mexico City Olympics also marked the first time that a woman was given the honor of carrying the Olympic flame to the opening ceremony. Enriqueta Basilio was so honored. At the Winter Games of that year, held in Grenoble (France), women athletes represented close to twenty percent of all participants.

Between 1940 and 1970, several world championships for women were held for the first time in sports outside the Olympic Games. These championships were developed in roller skating (1947), field handball (1949), water skiing (1949), gymnastics (1950), parachuting (1951), volleyball (1952), basketball (1953), Nordic skiing (1954), luge (1955), cycling (1958), shooting (1958), netball (1963), softball (1965), orienteering (1966), and cross-country running (1967).

In 1957 Althea Gibson succeeded in breaking the color barrier in tennis when she became the first black woman to win both the United States Open and the Wimbledon championships. The following year she repeated those victories.

The period between 1940 and 1970 saw the introduction of several regional games and competitions open to women. Women competed in the Pan-American and Asian Games as early as 1951. In 1965 women's track and field competitions were held in the first Africa Games. The British Empire Games, which had developed much earlier, continued to include women's competitions on a quadrennial basis. After World War II, these games were renamed the British Commonwealth Games.

## Post-War Developments in the United States

In the United States, a historic breakthrough in 1941 led ultimately to a change in physical education philosophy and to an increase in competitive activities for women. In that year Gladys Palmer, who was head of the women's physical education department at Ohio State University, issued invitations to other institutions for a National Collegiate Golf Tournament for Women. The collegiate physical education world, which generally opposed competition, was in an uproar. The same organizations that fought the participation of women in the Olympics issued resolutions against this tournament. Despite the protests, the tournament was a big success, with thirty-eight women competing. But Gladys Palmer paid a heavy price. She "was literally 'drummed out' of the profession because she had dared sponsor such an innovation."[19]

This first National Collegiate Golf Tournament for Women led to a change of the philosophy of women's athletics and to the demise of the informal play days. The National Collegiate Golf Tournament continued as an annual event and is held today under the sponsorship of the National Collegiate Athletic Association (NCAA). Thus the National Collegiate Golf Tournament is the oldest continuing competition for college women in the United States.

After the emergence of the National Collegiate Golf Tournament, attitudes began to change toward international competition as well. When there was no question that the Olympic Games would be revived after World War II, the National Section on Women's Athletics issued a report entitled "The Olympic Study Committee Report." The report "neither endorsed nor condemned the idea of women in Olympic competition but rather recommended certain standards."[20]

Together the tournament and the report marked the beginning of a gradual shift in attitude toward competitive women's sports in the United States. By the 1960s the pendulum had swung away from the focus on leisure and recreational activities in the direction of sanctioned competition.

In 1957 the American Association for Health, Physical Education and Recreation (AAHPER—now AAHPERD) requested that the United States Olympic Committee (USOC) include representatives from its Division for Girls and Women's Sports (DGWS) on those Olympic sports committees that governed women's activities. The USOC approved the request and in 1958 the Women's Advisory Board was created under the United States Olympic Development Committee. The term *advisory* was soon deleted and it became simply the Women's Board. After all the years of protests, resolutions, and silence about Olympic events, this board represented a dramatic step in the development of competitive sports for girls and women the United States.

In cooperation with the USOC, leaders in women's sport circles now began to sponsor National Olympic Institutes, which trained coaches and physical educators in the skills of Olympic sports and provided background information so their students would receive expert instruction. The institutes thus indirectly supported the training of potential female Olympic competitors, rather than deterring them from competition as educators had in the past.

Sponsored in part by a $500,000 donation from Doris Duke Cromwell (heiress of the Duke tobacco fortune), the first National Olympic Institute was held in 1963. Succeeding ones were held in 1965, two in 1966, and the last in 1969. Approximately 1,025 teachers took part in these five institutes and were charged with the responsibility to hold similar workshops in their respective areas. It is estimated that more than 100,000 teachers and recreation personnel attended these local coaching clinics. As for the effectiveness of the institutes, one observer believed that "the interest in women's sports generated by the five National Institutes and their influence on better quality of teaching and performance cannot be measured statistically, but will be clearly observed all over the world in the mirror of time."[21]

As a direct result of the institutes, many advances in women's competitive sports took place in the United States. Track and field and gymnastics, two sports that formerly were seldom found in girls' and women's programs, became common. National championships for women developed in several sports. In 1969 national championships were established in track and field and in gymnastics. As the women's program continued to expand on the college and university level, it clearly needed a more formally structured governing body. In 1971 the Association of Intercollegiate Athletics for Women (AIAW) was formed. It remained the governing agency of all women's intercollegiate athletics until it dissolved in 1982.

## WOMEN'S SPORTS COME OF AGE:
## 1970 TO THE PRESENT

Profound changes in women's sports took place during the 1970s. In the United States, the most significant development was federal legislation that mandated equal opportunities for women in physical education and sport. On the international level, most notably, gymnastics became a major women's sport, East Germany became a powerhouse in international competition, and drug use among female athletes became a major concern.

### Title IX

On July 1, 1972, the United States Congress passed a law known as Title IX of the Education Amendments of 1972. This legislation is considered the single most important influence on U.S. women's sports in the twentieth century. The law stated:

No person in the United States shall on the basis of sex, be excluded from participation in, be denied the benefits of, or be subjected to discrimination under any educational program or activity receiving Federal financial assistance.[22]

The effects of this federal mandate on women's athletic achievement, as well as on opportunities for women to participate in sports, were dramatic. In essence, Title IX ruled that women must be given equal opportunity to participate in all forms of sport and physical activity. It has resulted in enormous growth in both opportunities and programs for women on all levels. By the late 1970s, schools and colleges added major women's sports to their programs and hired women athletic directors, full-time women coaches, and female athletic trainers. Opportunities for women in professional sports increased, specialized sports camps were held for women, physical education classes became coeducational, and most importantly, an increasingly talented pool of women athletes began to emerge. Educational institutions cognizant of Title IX responded to female student athletes who were demanding equitable sports programs. By 1980 it was estimated that the average athletic budget for women on the college level had increased from less than 1 percent in 1972 to approximately 16 percent of the total athletic budget.[23]

However, despite the rapid advances in women's sports, implementation of the law was not easy, particularly on the college and university level. The NCAA immediately opposed Title IX's implementation and proposed that athletics be excluded from the mandate. The NCAA rationale is clearly expressed in a 1973 statement from Walter Byers, then executive director of the organization:

I think [Title IX] creates a crisis in intercollegiate athletics. . . . Impending doom is around the corner if these regulations are implemented. This regulation would entirely alter what has taken intercollegiate athletics 50 years to build and would dismantle our entire financial structure.[24]

During the early years of Title IX, the NCAA took numerous positions and made several proposals to either eliminate or modify the effects of the mandate. In 1975, having lost its battle, the NCAA announced it was ready to provide "services for all women-student athletes."[25] The announcement was made without either the advice or the approval of the Association for Intercollegiate Athletics for Women (AIAW), which at the time was the governing body for women's collegiate sports. Needless to say, a battle developed between the two groups over which one would be the governing body of college women's athletics. An article entitled "The Politics of Takeover" described the NCAA as "huge, powerful . . . moneyed and it lobbies in Washington, while the AIAW is small, idealistic, poor and politically naive."[26] Pressure from many factions forced the NCAA to drop its takeover move at that time. It is interesting to note that in protesting against Title IX, the NCAA spent more money lobbying against equal opportunity than it cost the AIAW to run seventeen national championships.[27]

In 1980 the NCAA announced it would sponsor women's championships for the 1981–1982 academic year. The AIAW had been staging national championships for women since 1971. It had also been successful in stopping previous proposals for NCAA-sponsored championships. In 1982, however, the NCAA won the battle, a victory that forced the demise of the AIAW. Since 1982 the NCAA has been the governing body of both men's and women's collegiate athletics.

In 1992 the NCAA released a study that reflected the amount of money Division I institutions spent on men's athletics in comparison to the amount spent on the women's program. Major findings of the study were: (1) although the total enrollment of men and women in Division I institutions was virtually equal, male athletes outnumbered female athletes by more than two to one, and they received twice as many scholarships; and (2) men's teams received three-fourths of the operating funds and more than 80 percent of recruiting funds.[28]

In 1993 the NCAA released a report from its Gender-Equity Task Force. Along with many other suggestions, the report recommended that (1) opportunities for participation by both males and females should be proportionate to their percentage of the undergraduate enrollment, and that all sports, including football, should be counted in the formula; (2) male and female athletes should receive equitable treatment in all areas of athletics, such as equipment, facilities, and so forth; and (3) the current scholarship allotment for women's sports should be increased with no increase in scholarships for men's sports.[29]

Although numerous advances have been made on all levels of women's sports, the issue of gender equity still remains. At the present time, a clear and concise definition of what constitutes gender equity is still under discussion. Although not fully accepted by all, the final report of the NCAA Gender-Equity Task Force, released in 1993, offered the following definition:

> An athletics program can be considered gender equitable when the participants in both the men's and women's sports programs would accept as fair and equitable the overall program of the other gender.[30]

## Women and the Olympic Games of 1972, 1976, and 1980

During the tenure of Lord Killanin as president of the IOC (1972–1980), the Olympic program for women expanded with the addition of four new sports. Killanin himself was instrumental in adding basketball, handball, rowing, and field hockey to the list of women's sports. Unlike his predecessor, Avery Brundage, Killanin was very supportive of women's sports.

In 1972, when the Olympic Games were held in Munich, Germany, the number of female participants exceeded 1,000 for the first time. A record number of 1,299 female athletes from sixty-one nations participated. As a reflection of the growing status of women's sports in Asia as well as the West, North Korea became the third Asian country to win an Olympic medal (after Japan and Taiwan). The sport of archery for women returned to the Olympics after being out of the program for fifty-two years. With new events in canoeing and track and field, the total number of women's events grew to forty-three. The Munich games of 1972 will also be remembered for the performances of a Soviet gymnast by the name of

Olga Korbut. The 4'11", 85-pound gymnast "stole the show" while winning gold medals in floor exercises and the balance beam.

In 1976 the Olympic Games moved back to North America and were held in Montreal, Quebec. The Montreal games were clouded by a boycott by African nations, but the boycott had minimal effect on the women's program. A total of 1,261 female athletes from sixty-five countries competed in the games. For the first time in the history of the modern Olympics, women represented over 20 percent of the total number of competitors. Three new sports (basketball, field handball, and rowing) were added to the women's program in this single year. The number of events for women grew to forty-nine. Most notably, women from only seventeen countries won Olympic medals in Montreal, illustrating the growing supremacy of female athletes from the communist countries. Although East Germany's Kornelia Ender won four gold medals and one silver medal in swimming, the heroine of the Montreal Olympics was a fourteen-year-old Rumanian gymnast, Nadia Comaneci. During competition, Comaneci scored an unprecedented total of seven perfect tens. Altogether, she won a total of five medals (three gold, one silver, and one bronze).

In 1980 the Olympic Games were held in Moscow. In spite of a boycott by many of Western countries that followed the lead of the United States, 1,112 female athletes from fifty-seven countries participated in the games. With the new sport of field hockey, women could now compete in a total of fifty events in eleven sports in the Summer Games. Three world records in track and field and six world records in swimming (all by swimmers from East Germany) were established at Moscow. East German women dominated the swimming competitions, winning twelve out of fifteen events, and capturing a total of twenty-six medals in swimming. Female athletes from Zimbabwe and Jamaica joined the list of countries winning an Olympic medal for the first time.

The 1980 Winter Games were held in Lake Placid, New York. In these games, 271 females from twenty-nine countries competed in a total of fourteen events. At Lake Placid, women from the Soviet Union and East Germany battled for supremacy, and female athletes from the People's Republic of China competed in the Winter Games for the first time.

## Doping and the Emergence of East German Supremacy

During the 1970s and 1980s, women's sports became clouded with problems associated with doping, particularly among female athletes from the East European communist countries. The problem of anabolic steroid use became so great that leading West German journalists referred to the Montreal Olympics in 1976 as the "Anabolics Games."[31]

The powerhouse of international women's sports in the 1970s and 1980s was the German Democratic Republic in East Germany. The great breakthrough of the East Germans first flashed on the world scene in 1973. In the swimming competitions at the Munich Olympics in 1972, the East German swimmers had achieved only mediocre results. One year later, the female swimmers from East Germany won thirteen gold medals in the first world championship for swimming, held in Belgrade. At the Montreal Olympics of 1976, East German female athletes gained an incredible twenty-five gold medals. Women competed in only forty-nine events in those games. There is little doubt that the success of the East Germans, followed closely by the success of athletes from the Soviet Union and other communist countries, was due to intensive planning and training by state officials, including the systematic doping of athletes. In the early 1980s, most experts estimated that up to 20 percent of female athletes, and a majority of the world's top athletes in track and field and swimming, used a performance-enhancing substance.[32]

In spite of the demise of East Germany as a separate state in 1989, East German female athletes continue to set world records, both in track and field and in swimming. The East Germans had obviously outdone their USSR sponsors and trainers.

## Women and the Olympic Games of 1984, 1988, and 1992

The years since 1980, when Juan Antonio Samaranch became president of the IOC, have seen unprecedented development in women's Olympic sports. (See Table 6.1.) The reasons behind this advance are still under discussion. Many believe that women's sports were added to the Olympics for purely economic reasons, while others hold that they were added for strictly political reasons. Regardless of the motives, twelve sports have been added to the women's Olympic program since 1980. Curling and ice hockey for women became part of the Olympics in the 1998 Winter Games, held in Nagano, Japan. Tae kwan do and the triathlon were added for the year 2000. With the addition of these sports, the total number of Olympic competitions open to women exceeds 40 percent. Today, only competitions in boxing, weight lifting, wrestling, baseball, and the modern pentathlon are closed to women in the Olympic program.

Los Angeles hosted the 1984 Olympic Games. Despite a boycott by countries aligned with the Soviet Union, the games were a huge success. A total of 1,567 women participated. America's Joan Benoit won the gold in the inaugural marathon race for women. America's Mary Lou Retton won the gold in all-around gymnastics. One of the more memorable incidents of the games occurred during the women's 3,000-meter race, when U.S. favorite Mary Decker and Great Britain's barefoot runner Zola Budd collided, allowing Rumania's Maricica Puica to win the gold medal.

The Winter Games of 1984 were staged at Sarajevo, Yugoslavia. A total of 274 women participated in the winter competitions. East German women swept the speed skating events. East Germany's Katarina Witt captured the gold medal in women's figure skating.

The 1988 Olympic Games were held in Seoul, Korea. For the first time, over 2,000 female athletes participated: a record total of 2,186 female competitors. Two new sports were added to the program, cycling and table tennis. The Seoul Olympics also marked the return of women's tennis after a sixty-four year

**TABLE 6-1  Development of the Olympic Program of Female Sports**

| | 1900 | 1904 | 1908 | 1912 | 1920 | 1924 | 1928 | 1932 | 1936 | 1948 | 1952 | 1956 |
|---|---|---|---|---|---|---|---|---|---|---|---|---|
| Golf | + | | | | | | | | | | | |
| Tennis | + | | + | + | + | + | | | | | | |
| Archery | | + | + | | | | | | | | | |
| Figure Skating | | | + | | + | + | + | + | + | + | + | + |
| Swimming | | | | + | + | + | + | + | + | + | + | + |
| Fencing | | | | | | + | + | + | + | + | + | + |
| Gymnastics | | | | | | | + | | + | + | + | + |
| Track and Field | | | | | | | + | + | + | + | + | + |
| Alpine Skiing | | | | | | | | | + | + | + | + |
| Canoeing | | | | | | | | | | + | + | + |
| Nordic Skiing | | | | | | | | | | | + | + |
| Speed Skating | | | | | | | | | | | | |
| Luge | | | | | | | | | | | | |
| Volleyball | | | | | | | | | | | | |
| Basketball | | | | | | | | | | | | |
| Field Handball | | | | | | | | | | | | |
| Rowing | | | | | | | | | | | | |
| Field Hockey | | | | | | | | | | | | |
| Shooting | | | | | | | | | | | | |
| Cycling | | | | | | | | | | | | |
| Table Tennis | | | | | | | | | | | | |
| Judo | | | | | | | | | | | | |
| Sailing | | | | | | | | | | | | |
| Badminton | | | | | | | | | | | | |
| Soccer | | | | | | | | | | | | |
| Softball | | | | | | | | | | | | |
| Curling | | | | | | | | | | | | |
| Ice Hockey | | | | | | | | | | | | |
| Tae Kwan Do | | | | | | | | | | | | |
| Triathlon | | | | | | | | | | | | |

absence. The tennis competition featured a lineup of highly paid professionals. Germany's Steffi Graf captured the gold medal in women's tennis singles. America's Jackie Joyner-Kersee dominated the women's heptathlon and long jump. American sprinter Florence Griffith Joyner won three gold medals in the 100 meters, the 200 meters, and the 400-meter relay. In swimming competitions East Germany's Kristin Otto gathered six gold medals.

**TABLE 6-1  continued**

| | 1960 | 1964 | 1968 | 1972 | 1976 | 1980 | 1984 | 1988 | 1992 | 1996 | 1998 | 2000 |
|---|---|---|---|---|---|---|---|---|---|---|---|---|
| Golf | | | | | | | | | | | | |
| Tennis | | | | | | | | + | + | + | + | + |
| Archery | | | | + | + | + | + | + | + | + | + | + |
| Figure Skating | + | + | + | + | + | + | + | + | + | + | + | + |
| Swimming | + | + | + | + | + | + | + | + | + | + | + | + |
| Fencing | + | + | + | + | + | + | + | + | + | + | + | + |
| Gymnastics | + | + | + | + | + | + | + | + | + | + | + | + |
| Track and Field | + | + | + | + | + | + | + | + | + | + | + | + |
| Alpine Skiing | + | + | + | + | + | + | + | + | + | + | + | + |
| Canoeing | + | + | + | + | + | + | + | + | + | + | + | + |
| Nordic Skiing | + | + | + | + | + | + | + | + | + | + | + | + |
| Speed Skating | + | + | + | + | + | + | + | + | + | + | + | + |
| Luge | | + | + | + | + | + | + | + | + | + | + | + |
| Volleyball | | + | + | + | + | + | + | + | + | + | + | + |
| Basketball | | | | | + | + | + | + | + | + | + | + |
| Field Handball | | | | | + | + | + | + | + | + | + | + |
| Rowing | | | | | + | + | + | + | + | + | + | + |
| Field Hockey | | | | | | + | + | + | + | + | + | + |
| Shooting | | | | | | | + | + | + | + | + | + |
| Cycling | | | | | | | | + | + | + | + | + |
| Table Tennis | | | | | | | | + | + | + | + | + |
| Judo | | | | | | | | | + | + | + | + |
| Sailing | | | | | | | | | + | + | + | + |
| Badminton | | | | | | | | | + | + | + | + |
| Soccer | | | | | | | | | | + | + | + |
| Softball | | | | | | | | | | + | + | + |
| Curling | | | | | | | | | | | + | + |
| Ice Hockey | | | | | | | | | | | + | + |
| Tae Kwan Do | | | | | | | | | | | | + |
| Triathlon | | | | | | | | | | | | + |

Earlier that year, the Winter Games of 1988 were held in Calgary (Canada). A record total of 313 women participated. East Germany's Katarina Witt again dominated the women's figure skating competition. America's Bonnie Blair won the gold medal in women's 500-meter speed skating.

The 1992 Olympic Games, held in Barcelona, Spain, attracted 2,708 female participants. Judo, badminton, and sailing were added to the program as new sports for women. Women competed in a total of 86 events. Due to the collapse of the Soviet Union, twelve former Soviet republics competed together as a unified team. Additionally, three former Soviet republics and several other countries competed for the first time as newly created independent nations. Women from South Africa competed in the Olympics after their twenty-eight-year exile. Results of the track and field competitions highlighted the truly global development of women's sports. Among the major accomplishments, Greece's Paraskevi Patoulidou won the women's 100-meter hurdles, thereby becoming the first Olympic track medalist from Greece since 1896. With a winning performance in the heptathlon, Jackie Joyner-Kersee maintained her title as the "greatest female athlete in the world." The 100-meter race was won by Gail Devers (USA). Hassiba Boulmerka from Algeria won the gold medal in the 1500 meters, and the Russian long-distance runner Valentina Yegorova won the marathon. Marie-Jose Perec from France won the gold medal in the 400-meter race. Zhang Shan, a Chinese skeet shooter, became the first woman to earn a gold medal in an open shooting event.

The 1992 Winter Games, held in Albertville, France, attracted a record number of 488 female athletes who competed in a total of twenty-three events. There were competitions in two mixed events as well. The 1992 Winter Olympics marked the last time that the Winter and Summer Games were held in the same year. Women's biathlon was added as a Nordic event. America's Bonnie Blair captured two gold medals in women's speed skating (500 meters and 1,000 meters). In figure-skating competition, America's Kristi Yamaguchi captured the gold medal.

Two years later, the 1994 Winter Olympic Games were held in Lillehammer, Norway. Following a definite pattern of increasing participation, a record number of 521 women competed in a total of twenty-five winter events. There were also competitions in two mixed events.

## The Emergence of Chinese Women in International Sports

Following the unification of West and East Germany in 1990, an extremely large number of sports scientists and coaches from the former East German state found themselves unemployed. Many of them went abroad to work, a significant number to the People's Republic of China. Their employment brought immediate improvement in that country's international sports standings. In the 1993 world championship in track and field, held in Stuttgart, Germany, Chinese female long-distance runners won three gold medals. In the following year, Chinese female swimmers gained fifteen gold medals in the world championship held in Rome. This line of success came to an abrupt end later that year, however, when a dozen Chinese athletes, many of them women, tested positive for doping activity at the Asian Games held in Japan. Following this doping scandal, Chinese long-distance runners suddenly disappeared from competition. Several of the Chinese female swimmers were barred from participation in the 1996 Olympic Games. In those games, female swimmers from the People's Republic of China gained a respectable but not "miraculous" three gold medals.

## The 1996 Olympic Games: The Games of the Women

The one hundredth anniversary of the modern Olympic Games was celebrated in Atlanta, Georgia (USA), in 1996. Many people feel that the Atlanta games should be called the "Games of the Women," because they attracted the largest contingent of female athletes ever assembled. Of the 10,744 athletes participating in the games, 3,684 were women—more than 30 percent. Appearing for the first time on the women's Olympic program were softball and soccer, bringing the total number of women's Olympic sports to twenty-one. Altogether, there were ninety-seven separate athletic events for women. There were also eleven open and mixed events, including competitions in badminton, yachting, equestrian, tennis, and shooting.

The American women garnered a total of nineteen gold medals in basketball, soccer, softball, track and field, gymnastics, tennis, shooting, and synchronized swimming. In the United States, their success was widely seen as evidence that Title IX had worked extremely well. The games also demonstrated that women's sports were becoming more and more global. An African woman became the first female from that continent to win the Olympic marathon. A woman from Kenya earned that nation's first medal by winning the 5,000-meter race in track and field. Syria, which had never won a gold medal at the Olympic Games, made history when a woman from that country won the heptathlon. The progress of women in developing countries was further illustrated by the presence of a woman shooter from Iran. She was the first Iranian woman since 1979 to participate in the Olympics.

The number of spectators who watched the Olympic Games in Atlanta was phenomenal. Many of the women's events were sellouts. It was reported that 76,481 spectators watched the final game in women's soccer between the United States and China, the largest crowd ever to see a sporting event between women in the United States.[33] Additionally, television provided live coverage of many of the women's competitions, thereby increasing by millions the number of people who watched women's sports.

## Women and the International Olympic Committee

Women's sports made considerable progress during the twentieth century, but the same cannot be said for the success of women in securing leadership positions in sports organizations. These organizations—especially international federations and committees—have traditionally been male dominated. This is especially the case in the International Olympic Committee (IOC). Prior to 1981, there had never been a female member of this governing body. The breakthrough occurred at the Olympic Congress in 1981 when two women were elected into the IOC. Pirjo Haggman of Finland and Flor Isava-Fonseca of Venezuela were both elected when vacancies were created by the departure of male members from those two countries. From 1981 to 1997, eight other women were elected as members: Mary Glen-Haig of the United Kingdom (1982), Princess Nora of Liechtenstein (1984), Anita DeFrantz of the United States (1986), Princess Anne of the United Kingdom (1988), Carol Ann Letheren of Canada (1990), Vera Caslavska of the Czech

Republic (1995), Dona Pilar de Borbon of Spain (1996), and Gunilla Lindberg of Sweden (1996).

While certainly a tribute to President Juan Antonio Samaranch, the progress of women's representation on the IOC has been small and intermittent. From 1990 to 1996, a period in which over forty men were elected for membership, only four women were added to the group. One previously elected member, Mary Glen-Haig, had to resign when she reached the then-required retirement age of seventy-five years. Thus, at the end of 1997, only nine women were members of the IOC, compared to 102 male members.

Despite limited representation in the IOC, women have made progress in positions of sports leadership in other Olympic-affiliated activity. Although not a member of the IOC, perhaps the most influential woman in international sports in the twentieth century was Monique Berlioux of France. She held the top position in the IOC's office in Lausanne from the later part of Avery Brundage's presidency until 1980. As long as the IOC presidents were in absentia from the Lausanne office, Madame Berlioux was the de facto administrator of the Olympic movement. It was only when Samaranch physically arrived in Lausanne, following his election to the IOC presidency in 1980, that the influence of Madame Berlioux declined. In 1985 Samaranch forced Madame Berlioux to retire from office, although he saw to it that she received a substantial settlement.

In 1997 Anita DeFrantz became the first woman to be elected a vice president of the IOC. She was to function in that capacity until 2001. Also, several women have served as presidents of their respective National Olympic Committees (NOCs). In 1996, in addition to Princess Nora and Vera Caslavska, women were serving as presidents of National Olympic Committees in Fiji, Georgia, Rumania, Canada, and Tonga. The vice president of the Iran Olympic Committee was a woman, and twelve other Olympic Committees had women secretaries in 1996.

Although not all of them are directly affiliated with the Olympic movement, five of the thirty-one international federations that govern sports (badminton, equestrian, netball, squash, and orienteering) have women presidents, and the field hockey, tennis, netball and water skiing groups have women in the post of executive director.

Opportunities for women to attain still more positions of leadership expanded when, in September 1995, the IOC executive office made a dramatic announcement. Recognizing the importance of equality between men and women in the Olympic movement, it made four proposals that were approved by the entire IOC in 1996.

> (1) the National Olympic Committees must reserve to women, by December 31, 2000, at least 10 percent of the offices in all their decision-making structures, such proportion to reach 20 percent by December 31, 2005; (2) the International Federations, the National Federations, and the sports organizations belonging to the Olympic movement are strongly invited to include by December 31, 2000, at least 10% of women in their decision-making structures, such proportion to reach 20 percent by December 31, 2005; (3) the subsequent stages to reach a strict enforcement of the principle of equality between men and women shall be determined from the

year 2001; and (4) the Olympic Charter will be amended to take into account the need to keep the equality between men and women.[34]

On an equally positive note, the IOC sponsored a World Conference on Women and Sport at its Lausanne headquarters in 1996. Attending were 220 participants from ninety-six countries. At the end of the conference, the participants adopted a list of recommendations "the aim of which was to promote women's role in the Olympic Movement and the sports world in general."[35] Two of the seventeen recommendations deserve mention. The first was to discontinue the controversial sex test that was adopted by the IOC in 1968. The second asked that the IOC call the 1996–2000 quadrennial the "Olympiad for Women."[36]

## Play for Pay: The Expansion of Women's Professional Sports

Prior to the 1970s, opportunities for women in professional sports were extremely limited. The Women's National Bowling Congress made prize money available to women, although it was a fraction of the amount that could be won by men. In 1943 a women's professional baseball league was established in the United States, primarily as a substitute form of entertainment while the professional male players were off fighting a war. The All-American Girls Professional Baseball League was established with four teams and eventually grew to eight teams, but it disbanded in 1954.

In 1943, professional opportunities also developed for women in golf with the establishment of the Women's Professional Golf Association (WPGA). Beginning in 1946, the WPGA began sponsoring open championships. In 1949 it reorganized as the Ladies Professional Golf Association (LPGA). The most prominent female professional golfer in the 1940s and early 1950s was Babe Didrikson Zaharias. The LPGA experienced major growth in both events and prize money during the 1950s. Following in the footsteps of Zaharias, Mickey Wright won ten major titles (four U.S. Open Championships, four LPGA Championships, and two tournaments for titleholders) between 1958 and 1963. Sweden's Annika Sorenstam earned over $1 million in prize money in both 1996 and 1997. As of 1997, the top earner in female professional golf was Betsy King; she won over $5.4 million in prize money during the 1990s.

In 1968 the doors for women to compete in professional sports opened wider with the introduction of open tennis and the subsequent development of professional tennis for women. A towering figure in the early years of women's professional tennis was Billie Jean King. In 1971 she was the first female athlete ever to earn over $100,000 in professional sports. As a vociferous advocate of equality for the female athlete, she became one of the most influential forces in shaping the future of women's sports. King, who had twelve grand slam titles to her credit (having won, at various times, the French, British, American, and Australian championship), fought for better if not equal prize money for women and was successful in doing so. While leading that fight, she became the recognized leader of female professional athletes in the United States.

The greatest number of grand slam titles ever acquired by a woman in tennis was achieved by Australia's Margaret Smith Court, who gained twenty-four titles in the years 1960–1973. She was followed by Germany's Steffi Graf, who gained twenty-one titles between 1987 and 1996. Court and Graf were also the only players who succeeded in scoring Grand Slams—winning the British, American, French, and Australian championships in a single year—since the introduction of open tennis in 1968. Court did so in 1970 and Graf followed her eighteen years later.

Accompanying the development in tennis and golf, other sports have moved toward professionalism as well. Attempts were made in 1978 to develop a professional basketball league for women. In that year the Women's Professional Basketball League (WPBL) was formed with eight teams, expanding to fourteen teams a year later. The league, which had limited spectator appeal and major financial problems, disbanded in 1982. In 1984 another attempt was made to organize a basketball league for women, the Women's American Basketball League (WABL), but it folded in the middle of its first year of operation. A similar unsuccessful attempt was made in 1991, with the formation of the Liberty Basketball Association (LBA). Because professional basketball failed in these attempts in the United States, many of the best U.S. players competed on professional teams in Europe.

In the late 1990s, however, women's professional basketball finally hit the big time with the formation of two leagues in the United States. The first of these, the American Basketball League (ABL), consisted of eight teams. It was financially supported by major sponsors and backed by a major television contract, only to fold in 1998 due to financial problems. The second league, the Women's National Basketball Association (WNBA), began its first year of play in 1997; it, too, was made up of eight teams. By piggybacking on the (men's) National Basketball Association's marketing power, the WNBA exceeded the league's expectations for attendance, television audiences, sponsors, and fan enthusiasm in its first year of operation.

During the 1990s, numerous other women's sports became professionalized, and several of the sport federations began offering cash prizes and payments to competing women athletes. Professional organizations in women's volleyball, women's figure skating, and other sports gained more influence The Women's Professional Volleyball Association in fact had been in existence since 1986. More recently, opportunities to compete in volleyball have grown to include women's beach volleyball. In late 1996 a Women's Professional Fast Pitch Softball League was established. In its inaugural year (1997), the league consisted of six teams, played a seventy-two game schedule, held play-offs, and conducted a title game. Although not established as a professional sport per se, women's track and field began offering cash prizes to successful athletes. At the present time, preliminary planning is under way for professional women's ice hockey and soccer.

The increasing value that society places on professional women's sports can be seen in the amount of money that female athletes earn. In 1971 Billie Jean King prided herself on becoming the first female professional athlete to earn over $100,000 a year in prize money. In the first nine months of 1997, the number one female tennis player in the world, seventeen-year-old Martina Hingas of Switzerland, had already made over $3 million. In that year Martina Navratilova headed the list of career earners with a total of about $20 million.

Thus, as we move into the twenty-first century, women have more opportunities to participate in a wider variety of sports than ever before. Women on all levels are actively participating in a variety of physical activities, driven by motives ranging from pleasure to profit.

## SUMMARY

Opportunities for women to participate in a significant number of sport programs did not develop until well into the twentieth century. Before 1800 opportunities for women to engage in sports were minimal. Although some women danced and engaged in physical activities, their involvement was often frowned on by society. This attitude prevailed during most of the nineteenth century as well. Victorian philosophy depicted the ideal woman as fragile, pale, and weak. Participation in vigorous activity was thought to violate the laws of nature. Even the medical profession believed that strenuous physical activity harmed a woman's ability to bear children. Thus most nineteenth-century women avoided energetic physical activity, engaging instead in such ladylike and socially acceptable activities as archery, croquet, bowling, tennis, and golf. These pastimes were especially popular among wealthy upper-class women in pursuit of leisure activity.

By the end of the nineteenth century, society's views began to change and the image of a healthy woman replaced the Victorian ideal. Exercise and physical activity were now considered beneficial to a woman's ability to do housework and bear children. Bicycling and swimming joined tennis and golf as popular sports for women. A handful of women even participated in the new team sports, notably basketball, field hockey, and track and field. Although opportunities were extremely limited, the seeds for women's participation in international sports also were planted during the mid- to late 1800s. Women were not, however, allowed to participate in the first modern Olympic Games in 1896.

During the twentieth century, programs and opportunities for women gradually increased. Advances in women's sports were made initially in the colleges and universities and on the international level. The women's colleges staged play days and sports days that included not only the traditional recreational sports, but the newly established team sports as well. Although the play days were successful in promoting opportunities for women to participate in sport, they frowned on serious competition and the "masculinization" of women's sports. The emphasis on competition between women in sports did not develop until well into the latter part of the twentieth century. Most of the advances in women's sports occurred during the last two decades of the twentieth century.

Throughout the 1900s, women's participation in international sports and in the Olympic movement showed slow but steady progress. More and more women's events were gradually added to the Olympic schedule. In the games of 1900, women were allowed to participate in only two events, golf and tennis. In the 1996 centennial games, women athletes participated in over ninety-seven separate events. However, the progress made by women in the international arena was not free of controversy and, at times, contempt.

At this time it is evident that women's sports have come of age. Opportunities abound for women of all ages to participate in a variety of sport programs on all levels. Programs for girls and women have mushroomed in public schools as well as colleges and universities. Opportunities for women to compete on the international level are at an all-time high. The increase in the number of women holding leadership positions in the international sport federations such as the IOC is notable. A number of women's professional sports leagues have emerged. As we enter the twenty-first century, there is little doubt that women's programs have made dramatic advances in participation, programs, and funding. Nevertheless, a number of gender issues still remain.

## STUDY QUESTIONS

1. How are women's sports in the twentieth century different from those of the nineteenth century?
2. Discuss methods an institution could employ to be in complete compliance with Title IX.
3. Is it appropriate or fair for athletic administrators to cut men's sports in order to add the required number of women's sports? If not, how could this measure be avoided?
4. Discuss the International Olympic Committee in relation to its women members.
5. Discuss the resolutions of the International Olympic Committee that by the year 2000, 10 percent of its members and members of the respective sport federations must be women. Since no sanctions have been stipulated for noncompliance, do you believe these are realistic goals?
6. In light of the success of the women Olympians at the 1996 Games in Atlanta, is it realistic to assume that each new Olympics will see more women entrants and more sports for women?
7. Discuss gender roles in the next millennium. Will there be more women administrators, coaches, and officials, or will men continue to dominate the athletic domain?
8. Analyze five sports magazines of the year 1990 and the year 1997, comparing the number of ads featuring women or pertaining to women.
9. Describe the achievements of ten men and ten women that greatly influenced twentieth-century sport.

## RECOMMENDED READINGS

Ashe, Arthur. *A Hard Road to Glory*. New York: Warner Books, 1988.

Cohen, Greta, ed. *Women in Sport: Issues and Controversies*. Newbury Park, CA: Sage Publications, 1993.

Gerber, E., J. Felshin, P. Berlin, and W. Wyrick. *The American Woman in Sport*. Reading, MA: Addison-Wesley, 1974.

Hult, J., and M. Trekell, eds. *A Century of Women's Basketball: From Frailty to Final Four*. Reston, VA: AAHPERD, 1991.

International Olympic Committee. "The Olympic Games and Women." *Olympic Review* 25, no. 5 (October-November 1995).

Lucas, John. *The Modern Olympic Games*. New York: A. S. Barnes, 1980.

Mechikoff, Robert A., and Steven G. Estes. *A History and Philosophy of Sport and Physical Education*, Boston: McGraw-Hill, 1998.

National Collegiate Athletic Association. *Achieving Gender Equity: A Basic Guide to Title IX for Colleges and Universities*. Overland Park, KS: NCAA, 1994.

National Collegiate Athletic Association. *Gender Equity Study*. Overland Park, KS: NCAA, 1992.

Nelson, R., and M. MacNee. *The Olympic Factbook*. Detroit: Visible Ink Press, 1996.

Von Borries, Eline. *The History and Functions of the National Section on Women's Athletics*. Baltimore, MD: The National Section on Women's Athletics, 1941.

Women's Division, National Amateur Athletic Federation. *Women and Athletics*. New York: A. S. Barnes, 1930.

## NOTES

1. Uriel Simri, *A Concise World History of Women's Sports* (Netanya, Israel: Wingate Institute for Physical Education and Sport, 1983), 12–13.

2. Jay Coakley, *Sport in Society: Issues and Controversies* (St. Louis: Times-Mirror, Mosby College Publications, 1994), 214.

3. Oliver Jensen, *The Revolt of American Women* (New York: Harcourt, Brace, 1952), 121.

4. M. Kuhn, *Michigan State: The First Hundred Years 1855–1955* (Michigan State University Press, 1955), 219.

5. James Naismith, *Basketball, Its Origin and Development* (New York: Associated Press, 1941), 161–170.

6. Senda Berenson, "Basketball for Women," *Physical Education* (1894): 106–109.

7. Mary Leigh, "Pierre de Coubertin: A Man of His Time," *Quest* 22 (June 1974): 19–24.

8. J. Findling and K. Pelle, *Historical Dictionary of the Modern Olympic Movement* (Westport, CT: Greenwood Press, 1996), 16.

9. *New York Times* (March 31, 1914): 98.

10. Pierre de Coubertin, "Les Femmes aux Jeux Olympiques," *Ula Revue Olympique* (July 1912): 109–111.

11. *Spaulding's Official Athletic Almanac for 1905* (New York: American Sports, 1905), 132.

12. During the 1920s, there was a three-way battle in the United States to control women's sports. The Amateur Athletic Union (AAU) was committed to a program emphasizing competitive sports. The Committee on Women's Athletics (CWA) of the American Physical Education Association (later the National Section on Women's Athletics) and the Women's Division of the

National Amateur Athletics Federation (NAAF) both supported programs that stressed participation by a broad range of women and girls, with limited competition.

13. Blanche M. Trilling, "The Playtime of a Million Girls or an Olympic Victory—Which?" *Women and Athletics* (New York: A. S. Barnes, 1930), 78.

14. *Athletic Handbook* (New York: American Sports Publishing Company, 1923), Foreword.

15. Mabel Lee, "The Case for and against Intercollegiate Athletics for Women and the Situation since 1923," *Research Quarterly* 2 (May 1931): 93.

16. Trilling, *Women and Athletics*, 84.

17. Trilling, *Women and Athletics*, 89.

18. "Things Seen and Heard," *Sportsman* 20 (October 1936): 18.

19. Celeste Ulrich, "Alexandria and the Gordian Knot," *Proceedings of the 50th Anniversary Convention of Southern District of AAHPER* (February 1977), 58.

20. E. Gerber, J. Felshin, P. Berlin, and W. Wyrick, *The American Woman in Sport* (Reading, MA: Addison-Wesley, 1974), 164.

21. S. Jernigan, "Mirror of Time: Some Causes for More American Women in Sport Competitions," *Quest* 22 (June 1974): 86.

22. U.S. Department of Health, Education, and Welfare, *HEW Fact Sheet* (June 1975), 1.

23. W. Leonard, *A Sociological Perspective of Sport* (New York: Macmillan, 1984).

24. E. Weber, "The Title IX Controversy," *Women Sports* (June 1974): 76.

25. R. Wiley, Letter to John Fuzek, President of the NCAA (May 12, 1975).

26. C. Hogan, "The Politics of Takeover," *Women Sports* (September 1974): 52.

27. C. Hogan, "NCAA and AIAW: Will the Men Score on Women's Athletics?" *Women Sports* (January 1977): 46.

28. A. L. Bryant, "Gender Equity in Intercollegiate Athletics," *The Chronicle of Higher Education* (February 17, 1993): 1.

29. J. Clemons, "Path for Gender Equity Outlined," Atlanta *Journal and Constitution* (May 19, 1993): E1.

30. National Collegiate Athletic Association, "Final Report of the NCAA Gender Equity Task Force" (July 26, 1993), 1.

31. Guenter R. Mueller and Dieter Kuehnle, *Moskauer Spiele* (Gütersloh: Sven Simon, no date), 160.

32. Simri, *A Concise World History of Women's Sports*, 148.

33. Michael Farber, "Score One for Women," *Sports Illustrated* (August 12, 1996), 72.

34. International Olympic Committee, *World and Sport—New Horizons* (September 26, 1995), printed document.

35. International Olympic Committee, *World Conference on Women and Sport* (Lausanne: International Olympic Committee, October 1996), 35.

36. Ibid., 36–57.

# CHAPTER SEVEN

# GLOBAL ISSUES IN THE PROFESSION OF PHYSICAL EDUCATION AND SPORT

## EARLE F. ZEIGLER

Almost everyone would agree that, like all other social institutions, competitive sport and physical activity ought to be organized and administered to make positive contributions to society. Some critics would say, however, that like religion in Marx's day, sport and physical education are an expensive "opiate of the masses." Today national and international competitive sports programs on all levels are plagued with violence, drug use, gambling, and other ethically questionable practices. Commercialization and labor issues are unresolved concerns. Physical education faces a severe, uphill struggle throughout the world. Whereas physical education once was required for most students in the United States and Canada, it is often now fighting to remain an elective offering in the curriculum. This decline has taken place even though we now have evidence that, in addition to enabling a person to live life more fully, steady involvement in the right kind of developmental physical activity will help a person to live longer.

What should we do about these issues and concerns? What *can* we do about them? These two questions must be addressed if the fields of sport and physical education are to make significant contributions to society. Before answering them directly, however, we must first be aware of three major concepts that will shape our world in the coming century and affect our planning.

We are all aware of technological advances in *communication*. From speech to the written word to mechanical reproduction of the printed word occupied all of history up until 500 years ago. Today we have relay space stations to bring us news and entertainment instantly and on a global scale. We have telephones, fax machines, and e-mail that put us instantly in touch with anyone else we choose. This vastly improved communication network can foster levels of international understanding and good will hardly dreamed of before. Yet it may also discourage people who learn about tragic happenings that our current institutions cannot deal with.[1] Better communication can also permit faster and more efficient communication of the dark side of the human spirit. So the question is, In what ways can advances in communications be used to improve our institutions and foster international cooperation? And what roles do sport and physical education play in this effort?

A second major concept is *diversity*. Cultural, racial, and ideological differences have always existed, but today they are much more an issue than ever before. Communication and transportation advances have made our world a global village in which we know all about our neighbors. The question is, How well can we get along with each other? Will decent behavior have to be enforced by a system involving B. F. Skinner's operant conditioning and behavior modification? To what extent will overpopulation and ideological disputes curb personal liberty? Skinner, writing in 1971, predicted that this would be the major issue of the twenty-first century. Our question here is whether sports and physical education can help us appreciate the talents and inherent value of those who are different.

A third major concept, *cooperation*, must also enter into our planning for the future. As suggested above, better communication and greater awareness of diversity make cooperation an imperative in today's world. Politicians and sport administrators have claimed for years that international sport fosters goodwill, besides giving both athletes and their home countries standing and recognition on the world scene. Yet many believe that competitive sport can do still more to expand the horizons of international cooperation. The question, of course, is how.

If the fields of sport and physical education are to contribute to better international communication, greater appreciation of diversity, and cooperation in social living, then they will need to improve, to reform, to clean up their act. But if they make this grand attempt, they are likely to find themselves strongly buffeted by economic forces and narrow ideologies. And they will be hindered by the split within their own ranks.

It may be true that significant change in education rarely comes from within. Yet professionals in sport and physical education have reached a point where they must search for consensus on their basic function as a profession. Only then can the profession advance and bring vital benefits to the public.

## THE PRESENT SITUATION

### A Good Life in Tomorrow's World

It was not so long ago that the idea of the "good life" beckoned us toward a coming age of leisure. But now we're not so sure about that. Twentieth-century progress in science and technology has been accompanied by retrogression or dubious progress at best in social and political affairs. The world is increasingly complex. Many leaders, along with the rest of us, must certainly be wondering how the whole affair can be managed.

Various pundits have tried to identify the major influences and trends that affect our world. In 1982, in a popular book entitled *Megatrends*, J. Naisbitt outlined "ten new directions that are transforming our lives." These trends were (1) the information society and the Internet; (2) "high tech/high touch"; (3) the shift to a world economy; (4) the need to shift to long-term thinking in regard to ecology; (5) the move toward organizational decentralization; (6) the trend toward self-help; (7) the ongoing discussion of the wisdom of participatory democracy as opposed to representative democracy; (8) a shift toward networking; (9) a reconsideration of the "north-south" orientation; and (10) the viewing of decisions as "multiple option" instead of "either/or." Ten years later, Aburdene and Naisbitt coauthored *Megatrends for Women.*

A list of ten issues facing political leaders was highlighted in the *Utne Reader* in an article titled "Ten Events That Shook the World between 1984 and 1994." These events included (1) the fall of communism and the continuing rise of nationalism; (2) the environmental crisis and the green movement; (3) the AIDS epidemic and the "gay response"; (4) continuing wars and the peace movement; (5) the gender war; (6) religion and racial tension; (7) the concept of "West meets East" and resultant implications; (8) the "Baby Boomers" coming of age and "Generation X" starting to worry and complain because of unmet expectations; (9) globalism and international markets; and (10) the computer revolution and the "specter" of the Internet.[2]

Add to these trends the ever-increasing, lifelong involvement of women in the workplace, politics, sports, organized religion, and social activism, and we begin to realize that a new world order is in store for us in the twenty-first century.

## General Intercultural Observations

Certain intercultural observations have direct implications for the field of physical education and sport. At the present time, a relatively small number of physical educators and even fewer coaches have an international orientation in regard to their chosen profession. The vast majority of physical educators and coaches in the United States seem to feel that "if anything worthwhile is going to happen, it will be here," and that "it had better be in English if you expect us to read it." This depiction may sound harsh, but these attitudes are prevalent and may cause harm in the future.

For this reason it is especially important to note that, since its inception, the International Council for Health, Physical Education, Recreation, Sport, and Dance (ICHPER-SD) has worked to broaden the horizons of professionals in the various fields of sport and physical activity. The founding of the International Society for Comparative Physical Education and Sport in 1968 marked a second thrust in this direction. It is through these efforts and similar ones that those in the profession of sport and physical education may be able to help civilization move a bit faster toward what Glasser (1972) called a "civilized identity society," a society in which the concern of humans will again—as Glasser theorizes—focus on such concepts as "self-identity," "self-expression," and "cooperation." Now, almost thirty years later, ecological concerns and economic interests often clash sharply, but it is possible—though far from probable—that humankind may yet reenter Glasser's civilized identity society.

As we contemplate the years ahead, what will all this mean to us who are interested in developmental physical activity in sport, exercise, and expressive movement for people of all ages and conditions? We have responsibilities in our own countries, of course, to help people appreciate the value of sport and physical education and to provide opportunities for physical activity. As physical educators and coaches, our role is to so guide education that everyone will understand the healthful and enjoyable benefits of developmental physical activity and sport.

## A Survey of the International Scene in Sport and Physical Education

In 1994 this author was asked by the organizers of the tenth International Scientific Congress of the International Society for Comparative Physical Education and Sports (ISCPES) to report on the current status of sport and physical education throughout the world. A survey undertaken in the development of that report yielded some interesting results that are summarized later in this section.

Prior to the survey, my initial assessment was that physical education and sport in educational institutions worldwide had deteriorated and would continue to do so in the years ahead. This view was based on the results of professional involvement of various types, the reading of many journals, and an extensive international correspondence carried on for many years. All these sources of information indicated that physical education had been reeling for years as a result of negative social forces. Additionally, persistent problems and issues have plagued competitive sports in every decade of the twentieth century.

Paradoxically, in the face of this decline and attendant problems, more was scientifically known than ever before about the potential beneficial effects that properly conceived developmental physical activity in exercise, sport, and related expressive movement could have on people of all ages and conditions. It did not, therefore, seem advisable for us in the profession to give up or to abandon the wisdom of striving to create a social situation in which the salutary effects of appropriate developmental physical activity would be introduced into all people's lives. However, we had to realize that society's need for developmental physical activity would be met if—and only if—(1) public support for our efforts was earned, and (2) highly trained leadership was made available to earn such public support and then to bring about these desirable educational and developmental outcomes.

The survey had two main purposes. The first was to carry out a preliminary analysis of global trends in physical education and sport. The second was to make recommendations regarding what the field should do in the immediate future. To accomplish these broad purposes, it was decided to follow a sequence of steps as follows: (1) to set the stage with a brief, general assessment of the international situation; (2) to obtain some specific reactions about what was happening in regard to physical education and educational sport in each of the thirty-three countries represented in the 1993 membership list of ISCPES; (3) to invite consideration of the future by offering one futuristic approach that had been recommended for coping with the "great transition" that the world has been undergoing; (4) while keeping separate the possible, probable, and preferable futures, to offer personal observations about how the knowledge already available to the profession of physical education and sport around the world might help in addressing the field's future; (5) to make recommendations for coping with the "modifications" that the field has undergone during the past thirty years to effect improved professional development; and (6) to delineate the basic considerations and strategies required to cope with the professional task ahead. The investigation therefore employed both historical method and broad descriptive methodology, as well as what may be called "philosophical assessment" as to the field's current direction and immediate future.

To determine the current status of sport and physical education in selected countries throughout the world, individuals from thirty-three countries drawn from the 1993 membership list of the ISCPES were contacted and asked to participate in the survey. In essence, the survey was designed to discover what professionals in the field were experiencing firsthand in certain countries in 1994.[3]

Educators from twenty of the thirty-three countries (60 percent of the countries) responded to the survey. The difficulty of developing scientific hypotheses from a survey of this type was recognized. Strictly speaking, hypotheses are statements about the relationship between variables. They also embody an understanding as to how such a relationship may be established. The results of the survey represented rather the opinion about the status of physical education and educational sport from one professionally minded person in each of the responding countries. Fortunately, the people who responded were representative of countries in all parts of the world, and they obviously made a sincere effort to respond to the questions raised.

Simple descriptive statistics were used to categorize and analyze the results.[4] The results were expressed in the following four categories: (1) substantial majority (76 to 100 percent); (2) majority (51 to 75 percent); (3) substantial minority (26 to 50 percent); and (4) unsubstantial minority (0 to 25 percent). As a result of this analysis, the survey yielded ten major findings.

First, to my surprise, a majority of the respondents believed that the physical education program in their country had, generally speaking, improved in the past decade. This finding was encouraging to an investigator whose thinking was undoubtedly influenced by the North American scene. Of course, in some countries, the original situation may have been quite poor, and the improvement modest.

Second, a substantial minority expressed the belief that the level of physical fitness had declined in their country. Only five individuals thought the level of physical fitness had improved, and a similar number felt it had stayed about the same.

Third, a substantial majority reported using the term *physical education* at the school level. Also, a majority indicated that they have not made a name change at the university level. It is apparent that name changes in universities during the past decade occurred in those institutions where the units are striving for academic status in a competitive environment. In the United States, at last count, upwards of 200 different names for physical education are used at the college and university level.

Fourth, the survey revealed that physical education was required in a substantial majority of the countries responding. The requirement ranged from a low of three years to a high of fourteen years. Only four countries—Canada, India,

Malawi, and the United States—reported having no national requirement in physical education.

Fifth, competitive sport of varying "intensity" is part of the overall physical education program in a majority of the schools. It is considered an extracurricular activity in a substantial minority of countries. It was not clear in this instance to what extent competitive sport was regarded an "educational experience" in the same way as what is typically called physical education. For a variety of reasons, this matter has not yet been resolved. It is certain, however, that in all countries competitive sport is available outside of school through private, semipublic, and public agencies.

Sixth, physical education and organized sport both come under the jurisdiction of a national ministry in a majority of the countries surveyed. In six countries physical education is considered an aspect of education, with education being the responsibility of a state or province within the country. The location of organized sport within governmental frameworks does not appear to follow any definite pattern. Physical education, on the other hand, is always located within the governmental bureau concerned with education.

Seventh, physical education counts for academic credit in a majority of the countries surveyed. The results here are not clear, because a great range in academic credit is granted (from no credit in seven countries to full acceptance as a tertiary entrance subject in a number of Australian states). Underlying this whole issue, of course, is the question of whether the physical education course experience and subsequent grade—especially when no theoretical component is included in the grade awarded for the course experience—should be averaged in with other course grades to determine an overall grade point average.

Eighth, as to the basic areas or activities generally included in the curricula at the elementary, middle, secondary, and university levels (such as fitness activities, sport skills, or rhythmic activities), it was not possible to classify the responses given to this question by each of the twenty respondents. However, the following generalizations are possible: (a) the curriculum and instructional methodology are fairly standard from country to country; (b) fundamental movement skills and games of low organization are standard at the elementary-school level; (c) sports skills instruction and fitness activities are introduced gradually at the middle-school level and continued on through the high-school level on either a required or elective basis; (d) a theoretical component in instructional programs is almost completely lacking, except in a few countries in specific states or provinces; (e) lifetime sport and physical recreation instruction is often offered in high schools; (f) extramural competitive sport between schools is offered only in Canada, Japan, Nigeria, and the United States; and (g) university programs, where offered, are largely elective and typically include voluntary sport and physical recreation and fitness-oriented activities.

Ninth, the respondents were almost unanimous in affirming that there was nothing highly unusual or unique in their countries' physical education curriculum or instructional methodology. This was a disturbing finding. For greater recognition within general education, increasingly sound theoretical material is necessary to undergird the skills instruction program. Australia and Canada report that in certain states or provinces highly sophisticated theory courses using textbooks have been introduced in the upper-level, high-school courses, the results of which are fully credited for university entrance. Also, Japan has been making extensive use of video cameras to provide sport-skill feedback to students at the high-school level.

Tenth, the present overall status of physical education was rated lower than other subjects in the curriculum by a substantial majority of the responding countries. Respondents from only two countries (Nigeria and Taiwan) believed that the status of physical education was equal to that of other subjects.

Finally, in response to a request for open-ended comments, respondents from six countries expressed the belief that physical activity's contribution to health would eventually help the field gain more recognition. Respondents from three countries felt that improved programs in teacher preparation were needed. Respondents reported that in two countries (Canada and the United States) legislation had significantly improved the level of adapted physical education. In one country (Australia) a recent national conference report about the prevailing situation in sport and physical activity had tended to improve the field.

## Further Research into the State of Sport and Physical Education Worldwide

The results of this 1994 survey include some interesting data but certainly not the full story in regard to the present world status of sport and physical education. Subsequently, it was decided to look for additional information on the most recent developments. Specifically, recent materials published in four internationally oriented journals (the *International Journal of Physical Education,* the *Journal of Comparative Physical Education and Sport,* the *European Physical Education Review,* and the *Journal of the International Council for Health, Physical Education, Recreation, Sport, and Dance)* were reviewed. The results of the review included significant information, both positive and negative, about recent developments.

Ken Hardman in 1995 published an excellent article on global trends in physical education.[5] The picture he presents is well documented and overall a bit depressing. While granting that his "various 'snap-shot' national scenarios presented may provide a somewhat distorted picture of physical education in the schools," Hardman does nevertheless make a solid case for the urgent need to redefine the parameters for twenty-first century conditions and needs, and to reshape the physical education system to meet those needs. Hardman's report includes brief statements about the status of physical education in Scandinavia (Sweden, Norway, and Finland), the Netherlands, Greece, Germany, the Czech and Slovak Republics, Scotland, England and Wales, a number of African countries (e.g., Kenya), Malaysia, the United States, Canada, and Australia. "The news is not good," even in England and Wales, where a "government-sponsored national curriculum was imposed in 1989 with physical education introduced as a statutorily required school subject for children aged 5–16."[6] The problem in England and Wales was that physical educators had no input into the deliberations prior to the announcement of the

national curriculum, and thus "economic viability" and not "educational desirabil-
ity" appeared to determine the time allotment for physical education. As Hardman
implies, the day for problem-solving, persuasion, and bargaining may have drawn
to a close, and the era of politicking has begun.

An article by John C. Andrews asks, "Is there a need for a continuing differ-
entiation between the terms *physical education* and *sport*?" Andrews, who was the
world president of the International Federation of Physical Education (FIEP) in
1995, came down strongly for the umbrella term *physical education and sport*.[7] This
umbrella term, rather than the separation of the terms *sport* and *physical education*,
is widely understood and used worldwide (this observation is based on the findings of the limited survey reported above). However, in the United States especially, it might be more appropriate to label it *physical education and educational sport*,
thus differentiating it from the overly emphasized commercial sport found in both
education and the public sector.

Further, Andrews reiterates several valid concerns, namely (1) the decrease
in curriculum time for instruction in physical education in the schools; (2) the
"confusion of multiple aims and directions;" (3) a growing gap between the
researcher and the practitioner; (4) inadequate public awareness and support; (5)
a murky relationship among the so-called allied professions; and (6) a widening
gap between physical educational and sport opportunities available in developed
and underdeveloped nations.[8]

A 1996 article by John Cheffers, "Sport versus Education: The Jury Is Still
Out," raises a highly interesting point.[9] Required physical education often seems
like work, whereas voluntary sport is more like play. Sport is even alluring, but
physical education is viewed as "dour" and "funereal."[10] With this as an introductory thought, Cheffers raises nineteen penetrating "sport-education statements"
and concludes with ten outstanding hypotheses for serious consideration by all
who are concerned with the future of physical education and sport. For example,
the fifth sport-education statement postulates that, "sports invite the short-cut,
cheating, drugs, gross egos. Education invites the same, but celebrates less." One
increasingly important hypothesis advanced by Cheffers is that "the essential
periphery (parents, press, business associates, and spectators) need also take
responsibility for their part in the total enterprise."[11]

Despite the serious condition of school physical education worldwide as
described in the above articles by Hardman, Andrews, and Cheffers, several
encouraging notes were sounded in other articles published in the four above-
noted journals. V. Roberts, for example, writing about "the success of school and
community sport provisions in Britain," reports "that in the years up to 1994,
Britain's schools were improving their sports facilities, that young people were
playing more sports in and out of school than in the past, that the drop-out rate on
completion of statutory schooling had fallen dramatically, that social class and gender differences had narrowed, and that by the mid-1990s, sports had higher youth
participation and retention rates than any other structured forms of leisure."[12] He
concludes with a plea that authorities not return to the earlier male-dominated,
"traditional games regime" that never held much attraction for young women.

Moving to the east, Z. Krawczyk explains that the "image of sport" in Eastern Europe has changed radically since the decline of communism. There is still significant concern for a responsible system of physical activity and sport for children and young people. Interestingly, Krawczyk also predicts that the promotion of elite sport will emerge again but that the money expended will be more in line with a depressed economy. Overall, because the situation is in a state of constant flux, Krawczyk does not see evidence confirming a future "strong recovery" overall in the entire region.[13]

In Australia, C. L. Saffici writes about a successful initiative in physical education there called Aussie Sport. The two main philosophic stances of this program for boys and girls are "sport for all" and "fair play." "The hope is that people who find sport attractive will continue to have active lifestyles, and thus be able to decrease the likelihood of suffering from cardiovascular disease and/or low back problems."[14] A further objective of this program is to involve an increasing number of elementary school teachers over and above the physical education specialist.

Julian U. Stein offers an uplifting report of the Third Paralympic Congress and the Atlanta Declaration of People with Disabilities.[15] Both followed after the 1996 Olympic Games in Atlanta. The declaration expresses such a grand vision of the rights of "people with disabilities" that it should be enlarged and framed in the office of every physical educator worldwide. It reminds us that programs of physical education and sport for normal, accelerated, and special populations must be ever cognizant of the need to strike a balance that recognizes the inborn rights of all.

D. Penny and D. Kirk demonstrate serious concern in a 1996 article comparing national curriculum developments in Australia and Britain. They observe that recent trends in curriculum development appearing in "a climate of low morale among some sections of the physical education profession in the face of public criticism and amidst constrained and pressured contexts appear to be encouraging a tendency toward backward looking conservatism rather than forward looking experimentation and risk taking"[16] The authors deplore efforts in these two countries to return to "the good old days of yore" emphasizing a traditional sport-based and subject-focused rationale for physical education.

Overall, physical education and sport as a subject in general education programs is confronted today with a paradox. At the very time when scientific evidence is available to make the case for the health benefits of a sound program of required and voluntary developmental physical activity, economic restraints and public criticism of the physical activity programs in most countries are making progress extremely difficult.

## The State of Sport and Physical Education in Canada and the United States

At the present time, education at all levels in the United States and Canada, including school programs in sport and physical education (not necessarily competitive sport), is facing crises from without and within. The level of support for education is diminishing, and yet at the same time the pressure is on to achieve high academic test scores comparable to those in other lands. A thrust toward

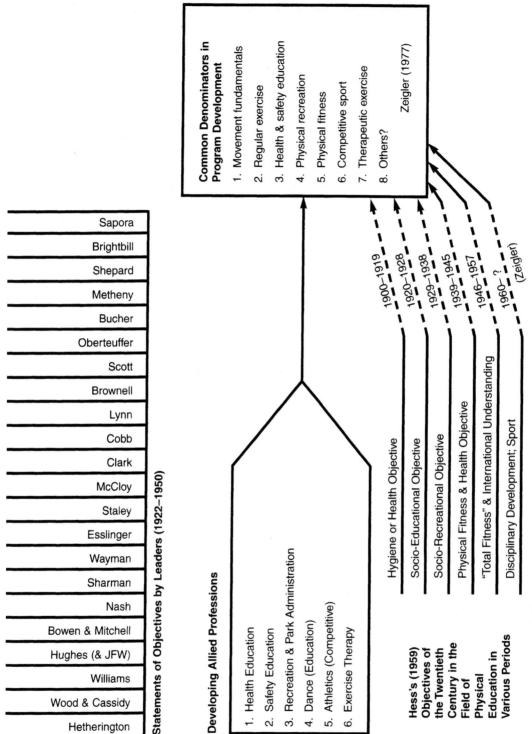

Statements of Objectives by Leaders (1922–1950)

Sapora
Brightbill
Shepard
Metheny
Bucher
Oberteuffer
Scott
Brownell
Lynn
Cobb
Clark
McCloy
Staley
Esslinger
Wayman
Sharman
Nash
Bowen & Mitchell
Hughes (& JFW)
Williams
Wood & Cassidy
Hetherington

**Common Denominators in Program Development**

1. Movement fundamentals
2. Regular exercise
3. Health & safety education
4. Physical recreation
5. Physical fitness
6. Competitive sport
7. Therapeutic exercise
8. Others?

Zeigler (1977)

**Developing Allied Professions**

1. Health Education
2. Safety Education
3. Recreation & Park Administration
4. Dance (Education)
5. Athletics (Competitive)
6. Exercise Therapy

**Hess's (1959) Objectives of the Twentieth Century in the Field of Physical Education in Various Periods**

Hygiene or Health Objective — 1900–1919
Socio-Educational Objective — 1920–1928
Socio-Recreational Objective — 1929–1938
Physical Fitness & Health Objective — 1939–1945
"Total Fitness" & International Understanding — 1946–1957
Disciplinary Development; Sport — 1960–?

(Zeigler)

FIGURE 7.1  Twentieth-Century Program Developments in Physical Education.

school privatization is supported by concern over declining test scores and people's desire to provide safer environments for their children as the breakdown of public order continues. All this has occasioned a traditionalist or fundamental philosophy of education to surface more strongly. A "return to essentials" approach prevails, especially in the hard sciences and mathematics.

. As mentioned earlier, the field of physical education and sport is facing a severe, uphill struggle. Physical education, once required, now often must fight to remain as even an elective offering at many schools, colleges, and universities in North America. Yet now we also have evidence that, in addition to enabling a person to live life more fully, steady involvement in the right kind of developmental physical activity will help a person to live longer.

What can be done to improve the situation? As early as the 1960s, reasonably balanced development in the field of physical education was envisioned, but whether this movement will result ultimately in a more significant professional development for the field remains to be seen. Because there have been so many different interpretations with varying and at times conflicting emphases, the aims and objectives of physical education and its allied professions in the twentieth century in North America should be reviewed as we enter the next century. The specific objectives listed as "common denominators" in Figure 7.1 are probably accepted by the majority in our field and those in allied professions. If this listing of common denominators is acceptable, then this presumed agreement—having come about gradually over a period of decades—has presumably guided the approaches, emphases, and courses of action pursued by scholars and researchers over the past fifty years.

During the first half of the twentieth century, leaders in physical education and sport espoused a plethora of objectives for the field as they sought to make a case for greater or lesser "intrusion" into the school, college, and university curricula. Because of their typically defensive posture—a stance almost automatically assumed still today by the large majority—leaders felt it necessary to proclaim that an excellent health and physical education program could produce truly remarkable results in children and young people. However, the evidence to support the arguments for these presumed accomplishments was unavailable in sufficient quantity or quality. Missionary zeal was used to make up for the lack of supporting scientific data. Be that as it may, these educators, many of whom are listed in Figure 7.1, were dedicated leaders with a grand vision for the future of their chosen profession—and they did point the way for the coming generation.

We could categorize and then enumerate the various objectives proposed for the field, and the resultant list would be an impressive picture of our field's potential educational contribution. Our professional task today, however, is to ascertain in an ever more scholarly and scientific manner what the results of planned, developmental physical activity in exercise, sport, and related expressive movement actually are under a myriad of conditions. Additionally, we need to become ever more alert in our interpretation of the various social forces affecting program development for the normal, accelerated, and special populations for all ages (Zeigler, 1989).

In the late 1950s, F. A. Hess completed a study in which he investigated the objectives of physical education in the United States from 1900 to 1957 in light of certain historical events. The major objectives of the various periods, as identified by Hess, are shown at the bottom of Figure 7.1.[17] While we must grant a certain subjectivity to this type of historical analysis, Hess's investigation nevertheless offers a point of departure when we seek to compare (1) the results of Hess's study, (2) the stated objectives expressed by the various leaders listed, (3) the influence of the several (now) allied professions that were growing rapidly between 1900 and 1950, and (4) the pivotal social forces operative in the society.

The influence of allied professions on the objectives of physical education is an interesting question in itself. Each of these professions had dedicated adherents who were working to have their embryonic profession represented well and fairly within the health and physical education curriculum of the first half of the century. Since the middle of the century, they have looked forward to the day when separate, fully independent status might be granted to their particular field (or subject matter) with resultant increased curricular time allotment. These allied professions have been identified as (1) health education; (2) safety education (including driver education); (3) recreation and parks administration; (4) dance (education); (5) competitive athletics including interscholastic, intercollegiate, intramurals, and recreational sports, with the last now striving for its own professional identity under the name (as a significant number want to call it) of "campus recreation"; and (6) therapeutic exercise including adapted or special physical education.

# SOCIAL FORCES AND PROFESSIONAL CONCERNS AFFECTING PHYSICAL EDUCATION AND SPORT

In most histories of physical education and sport, the author guides the reader through a chronological narrative with relatively little attempt to interpret the material. This approach is undoubtedly helpful, but it has its limits. A fuller understanding requires a more interpretive approach.

## Social Forces or Influences

At least six pivotal social forces or influences, identified by John S. Brubacher (1966) as "persistent, historical problems," have continually affected society. As such, each of them has directly or indirectly influenced physical education and sport in most countries worldwide. These social forces have been delineated as (1) the influence of values and norms; (2) the influence of politics; (3) the influence of nationalism; (4) the influence of economics; (5) the influence of religion; and (6) the influence of ecology.

More recently the present author has added two more social forces to this list. These are the influence of science and technology and the influence of a concern for peace.[18]

## Professional Concerns

Ten problems in the field of sport and physical education have persisted histori-cally as professional concerns.[19] Each of these problems has also been influenced by the social forces identified by Brubacher. The following is a listing of the iden-tified problems and concerns. Space does not permit more than a mere listing of each of the ten problems. However, the final problem—the influence of the idea of progress—is discussed in more detail.

**1.** The first persistent problem in the field of sport and physical education is the *curriculum*. Questions relating to the nature and extent of the program in phys-ical education and sport have consistently plagued the profession.

**2.** The second professional concern is *methods of instruction*. The manner in which content is to be delivered to effect the most positive results has consistently been a source of controversy and disagreement.

**3.** *Professional preparation* for service is the third professional concern. Ques-tions relating to the nature and extent of professional education and the training of physical educators and coaches remain unanswered.

**4.** *The concept of the healthy body* is the fourth professional concern. Concepts relating to the role that sport and physical education play in meeting societal health needs have constantly changed throughout history.

**5.** *The place of sport, exercise, and related expressive activity in the lives of women, eth-nic minorities, and the disabled or other special populations* is the fifth professional con-cern. It may seem odd to list these three segments of the population under one heading, but each—for one reason or another—has been denied equal access to the benefits that come from full participation in physical education and educa-tional sport.

**6.** The sixth professional concern is the *role of dance* within the physical edu-cation and sport curriculum. The question of whether dance should be considered separately as an important aspect of the human movement experience has remained a major professional concern.

**7.** *The use of leisure*—especially involvement with developmental physical activity—is the seventh professional concern. The role of leisure in a society has always been influenced by the prevailing educational philosophy of the time.

**8.** The eighth professional concern is the perplexing matter of *amateur, semipro-fessional, and professional sport*. The relationship of these three subdivisions of sport to one another, to the educational system, and to the entire culture must be fully under-stood before improvements can be made in the light of changing circumstances.

**9.** *The role of management or administration* is the ninth professional concern. What should the educational training and role be for those involved in the man-agement of programs in sport and physical education?

**10.** *The idea of progress*, the tenth and final professional concern, can be viewed from two standpoints. First, it is a concern that relates closely to the val-ues that a society holds for itself and, therefore, it can be a greater or lesser influ-ence. Second, it can also be seen as a professional concern for every professional in physical education and sport.

Any study of history inevitably forces a person to conjecture about human progress. Certainly there has been change through time, but can this be called progress? Have changes made things better? Criteria by which progress may be judged vary from one culture to another. It is true, of course, that humans have become more adaptable over time and can cope with a variety of environments. It is probably safe to call this progress. But progress in physical education and sport must be defined by culturally determined criteria. Hopefully, with greater global communication among members of the profession, agreement on many of these criteria will be possible.

## Changes in the United States and Canada

The field of physical education and sport has changed a great deal in the twentieth century—through its own efforts and those of other professions—particularly in the United States and Canada. Some of the more significant modifications include the following:

1. *We now don't know exactly what we stand for.* In the past the field of physical education sought to be all things to all people. Pretty soon, however, we won't even be certain whether push-ups and jogging still belong in the field. What is the major focus of physical education and sport at this time?

2. *All kinds of name changes are being made* to describe what people think the field is doing or should be doing, not to mention how it can camouflage the "unsavory" connotation of the term *physical* education. Thus the academic field of physical education is becoming kinesiology, human kinetics, ergonomics, exercise and sport science, sport management, sport studies, kinanthropology, or what have you.

3. The advent of Sputnik in the late 1950s; the subsequent "race for the moon" and how science and technology generally have affected education; the devastating criticisms of the presumed academic content of physical education curricula; and the subsequent almost frantic drive since for a body of knowledge for the field that is based on solid scientific and scholarly investigation—all have placed us in a curious position as a profession. *We really don't know where or what our body of knowledge is.* Nowhere is it available to us in a series of ordered principles or generalizations based on an accepted taxonomy of subdisciplinary and subprofessional specializations.

4. Today, *professionals in the field are not supporting their own professional organizations well enough,* neither on the state and provincial level nor on the national level in the United States and Canada. As a result, the professional organizations are struggling with insufficient funding and are incapable of meeting the many demands being made by practitioners.

5. *An ever-widening gap is developing between the societies for what might be called related-discipline sport and exercise and the established profession of physical education and sport.* The reference here is to those in the United States who belong to the National Association for Sport and Physical Education (NASPE); the American Association for Active Lifestyles and Fitness (AAALF); the National Association for Girls and

Women in Sport (NAGWS); and the American College of Sports Medicine (ACSM). We also find the North American Society for the Sociology of Sport (NASSS), the North American Society for Sport Management (NASSM), the Philosophic Society for the Study of Sport (now IPSSS), the Association for the Study of Play (ASP), the North American Society for Sport History (NASSH), and many other professional associations who apparently could not care less, to put it bluntly, what happens to the field of physical education and sport. In recognition of the proliferation and splintering of these specialized societies, W. Sparks in 1992 issued a plea to these "specialists" to consider integrating more closely with the profession.

**6.** In the early 1970s, the College Entrance Examination Board (CEEB) in the United States established a commission that eventually recommended that *much greater weight and consideration in entrance requirements should be allotted to certain important qualities and attributes over and above the traditional verbal factor and mathematical factor (such as sensitivity and commitment to social responsibility, political and social leadership, and ability to adapt to new situations).* There is no evidence, however, that we have stressed, or even understood to any degree, whether physical education majors originally possess or subsequently achieve knowledge, competence, or skill in any of the nine vital components recommended by the CEEB. In Canada there never was any effort made in this regard. The academic average is now the only factor in deciding whether a student may enter a Canadian university, and in Ontario there is also talk of bringing back provincial-level examinations and standardized testing.

**7.** *Another unacceptable series of gaps* that is developing is among (a) the people in physical education concerned with bioscience; (b) those investigating the social science and humanities aspects of the discipline; (c) a third group concerned with the professional preparation of physical educators and with what might be called the subprofessional aspects of the field (such as curriculum, instructional methodology, supervision, and management); (d) a group of professionals promoting professional training in sport management; and (e) professional practitioners who themselves are often divided among the physical educator, the coach, and the dance teacher.

**8.** A further disturbing development is taking place. For several reasons, at least one of which can be blamed on physical education professionals, *the influential and highly volatile area of competitive sport has become a playground for several allied professions and related disciplines.* Many of these people became aware of the ever-increasing popularity of physical fitness and competitive sport and are tackling "our" problems in a piecemeal fashion, often without full awareness of sport and physical education's broad domain and outlook. Here we are referring to the relatively recent identification of the recreation profession with highly competitive sport and physical fitness (and most recently, sport management), the presence of health educators in exercise science, the involvement of physiotherapists in adaptive (special) physical education, the developing relationship between business administration and sport management and/or intercollegiate sport, and, of course, the gradually awakening interest of historians, philosophers, sociologists, psychologists, anthropologists, physiologists, medical professors, biomechanics specialists, and others in competitive sport. All these people could readily help the mission of physical education rather than ignoring it or putting it out of business.

**9.** Steadily but surely, because physical education has been struggling to acquire an "academic image" ever since it was criticized sharply by James J. Conant in the 1960s,[20] *a larger wedge than ever has been driven between physical education and intercollegiate athletics.* (Of course, the relatively small but highly visible segment of intercollegiate sport that may be called "big-time, commercial, intercollegiate athletics" has been subject to all sorts of abuses throughout this century and is to all intents and purposes out of educational control.) This gap has been highly unfortunate for the profession of physical education and will ultimately be so for the intercollegiate athletic program as well. A relatively small group of pressure-driven administrators and coaches has exploited the professionals in physical education and sport and many of their colleagues in other disciplines as well, not to mention the unethical way in which many so-called scholar-athletes have been sacrificed along the way (note the extremely large percentage of black athletes who have not graduated). This wedge between physical education and intercollegiate athletics has been most unfortunate for all concerned.

**10.** Finally, *an uneasiness or malaise in U.S. and Canadian physical education has developed over the past thirty-plus years.* Some appear ready and willing to write off physical education entirely. *Many in the field are losing their will to win.* In the final analysis this last development could be the most devastating of all the changes we have enumerated.

Certainly physical education and sport in the United States and Canada are being buffeted about by many conflicting social forces. Also, we seem to have more than our share of "that vast majority of people who either watch things happen, or don't even know that anything is going on." Thus we can legitimately ask, "Can we possibly take control of our professional destiny?" Can we become better able to help our field make a difference, both in education and in the larger society? In other words, are we as a profession capable of becoming strong men and women who, rather than merely reacting to social forces, are able to adapt reality to our own ends to the greatest extent possible?

## WHAT THE PROFESSION SHOULD NOT DO IN THE IMMEDIATE FUTURE

Before recommending what we should do as we move into the twenty-first century, it might be just as important to consider briefly *what needs to be avoided.* First, we must avoid a rigid philosophical posture. Maintaining a certain degree of flexibility will be difficult for those who have worked out definite, explicit philosophic stances for themselves. For those who are struggling along with an implicit sense of life (as defined by Rand, 1960), having philosophic flexibility may be even more difficult—they don't fully understand where they are "coming from." All of us know people for whom Toffler's (1970) concepts of "future shock" and subsequent "third wave world" have become a reality. Life is stressful for those who cannot adapt.

Second, we must avoid both naive optimism and despairing pessimism. What we should assume is a philosophical stance of positive meliorism—a belief that steady improvement in the quality of life is possible if we work at it. This second "what to avoid" item may seem to contradict the recommendation above concerning flexibility in philosophical approach. Blind pessimism and blind optimism, though, no matter how attractive they may seem, are really traps for the unwary.

Third, we should avoid "opportunities" presented by those who want to cut back on individual freedom in the "best interests" of all. As professionals in sport and physical education, we should strive for just the right amount of freedom both in our own lives and in professional affairs. Freedom for the individual may be a fundamental characteristic of a democratic state, but such freedom as may prevail in various countries today had to be won inch by inch. There are always those in our midst who think they know what is best for the rest of us, and who seem anxious to take away our hard-won freedoms. We must zealously guard our freedom to teach responsibly what we will in sport and physical education, and conversely the freedom to learn what we will.

A fourth pitfall to avoid is succumbing to certain negative aspects inherent in the various social forces capable of influencing our culture and everything in it (including, of course, sport and physical education). In other words, we should not allow some social force to twist life out of balance. Consider nationalism and how an overemphasis on it can destroy a desirable world perspective and even bring about isolationism and xenophobia. Another negative social force is capitalistic economic practices that ride roughshod over the environment. "Bigger" may be appealing, but it is not necessarily "better" in the final analysis.

Fifth, moving specifically back to the realm of education, we must be careful that our field does not contribute to a fundamental anti-intellectualism in the United States. On the other hand, intelligence or intellectualism for its own sake is far from being a balanced answer to our problems. As long ago as 1961, Brubacher asked for a "golden mean" between cultivation of the intellect and cultivation of a high degree of intelligence because this kind of balance is needed as "an instrument of survival" in the Deweyan sense.[21]

Sixth, and finally, despite the current cry for a "return to essentials," we should avoid imposing a narrow academic approach on students in a misguided effort to promote the pursuit of excellence. One is continually amazed and discouraged by decisions concerning admission to undergraduate sport and physical education programs made solely on the basis of numerical grades—in essence a narrowly defined concept of academic proficiency. We should not throw out academic testing, of course, but we should by all means broaden the evaluation made of candidates by assessing other dimensions of excellence they may have. In addition to motor performance, we should evaluate such dimensions as "sensitivity and commitment to social responsibility, ability to adapt to new situations, characteristics of temperament and work habit under varying conditions of demand," and other such characteristics and traits as recommended in 1970 by the Commission on Tests of the College Entrance Examination Board.[22]

# WHAT THE PROFESSION SHOULD DO
# IN THE IMMEDIATE FUTURE

The field of physical education and sport has reached a point where it must act to preserve its professional identity. By doing so, it can best serve its various constituencies. The following recommendations combine current concerns—directly related to the changes or "modifications" that have taken place in recent decades in the United States and Canada—with specific actions. The field of physical education and sport should actively reach out to seek a world consensus on these recommendations. If agreement can be achieved, then we, as dedicated professionals, could take rapid and strong action through our national and international professional associations, while at the same time welcoming any assistance we can obtain from allied professions and related disciplines. The recommended actions are as follows:

**1.** *Develop a sharper image.* In the past the field of physical education and sport tried to be all things to all people. At present it does not know exactly what it does stand for. We should sharpen our image and improve the quality of our efforts by focusing primarily on developmental physical activity—specifically, human motor performance in sport, exercise, and related expressive movement. As we sharpen our image, we should make a strong effort to include those who are working in the private agency and commercial sectors. At the same time, we should extend our efforts to promote the finest type of developmental physical activity for people of all ages whether they be members of "normal, accelerated, or special" populations (Zeigler, 1997).

**2.** *Change our profession's name.* The ongoing struggle to find and agree on a name for our field has brought us to a state of utter confusion. All sorts of name changes have been proposed or implemented to (a) explain what people think we are doing or ought to be doing, or (b) camouflage the presumed unsavory connotation of the term *physical education,* which evidently conjures up the notion of a dumb jock going through mindless motions. Instead, we should continue to focus primarily on developmental physical activity while moving as we can toward an acceptable working term for our profession. In so doing, we should keep in mind any profession's dual nature in that it has both theoretical and practical aspects.

At the moment we are called physical education and sport quite uniformly around the world. An alternative term, *sport and physical education,* is now recommended by the National Association for Sport and Physical Education (NASPE) to describe the professional entity in the United States. The terms *physical education and sport* and *sport* are more popular in other countries that identify with the Western world. In Canada the professional entity is still titled physical and health education. It seems apparent that no one of these names, or combination of names, is going to make it in the long run.

There is no question that the time is overdue for us to bring our field's image into sharper focus for the sake of our colleagues and students, not to mention the public. What is needed, therefore, is that we should call ourselves by a name that bespeaks what it is that we study and what we stand for professionally. Perhaps the name arrived at by the American Academy of Kinesiology and Physical Education, namely *kinesiology and physical education* is more appropriate, but only in reverse order. *Physical education and kinesiology* is an all-encompassing term that refers to the theory of human motor performance in developmental physical activity in exercise, sport, and expressive movement for people of all ages and conditions. This theory is based increasingly on scholarly and research endeavors of a high order. We could also consider naming our field *human motor performance*, but this may not sound sufficiently academic for some. The terms *kinesiology* and *human kinetics* are looming in both the United States and Canada as new names for the undergraduate degree program. *Movement arts and science* has possibilities as well. The term *kinesiology* has been in the dictionary for decades, but we would have to broaden the definition in one sense and narrow it in another. In determining the most appropriate name for our profession, it is imperative that we remember that what we are fundamentally involved with is *developmental physical activity in sport, exercise, and related expressive movement*—and that's it!

**3.** *Develop a tenable body of knowledge.* As professionals we must possess the requisite knowledge, as well as competencies and skills, to provide developmental physical activity services of a high quality to the public. Inasmuch as various social forces and professional concerns have placed us in a position where we don't know where or what our body of knowledge is, we should strongly support the idea of disciplinary definition and the continuing development of a body of knowledge based on such a consensual definition. From this must come a merging of tenable scientific theory in keeping with societal values and computer technology so that we will gradually, steadily, and increasingly provide our members with the knowledge they need to perform as top-flight professionals.

In the early 1970s, a taxonomy that included both the professional and the scholarly dimensions of developmental physical activity in exercise, sport, and related movement was developed by Huelster and Zeigler (Zeigler, 1977). This taxonomy represented a balanced approach between the subdisciplinary areas of our field and what might be identified as the subprofessional or concurrent professional components as explained above. As part of an effort to close a debilitating rift in the field, a taxonomical table was developed to explain the proposed areas of scholarly study and research using our nomenclature (sport and physical education terms only) along with the accompanying disciplinary and professional aspects. Eight areas of scholarly study and research, correlated with their respective subdisciplinary and subprofessional aspects, were included (see Table 7.1). Most important, the names selected for the eight areas of scholarly study and research *do not include terms that are currently part of the names of, or the actual names of, other recognized disciplines* and that are therefore usually identified with those other (related) disciplines by our colleagues and the public.

Thus, it is extremely important that we promote and develop *our own discipline* of physical education/kinesiology (or whatever it is called eventually) and *our own profession* of sport and physical education as described above. At the same time, we must work cooperatively with related disciplines and allied professions to the extent that they express interest in our objectives. By continuing to speak of the *sociology* of sport, the *physiology* of exercise, the *psychology* of sport, and so on,

**TABLE 7.1 Scholarly and Professional Dimensions of Developmental Physical Activity in Exercise, Sport, and Related Movement**

| AREAS OF SCHOLARLY STUDY AND RESEARCH | SUBDISCIPLINARY ASPECTS | SUBPROFESSIONAL ASPECTS |
|---|---|---|
| I. Background, meaning, and significance | History<br>Philosophy<br>International & comparative study | International relations<br>Professional ethics |
| II. Functional effects of physical activity | Exercise physiology<br>Anthropometry & body composition | Fitness & health appraisal<br>Exercise therapy |
| III. Sociocultural and behavioral aspects | Sociology<br>Economics<br>Psychology (individual & social)<br>Anthropology<br>Political science<br>Geography | Application of theory to practice |
| IV. Motor learning and control | Psycho-motor learning<br>Physical growth & development | Application of theory to practice |
| V. Mechanical and muscular analysis of motor skills | Biomechanics<br>Neuroskeletal musculature | Application of theory to practice |
| VI. Management theory and practice | Management science<br>Business administration | Application of theory to practice |
| VII. Curriculum theory and program development | Curriculum studies | Application of theory to practice |

VII. General education; professional preparation; intramural sports and physical recreation; intercollegiate athletics; programs for special populations (e.g., the disabled) including both curriculum and instructional methodology.

| VIII. Evaluation and measurement | Theory about the measurement function | Application of theory to practice |
|---|---|---|

the time is ever closer when these other disciplines and professions will awaken to the importance of what we believe to be our professional task. That task is the gathering and dissemination of knowledge about developmental physical activity through the media of sport, exercise, and related expressive movement, and the promotion of developmental physical activity to the extent that such furtherance is socially desirable.

Without this cooperative collaboration, the end result of the multidisciplinary splintering of our field of sport and physical education will be a mishmash of isolated findings by well-intentioned, scholarly people who do not fully understand the larger goal toward which our profession is striving. Also—and this is vital for us—we will be destined to perpetual trade status—not professional status—as perennial jacks of all trades and masters of none.

**4.** *Support our own professional associations.* Inasmuch as there is insufficient support of our own professional associations for a variety of reasons, we need to develop voluntary and mandatory mechanisms that relate membership in professional organizations both directly and indirectly to stature within the field. We must commit ourselves to promote the welfare of professional practitioners who serve the public in areas that we represent. Incidentally, it may be necessary to exert pressure to encourage people to give first priority to our own groups (as opposed to those of disciplinary-oriented societies, related disciplines, and/or allied professions). The logic behind this dictum is that we must first survive as a profession if we are to carry out our mission.

**5.** *Improve professional licensing.* Although the status of most teachers/coaches in the schools, colleges, and universities is seemingly protected by the teaching profession, we should move rapidly and strongly to seek official recognition of our endeavors in public, semipublic, and private agency work and in commercial organizations relating to developmental physical activity through professional licensing at the state or provincial level. Further, we should encourage individuals to register voluntarily as qualified practitioners at the federal level in their countries.

**6.** *Establish harmony within the profession.* An unfortunate series of gaps and misunderstandings has developed among those in our field concerned primarily with the bioscientific aspects of human motor performance, those concerned with the social science and humanities aspects, those concerned with the general education of all students, and those concerned with the professional preparation of physical educators/coaches, managers, scholars, and scientists—all at the college or university level. All these essential elements in the profession need to work toward greater balance and improved understanding among themselves.

**7.** *Maintain harmony among the allied professions.* Keeping in mind that the field of physical education and sport has spawned a number of allied professions, we should strive to comprehend what they claim to do professionally and where there may be a possible overlap with what we claim to do. Where disagreements prevail, they should be ironed out to the greatest extent possible at the national level in all countries of the world.

**8.** *Improve the relationship with competitive sport.* In those relatively few countries where, within educational institutions, the commercialization of sports is a basic factor in the continuance of sporting competition, an ever-larger wedge is being driven between the physical education program and that of competitive sport. Such a rift serves no positive purpose and in fact is contrary to the best interests of both groups. In these countries, *the organized sport and physical education profession should work for greater understanding and harmony with those who are primarily interested in promoting* *highly organized, often commercialized sport.* At the same time it is imperative that we do all in our power to keep competitive sport in sound educational perspective within schools, colleges, and universities where it is presently offered.

**9.** *Improve the relationship with intramurals and recreational sports.* Intramurals and recreational sports are presently in transition. They are mainstays at the college and university level, but for several reasons intramurals have not taken hold yet at the high-school level, generally speaking. This is true even though intramurals have a great deal to offer the large majority of students in what may truly be called recreational (and arguably educational) lifetime sport. Also, a minority of college administrators would like to adopt the term *campus recreation* as an official designation, but there is no consensus on whether this is appropriate or whether an effort should be made to encompass all recreational activities on campus within the sphere of what is now typically intramurals and recreational sports only.

Everything considered, it is recommended that intramurals and recreational sports remain within the sphere of the physical education and sport profession. At the same time, it is impractical and inadvisable to attempt to subsume all noncurricular activities on campus under one department or division. Departments and divisions of physical education and sport ought to work for consensus on the idea that intramurals and recreational sports are cocurricular in nature and deserve regular funding as laboratory experience in the same manner that general education course experiences in sport and physical education receive funding for instructional purposes.

**10.** *Guarantee equal opportunity.* As a profession we should move positively and strongly to promote equal opportunity for women, minority groups, and special populations (such as those with disabilities).

**11.** *Develop a physical education and sport identity.* In addition to the development of allied professions (such as school health education) in the second quarter of the twentieth century, our field witnessed the advent of a disciplinary expansion in the 1960s that was followed by a splintering of many of the various "knowledge components" and subsequent formation of many different societies nationally and worldwide. These developments have weakened the field of physical education and sport. Thus, it is now more important than ever that we hold to the physical education and sport identity and support those who are developing our profession's undergirding body of knowledge. At the same time, we should reaffirm, but also delineate ever more carefully, our relationship with allied professions.

**12.** *Explore the competency approach.* The failures and inconsistencies of established education have become apparent to all of us. As a profession, therefore, we need to explore the educational possibilities of the competency approach as it might apply to general education, to professional preparation, and to all aspects of our professional endeavor in public, semipublic, private, and commercial agency endeavors.

**13.** *Manage the enterprise.* All professionals in physical education and sport are managers—but in various ways and to varying degrees. The "one course in administration" approach of earlier times that included no laboratory or internship experience was not sufficient. There is an urgent need today to utilize a competency approach in the preparation (as well as in the continuing education) of those who will serve as managers either in educational circles or elsewhere, promoting exercise and sport in the society at large.

**14.** *Concentrate on ethics and morality.* In the course of development of the best professions, the various embryonic professional groups have become conscious of the need for a code of professional ethics—that is, a set of professional obligations that are established as *norms* for practitioners in good standing. Our profession needs both a universal creed and a reasonably detailed code of ethics. Such a move is important because, generally speaking, ethical confusion prevails throughout the world. Development of a sound code of ethics, combined with steady improvement in the three essentials of a reputable profession (namely, an extensive period of training, a significant intellectual component that must be mastered before the profession is practiced, and recognition by society that the trained person can provide a basic, important service) would soon place us in a much firmer position to claim that our profession is both useful and respectful (Zeigler, 1984).

**15.** *Reunify the profession's integral elements.* There now appears to be reasonable agreement that what is now called the field of physical education and sport is concerned primarily with developmental physical activity as manifested in human motor performance in sport, exercise, and related expressive movement. We therefore need to work for the reunification of those elements of our profession that should be uniquely ours within our disciplinary definition.

**16.** *Develop cross-cultural comparisons and international understanding.* Professionals in North America have done reasonably well in the area of international relations, thanks to the solid efforts of a number of dedicated people over a considerable period of time. However, we need to increase our efforts to make cross-cultural comparisons of physical education and sport while reaching out for greater understanding and cooperation in all parts of the world. Better understanding of the implications of the concepts of communication, diversity, and cooperation will help our profession develop ways in which to contribute significantly to a better life for all and a more peaceful world. (See Chapter 8, which includes a recommended approach to multicultural ethics in physical education and sport.)

**17.** *Recognize permanency and change.* The original "principal principles" proposed for physical education and sport by Steinhaus in 1952 (see also Zeigler, 1994b) can now be expanded significantly and applied logically to our professional endeavors. We therefore need to emphasize that which is timeless in our work, while at the same time accepting the inevitability of certain societal change.

**18.** *Improve both the quality and length of life.* Since our field is unique within education and in society, and since the good life and professional success involve so much more than verbal and mathematical skills, we are in a good position to emphasize strongly—and should emphasize—that education is a lifelong enterprise. Further, we need to make it known, both inside and outside educational institutions, that both the quality and length of life can be improved significantly through achieving a high degree of kinetic awareness and through lifelong involvement in sport, exercise, and related expressive movement.

**19.** *Reassert our will to win.* The developments of the past forty years have created uneasiness within the profession and doubts as to whether we have the will to achieve a professional status that is well-defined and highly respected. We therefore need to pledge ourselves to greater efforts in our professional endeavors. Ours is a high calling because we seek to improve the quality of life for all people on earth through the finest type of human motor performance in sport, exercise, and related expressive movement (Zeigler, 1990).

## CONCLUSIONS AND RECOMMENDATIONS: THE PROFESSIONAL TASK AHEAD

Reflecting on all that has been discussed above, what makes up our task in relation to the profession? What are our responsibilities?

First, we should understand why we have chosen this profession, why we dedicate ourselves to the study and dissemination of knowledge, competencies, and skills in developmental physical activity in sport, exercise, and related expressive movement. Concurrently, we need to determine exactly what it is that we are professing.

Second, as either present or prospective practitioners, we should all search for young people who possess the attributes needed for success in our field. We need to be alert for people who will develop lifelong commitments so that our profession can achieve its potential through the implementation of democratically agreed-upon goals. We should also be ready to encourage young people to serve in the many alternative careers in sport, exercise, dance, and recreative play that are becoming increasingly available.

Third, we must make quality the first priority of our professional endeavors. Our personal involvement and specialization should include a high level of competency and skill undergirded by solid knowledge about the profession. We should also be willing to defend our professional task as being as important as any other in society. Indecision, halfhearted commitment, imprecise knowledge, and general unwillingness to stand up and be counted in debate with colleagues and others do great harm to our profession. Willingness to debate should also extend to appropriate public occasions.

Fourth, the obligation is ours. If the profession is to reach its potential, we must sharpen our focus and improve the quality of our professional effort. Only in this way will we be able to guide the modification process that the profession is currently undergoing so that the changes work toward the achievement of high professional goals. We have the opportunity to employ exercise, sport, and related expressive movement to make life more healthful, more pleasant, more vital for people everywhere. But we cannot do so unless we tend to the health of our own profession.

You may at this point be saying to yourself: "Fine, but how can we begin to implement these 'what to do' items to help our developing profession achieve its lofty goals? We are currently mired in a state of semirigidity!" Well, every great enterprise is conceived first in the mind of one individual, and the work is done by individuals working together. Some wise person is purported to have said, "If you want to accomplish something big in this life, do not expect people to roll stones out of your path; in fact, do not be surprised if they heap boulders in your way." It is not anticipated that tremendous boulders will be heaped on our path, but a few stones are likely to be there. The political and social powers that be are not going to say, "Congratulations, you've got the answer to the world's plight! Here's a billion dollars to organize, develop, and begin the administration of a worldwide plan to make the field of physical education and sport a full-fledged, respected profession."

Nevertheless, without trying to guess where any specific stumbling blocks might loom in our path, we can consider four processes proposed by March and Simon.[23] These steps, taken in sequence, can help us in reaching any objective, whether immediate or long range.

**1.** *Problem-solving.* We have proposed a problem for our profession to resolve. We must move as soon as possible to convince others that our proposal is worthwhile. Part of our approach includes assuring others that the objectives are operational (that is, that their presence or absence can be tested empirically as we progress). In this way, even if sufficient funding were not available—and it well might not be—the various parties to the success of the venture would at least have agreed-upon objectives. However, with a professional task of the magnitude we have proposed, it is quite possible that universal consensus on objectives will not be achieved initially. But it can be instituted—one step at a time.

**2.** *Persuasion.* For the sake of argument, assume that our objectives are not shared by the others whom we need to convince, people who are either directly or indirectly related to our own profession or are in allied professions or related disciplines. If the stance of the others is not absolutely fixed or intractable, then this second step of persuasion can (should) be employed on the assumption that *at some level* our objectives will be shared and that disagreement over subgoals can be mediated by reference to larger common goals. Influencing specific leaders in each of the various "other" associations and societies with which we are seeking to cooperate can be a most effective technique for bringing about attitude change in the larger membership of our profession everywhere.

**3.** *Bargaining.* If the process of persuasion is successful, then the parties concerned can return to the problem-solving level, identified as step one. However, if the second step (persuasion) does not work, it becomes necessary to move along to the third stage of this theoretical plan, namely the process of bargaining. At this point there is still disagreement over the operational goals proposed at the problem-solving level (the first stage). Now the people who want change have a difficult decision to make: do we attempt to strike a bargain, or do we give up and go it alone?

The problem with the first alternative is that bargaining implies compromise, and compromise means that each group involved will have to surrender a portion of its claim, request, or argument. The second alternative may seem more desirable, but following it may mean eventual failure in achieving the final, most important objective. Arriving at the bargaining stage and then selecting either of the two alternatives is obviously much less desirable than settling the matter at either the first or second stage.

**4.** *Politicking.* Implementation of the fourth stage (or plan of attack) is necessary only if the action proposed in the first three stages has failed. At this point the participants in the discussion cannot agree in any way about the main issue. The strategy now is that the change agent—in this case our recognized profession—has to somehow expand the number of parties or groups involved in considering the proposed project. The goal is to include potential allies so as to improve the chance of achieving the desired final objective. Employing so-called power politics is tricky, however, and it may backfire on the group bringing such a maneuver into play. However, this is the way the world (or society) works, and the goal may be worth the risk or danger involved. We hope that continued politicking of this kind will not be necessary in the development of our profession, as it is time-consuming and often divisive. We should certainly consider whether this type of operation would do more harm than good (in the immediate future at least).[24]

Worldwide improvement in the professional status of physical education and sport will not come easily. It can only come through the efforts of professional people making quality decisions, through large numbers of ordinary people being motivated to change their sedentary lifestyles, and through our professional assistance in guiding people as they strive to become more physically active. Our mission is to bring excellence and a spirit of dedication to all our professional endeavors.

## SUMMARY

Sport has grown to become a major social institution throughout the modern world. As such, the various forms of organized sport and physical activity need to be assessed for their contributions and impact on society. At the present time, programs of competitive sport on both the national and global level are faced with a myriad of societal issues and concerns. Problems of violence, drug use, gambling, commercialization, the circumvention of rules, professionalism, and other ethically questionable practices abound. School programs of physical education throughout the world face serious challenges. These challenges have often led to the curtailment of physical education in the school curriculum or even its elimination. As the world enters the twenty-first century, there is an urgent and pressing need to examine and ultimately to reshape competitive sport and physical education programs.

The concepts of communication, diversity, and cooperation are integral aspects of the present world's quest for the "good life." Recognition of these concepts is paramount in planning the future of sport and physical education. The influences of conflicting values, politics, nationalism, economics, religion, ecology, and technology have historically caused persistent societal problems. Historically, programs in competitive sport and physical education have been significantly influenced by these forces. Programs in sport and physical education have been persistently plagued by concerns associated with curriculum content; methodology; interrelationships among physical education, athletics, health, recreation, dance, and the exercise and sport sciences; problems of amateurism and professionalism; the training of teachers, coaches, and administrators; and finally and most important, with questions relating to the meaning and value of sports.

The field of physical education and sport must become better defined and more focused. Once defined, it will present a much clearer image to society. The processes of problem-solving, persuasion, bargaining, and politicking may be needed if society is to accept the importance of the sport and physical education profession. Changing the public's perception of physical education and sport is the responsibility of professionals in the field.

## STUDY QUESTIONS

1. Discuss the statement that, "As is the case with all other social institutions, sport should be so organized and administered that it makes a positive contribution instead of serving—as appears to be the case too often today—as an expensive opiate for the masses."
2. How would you define "the good life"? Are the chances of you enjoying the good life getting better or worse? Which current megatrends or events may affect your realization of such a goal? In what ways can developmental physical activity in sport and exercise contribute to a better life?
3. Reflecting on the findings from the author's preliminary survey of conditions in our field in twenty countries, did any of the questionnaire results surprise you? If so, which ones? Are you generally encouraged or discouraged by the results of the survey? Also, keeping in mind the gist of the other articles reviewed by the author, what stance do you think that a young physical educator should take? For example, do you feel that the field should promote establishment of a physical and health education requirement at all educational levels? If so, what would be the best way to go about reaching this objective? If not, just what should we do?
4. In Hess's 1959 study, he suggested certain themes that seemed to be representative of our field's long-range goals during various time periods in the twentieth century. Keeping in mind the theme for the 1960s ("disciplinary development; sport") suggested by the present author in Figure 7.1, does this make sense to you in the light of recent developments? What might be the theme for the 1980s and 1990s as you see it at the present?
5. Explain what the author means by social forces or influences as opposed to professional concerns. Discuss briefly an example in each category. Can you think of additional "forces" or "concerns" that might be added to these lists?
6. What is meant by the author's position that the field needs to be brought into "sharper focus" as it seeks to present a "clearer image" to the public? If you do not agree that a clearer image is needed, explain why you think that in U.S. colleges and universities the various departments relating to our field are functioning with upward of 200 different individual names? Would changing the field's name by consensus help the situation? What name would you give the field?

**7.** Do you feel overwhelmed or discouraged by all the steps or changes that the author feels are needed in the immediate future to achieve greater recognition for our field? Review the suggested steps/changes briefly, and then place them in the order of priority that you feel would help accomplish an improved status more effectively or efficiently. Justify your priorities briefly.

**8.** Discuss some of the conclusions and recommendations arrived at in this chapter on global issues and concerns in physical education and sport.

## RECOMMENDED READINGS

Aburdene, P., and J. Naisbitt. *Megatrends for Women.* New York: Villard Books, 1992.

Asimov, Isaac. "The Fourth Revolution." *Saturday Review* (October 24, 1970): 17–20.

Brubacher, John S. *A History of the Problems of Education.* 2nd ed. New York: McGraw-Hill, 1966.

Glasser, W. *The Identity Society.* New York: Harper and Row, 1972.

Naisbitt, J. *Megatrends.* New York: Warner, 1982.

Northrop, F. S. C. *The Meeting of East and West.* New York: Macmillan, 1946.

Rand, A. *The Romantic Manifesto.* New York: World Publishing, 1960.

Shea, E. J. *Ethical Decisions in Physical Education and Sport.* Springfield, IL: C. C. Thomas, 1978.

Skinner, B. F. *Beyond Freedom and Dignity.* New York: Alfred A. Knopf, 1971.

Sparks, W. "Physical Education for the 21st Century: Integration, Not Specialization." *NAPEHE: The Chronicle of Physical Education in Higher Education* 4, no. 1 (1992): 10–11.

Steinhaus, A. H. "Principal Principles of Physical Education." *Proceedings of the College Physical Education Association.* Washington, DC: AAHPER, 1952: 5–11.

Toffler, Alvin. *Future Shock.* New York: Random House, 1970.

Zeigler, Earle F. *Ethics and Morality in Sport and Physical Education.* Champaign, IL: Stipes, 1984.

Zeigler, Earle F. "From One Image to a Sharper One." *The Physical Educator* 54, no. 2 (Spring 1997): 72–77.

Zeigler, Earle F. "Philosophical Perspective on the Future of Physical Education and Sport," in R. Welsh, ed. *Physical Education: A View Toward the Future.* St. Louis: C.V. Mosby, 1977: 36–61.

Zeigler, Earle F. "Physical Education's 13 Principal Principles." *Journal of Physical Education, Recreation and Dance* 65, no. 7 (September 1994b): 4–5.

Zeigler, Earle F. *Sport and Physical Education: Past, Present, Future.* Champaign, IL: Stipes, 1990.

Zeigler, Earle F. *Sport and Physical Education Philosophy.* Carmel, IN: Benchmark, 1989.

## NOTES

1. Isaac Asimov, "The Fourth Revolution," *Saturday Review* (October 24, 1970): 17–20.

2. "Ten Events That Shook the World between 1984 and 1994," *Utne Reader* 62 (March/April 1994): 58–74.

3. Each person selected for participation in the survey was sent a pretested questionnaire designed to elicit answers to selected questions that would afford insight to the main problem of this investigation. By the very nature of this sample, no claim can be made in regard to the accuracy of the sum of the findings. However, the author reasoned that the responses obtained would "fortify" to a degree his theory on the question of global trends in physical education and sport programs in educational settings.

4. The survey was structured around various "status" subproblems that could easily be phrased as questions. Then, using simple descriptive statistics with the results expressed in categories relating to percentage values determined, the data gathered were numerically tabulated and

the responses were summarized by percentage values based on the predetermined questions. The results from each question asked were followed immediately by discussion related to each question. With several questions it was possible to double up with responses that were closely related.

5. Ken Hardman, "Present Trends in the State and Status of Physical Education," *International Journal of Physical Education* 32, no. 4 (1995): 17–25.

6. Ibid., 19–20.

7. John C. Andrews, "Physical Education and Sports of Children and Youth: F.I.E.P. Policy and Action," *International Journal of Physical Education* 32, no. 4 (1995): 26.

8. Ibid., 28.

9. John Cheffers, "Sport versus Education: The Jury Is Still Out," *International Journal of Physical Education* 33, no. 3 (1996): 106–109.

10. Ibid., 107.

11. Ibid., 109.

12. V. Roberts, "Youth Cultures and Sport: The Success of School and Community Sport Provisions in Britain," *European Physical Education Review* 2, no. 2 (1996): 105.

13. Z. Krawczyk, "Image of Sport in Eastern Europe," *Journal of Comparative Physical Education and Sport* 18, no. 1 (1996): 9.

14. C. L. Saffici, "Aussie Sport: A Physical Education Initiative," *Journal of the International Congress for Health, Physical Education, Recreation, Sport and Dance* 32, no. 4 (1996): 52.

15. Julian U. Stein. "Third Paralympic Congress and the Atlanta Declaration of People with Disabilities," *Journal of the International Congress for Health, Physical Education, Recreation, Sport and Dance* 33, no. 1 (1996): 41–44.

16. D. Penney and D. Kirk, "National Curriculum Developments in Physical Education in Australia and Britain: A Comparative Analysis," *Journal of Comparative Physical Education and Sport* 18, no. 2 (1996): 35–36.

17. F. A. Hess, *American Objectives of Physical Education from 1900 to 1957 Assessed in Light of Certain Historical Events* (Ph.D. dissertation, New York University, 1959). It was next to impossible for Hess to achieve historical perspective for the 1950s, of course, but he could certainly list several "leading" objectives, which he did with reasonable accuracy. One should also not forget the overlapping nature of these objectives from one period to another.

18. Earle F. Zeigler, ed., *Physical Education and Kinesiology in North America: Professional and Scholarly Foundations* (Champaign, IL: Stipes, 1994), 25–26.

19. Earle F. Zeigler, ed., *History of Physical Education and Sport* (Champaign, IL, Stipes, 1988), 292–300.

20. James J. Conant, *The Comprehensive High School: A Second Report to Interested Citizens* (New York: McGraw-Hill, 1967).

21. John S. Brubacher, "Higher Education and the Pursuit of Excellence," *Marshall University Bulletin* 3, no. 3 (1961): 7–9.

22. "Report by the Commission on Tests of the College Entrance Examination Board," *New York Times* (November 2, 1970).

23. J. G. March and H. A. Simon, *Organizations* (New York: Wiley, 1958), 129–131.

24. Earle F. Zeigler, *Assessing Sport and Physical Education: Diagnosis and Projection* (Champaign, IL: Stipes, 1986), 260–262.

# CHAPTER EIGHT

# A MULTICULTURAL APPROACH TO ETHICS IN SPORT AND PHYSICAL ACTIVITY

## EARLE F. ZEIGLER

Ethics is a value system pertaining to standards of conduct and to moral judgment. As such, it is concerned with determining whether a moral action is right or wrong. When speaking of ethics in sport, we examine sport actions in light of moral consciousness.

In this chapter, ethics in sport and physical activity will initially be assessed from a U.S. and Canadian perspective and then placed in a global perspective. Ethical issues in sport and physical activity are in the news almost daily. Although the situations cited in this chapter took place in the United States during just two discrete time periods, (1) a brief period in the mid-1980s and (2) a similar short period in the 1990s, it should be evident that they are but examples of an ongoing problem that requires serious examination.

The premise of this chapter, therefore, is that there is an urgent need for those of us involved in programs of competitive sport and related physical activity to develop a greatly improved approach to ethics. This is true whether we are athletes, coaches, athletic administrators, game officials, teachers, students, educational administrators, governing board members, the sports media, local citizens, state or provincial legislators, or citizens of any nation.

A plan to improve sport ethics should be developed in two ways. First, the plan should provide for teaching ethics and morality to present and future athletes. Second, the subject of ethics should be a requirement in the professional preparation programs in which sports coaches and physical educators are trained.

In this chapter we discuss the following topics sequentially: (1) a brief introduction to current ethically related events in sport; (2) a brief review of the importance of viewing social conditions globally; (3) a comparison of the moral mentality in those parts of the world known broadly as East and West; (4) the major philosophical approaches to ethical decision-making in the Western world in the twentieth century; (5) the way in which ethical instruction is typically handled in Canada and the United States; and (6) reasons why we need to have both a personal and a professional understanding of applied ethics. In the second half of the chapter, the discussion continues with: (7) published material on ethics in the fields of sport, physical education, and recreation; (8) a way in which certain ideas promulgated by Kant, Mill, and Aristotle might be employed in a three-pronged approach to ethical decision-making; (9) how this approach can be merged with a jurisprudential (law-court) argument; (10) a sample case involving a head football coach who discovers illegal drug-taking on his team; (11) the possible cross-cultural applicability of the proposed model for applied ethics; and (12) several reasonable conclusions for consideration in the immediate future.

## ETHICALLY RELATED EVENTS IN SPORT

In January 1985 it was disclosed that six, and possibly nine, members of the unusually successful United States Olympic Cycling Team had blood-boosting transfusions shortly before the 1984 Summer Games.[1,2] No sooner had this highly questionable—but not yet illegal—act been condemned by United States Olympic Committee officials when evidence of drug-taking was reported in a Clemson University situation that had come to light in October 1984 as a result of the tragic death of Augustinius Jaspers.[3] Evidently, thousands of doses of illegal drugs had been distributed throughout the Southeastern Conference from a source in Tennessee to those who were willing to take the risk. What made this case even more egregious was the role of athletic coaches in the drug distribution. As it developed, this was only the beginning of a series of most disturbing news stories. Three coaches at Clemson who had resigned because of direct involvement with the drug distribution were indicted. Further, the president of the university felt it necessary to resign when the institution's trustees denied him the right to reorganize the athletics program and reassign the athletic director.[4]

In March 1985, the results of a limited survey of 3,000 university athletes in the United States were published. This survey, which had been supported by the National Collegiate Athletic Association, reported that 27 percent of college and university athletes smoked marijuana and 12 percent used cocaine. It was explained that the percentages were roughly the same as those in a national survey of other Americans in the same age group.[5]

On March 25, 1985, it was announced that a plan would be recommended to the Executive Committee of the United States Olympic Committee urging official testing for illegal drugs of the top three finishers and others selected at random at every major competition up to the 1988 Olympic Games.[6] One day later, on March 26, a story broke that point shaving in basketball at Tulane University was being investigated by a grand jury.[7] This was soon followed by the resignation and subsequent indictment of the Tulane basketball coach.[8] A subsequent announcement was made that the president of the university had recommended that the men's basketball program be dropped immediately.[9]

On April 5, 1985, at the third annual Journalists' World Games held in Quebec City, Canada, Gilles Neron, the executive director of the Quebec Sports Safety Board, sharply criticized the then current situation in competitive sport. He stated that "the ignorance of fair play and the essence of sport, the absence of a philosophy of sport and disrespect for the rules of the game are the fundamental reasons for the present decadence in sport."[10] At the same meeting, Paul Palango, sports editor of the *Toronto Globe and Mail*, "suggested that 'the sports industry, a powerful social, economic, and political force,' was responsible for masking the harm done to children in such 'contact and combat' sports as hockey, football, and boxing. 'Even we journalists are co-conspirators."[11]

Also on April 5, the president of Indiana University, who was then chairperson of the Presidents Commission appointed by the NCAA, announced that intercollegiate athletics was out of control in the some hundred colleges and universities involved in highly commercialized sport competition. The group declared a "crisis in integrity," a conclusion echoed by the president of the NCAA, who said that the NCAA Executive Council had approved the transmission of the commission's recommendations to the entire organization for a roll-call vote at a special convention.[12] The recommendations included stiff penalties against those institutions where major infractions occurred.

On April 7, the *New York Times* reported that "commentary, suspicion, and paranoia were flowing forth" at Arizona State University, Tempe, because "on March 22, the *Arizona Republic* reported that some unnamed Arizona State University baseball players had been prescribed an antidepressant drug called Nardil by a psychiatrist who served as a consultant to the athletic department."[13] On April 22, the Vanderbilt University strength coach, indicted in a steroid drug conspiracy, resigned after a Tennessee Bureau of Investigation probe led to a 97-count criminal charge against him.[14]

On April 30, the Metro Conference confirmed that it had notified the NCAA of possible violations concerning two of its basketball players, Keith Lee and William Bedford, in regard to working during the school year (which was prohibited) and the use of a car provided by a local "booster," a practice that also was forbidden.[15] On May 2, Willis Reed resigned as basketball coach at Creighton University, stating, "If you're going to stay in college basketball and be successful, you'll have to do some things that I can't do—that I won't do!"[16,17]

On May 3, the University of Washington athletic director ordered an investigation to determine whether university track athletes had been using steroids and other prescription drugs during the 1970s.[18] On the same day, the following items were reported in *USA Today*. The Illinois State basketball coach reported suspected rules violators in the Missouri Valley Conference. Tulane University withdrew from the Metro Conference after a unanimous vote against it by the Metro Conference Joint Committee. The president of Memphis State (now the University of Memphis) stated that the rules governing college athletics should be changed to allow monthly cash payments to student-athletes.[19]

Jumping ahead ten years to the mid-1990s, a review of ethically related sport occurrences in the news indicates that the situation did not improve. If anything, it seemed to have worsened since the mid-1980s. And the events in 1985 and in the mid-1990s that are mentioned here appear to be just the tip of the iceberg. At any rate, the following series of incidents was collected at random primarily from the *New York Times* from late 1995 to "the bite of the century" in mid-1997.

On November 26, 1995, an article titled "Not Sweet, and Not a Science," reported on the growing popularity of a new sport called extreme, or ultimate, fighting. This new sport resembles video games such as Mortal Kombat, which features bare-knuckled encounters between fighters who can punch and kick with abandon while obeying only one cardinal rule: no eye-gouging![20]

On December 3, 1995, the *New York Times* reported that more than 20 years after Congress decided that opportunities for men and women in intercollegiate athletics must be equal, the U.S. Department of Health, Education, and Welfare published a new set of rules requiring colleges and universities to make annual reports on expenditures available for both men's and women's intercollegiate athletics. The new reports were deemed necessary because many of these institutions were still not complying with the Title IX legislation from the 1970s.[21]

On December 28, 1995, the *New York Times* reported on the "Great Snowball Bombing." This incident had taken place a few days earlier when literally thousands of fans at a football game first took to throwing snowballs at each other but later switched to throwing snowballs at the people on the playing field, with resultant injuries. As a result seventy-five people were barred for life from the stadium, and charges were filed against one spectator who was identified from a newspaper photo.[22]

The following day, Barra's piece in the *New York Times* titled "Sentenced to Play Football" reviewed a case at the University of Nebraska in which a football star battered his girlfriend to the floor in her apartment and then dragged her down three flights of stairs to the street. The athlete's arrest and subsequent suspension from the team ended after he had missed six games and the University "sentenced" him only to "mandatory counseling, community service, and attendance at all classes."[23]

After a century in which many institutions of higher education in the United States have been "dogs wagged by athletic tails," an editorial in the January 23, 1996 issue of the *New York Times* stated that "the N.C.A.A. Gets It Right." This editorial celebrated the fact that "after a 10-year power struggle within the National Collegiate Athletic Association—the group that sets rules for undergraduate sports—college presidents have won a big victory in their campaign to control runaway athletic programs." Of course, this doesn't mean that the battle has been won; it is just being fought on a more level battlefield. The editorial concluded, "The presidents will need energy, courage and their trustees if the effort is to succeed."[24]

Moving from the general to a more specific item, a first-year student at Virginia Polytechnic and State University claimed in February 1996 that she was raped by two freshman football players in her dormitory. The university's evidently lax approach to the incident occasioned a groundbreaking lawsuit against the two athletes and the university. The case became a civil rights issue under the 1994 Violence Against Women Act.[25]

Mixed in with this litany of unsavory practices relating to sport was a heartening article that appeared in the March 20, 1996 issue of the *New York Times*. It stated that "if we need any further evidence that golf is an oasis of integrity in a sports desert of mendacity, it came this past weekend." This startling event was Jeff Sluman's disqualification of himself from the Bay Hill Invitational Gold Tournament. Why had he done so? He did this simply because he believed, but was not certain, that he had broken a tournament rule the day before by taking an improper drop—in this case retrieving his ball from the water and dropping it in a so-called drop zone.[26] The point of mentioning this incident is simply that deliberately living up to a rule in sport—especially when not being observed—or even upholding the spirit of a rule is such an anachronism today that it was featured in one of the country's leading newspapers.

Moving to a different aspect of sport ethics, the legendary baseball player Hank Aaron, writing on the fiftieth anniversary of the first black's admission to the major leagues, decried the current lust for money in sport. Stated Aaron:

> The result is that today's players have lost all concept of history. Their collective mission is greed. Nothing else means much of anything to them. As a group, there's no discernible social conscience among them; certainly no sense of self-sacrifice, which is what Jackie Robinson's legacy is based on. . . . People wonder where the heroes have gone. Where there is no conscience, there are no heroes.[27]

In a 1997 study, 195 out of 198 athletes stated that they would take illegal, performance-enhancing substances if they were guaranteed that (1) they would not be caught, and (2) they would win. When researchers extended the guarantee of winning and not being caught to a period of five years, with the added proviso that the athlete would die from the side effects of the drugs consumed, 50 percent said they would still take them. M. Bamberger and D. Yaeger, writing in *Sports Illustrated*, concluded that the availability of hundreds of substances has caused athletes, "aware that drug testing is a sham," to "seem to rely more than ever on banned performance enhancers."[28]

In a second article in the same issue of *Sports Illustrated* titled "Under Suspicion," Bamberger related the tale of a swimmer from Ireland named Michelle Smith. "After winning three gold medals in Atlanta, Michelle Smith should be a big star—but too many people believe that her victories were drug-aided." The suspicion is that at age 26 her accomplishments were literally incredible because at that age "most female swimmers are a half decade beyond their best performances."[29]

We end this capsule review of ethical situations in sports with an article appearing in the *New York Times* on July 3, 1997. In an article titled "Fury and Fine Lines," Joyce Carol Oates discussed what has facetiously been labeled "the bite of the century." In this event, which might have been called the "bites of the century," boxer Mike Tyson twice bit the ear of Evander Holyfield, his opponent in a heavyweight championship fight. Commenting on this horrible act, Oates wrote, "It is now clear that Mike Tyson was not inspired to fight bravely and more dangerously than before." Rather, Ms. Oates declared that by his action "Tyson has provided us with an iconic moment."[30] So be it; the sporting world marches on. . . .

All these ethically related issues and incidents are mild compared to other twentieth-century athletic transgressions that we might have considered. Even the strongest supporters of competitive sports recognize that sport is a powerful social force that has somehow gotten off track. Our organized programs of sport and physical activity *must* encourage and perhaps enforce more positive behavior. Sport must *be socially useful*, or else, in the course of time, an ethically conscious society will decide to eliminate it.

## THE IMPORTANCE OF VIEWING SOCIAL CONDITIONS GLOBALLY

This brief section summarizes some of the concepts previously discussed in Chapter 7. Competitive sport, as we all realize, has worldwide impact. It should accordingly be so organized and administered that it makes a contribution to what Glasser (1972) has called civilized identity society—a state in which the concerns of humans will again focus on such concepts as self-identity, self-expression, and cooperation. Postulating that humankind has gone through three stages of society already (primitive survival society, primitive identity society, and civilized survival society in which certain groups created conflict by taking essential resources from neighbors), Glasser believes that the world should try to move as rapidly as possible into a role-dominated society so that life as we know it on earth can continue.

Interestingly, Kaplan (1961), after a worldwide study a bit earlier, discovered that people's hopes and ideals are really not that dissimilar. In an analysis that lends credence to the work of Glasser, Kaplan found recurring world movements toward rationality, activism, humanism, and preoccupation with values. To bring about a world in which these themes prevail, it will be necessary to establish in the years immediately ahead the fundamental importance of such vital societal concepts as communication, diversity, and cooperation.

As discussed in Chapter 7, the concept of *communication* is a vital component of life in the twenty-first century. The telecommunication age is bringing about a type of international personal relationship hitherto undreamed of (Asimov, 1970). It is imperative that this vastly improved communication network be employed to foster international understanding and goodwill. International sport competition has an obvious role to play in this undertaking.

*Diversity* is an equally important aspect of the new millennium. People on earth are a diverse lot characterized by a variety of ideologies and beliefs, and this diversity has many positive qualities both individually and collectively. However, despite these natural and often desirable differences, will it be necessary to regulate people's actions more stringently, as Skinner (1971) suggested, because of overpopulation and ideological issues? This question has major implications for competitive sport and physical education.

Third, the concept of *cooperation* must enter into our planning for the future in sport and physical education. Cooperation implies working together for a common purpose or benefit. As the world grows "smaller," the importance of international relations and cooperation becomes greater. Politicians and sport administrators have claimed for years that competition in international sport fosters goodwill. Now it is more important than ever for sport and physical education to work vigorously toward this goal.

## MORAL MENTALITY OF THE EAST AND WEST

Keeping in mind that this chapter is aimed at putting the question of sport ethics in world perspective, it is important at this point to make a brief comparison of the moral mentality of the East and the West. A reasonable, but possibly oversimplified, approach to such a comparison was offered by Northrop (1946), who wrote of the "intuitive mind" of the East and the "logical mind" of the West.

He explained that Eastern morality tends to be provisional because people believe that ultimate guidance comes from a source infinitely greater than any of the various moral constructs of mere man. The assumption is that morality is implicit in the nature of things, whereas the ethical approaches of the West have been devised by fallible men and women. Interestingly, citizens of both the East and the West have figured out ways of "getting beyond" what has been called normative ethics. The East traditionally has done this by blurring the distinction between philosophy and religion (that is, the highest form of guidance comes from a supra-moral source). Thus in the East an overriding mysticism warns the individual against becoming bound by man-made normative standards.

The West has developed other types of "escape routes" from normative ethics. Existentialism, for example, says that a person is free to establish his or her own personal essence, an approach that is definitely antinormative. Psychoanalysis helps a person to shed feelings of guilt for possibly unethical actions taken in the past (or inflicted upon him or her). A third escape route, or means of accommodation, could be the adoption of a particular ideology as a leading influence in one's life, a commitment that could well lead the person to commit unethical actions contrary to the prevailing values of the culture. If none of these means of accommodation is sufficient, then still others are available. In recent decades, perhaps the leading approach in the West has been a metaethical or analytic approach that downplays normative ethical standards because of their uncertainty.

## APPROACHES TO ETHICAL DECISION-MAKING IN THE WEST

There are many philosophical approaches to ethics. Six are listed here as being representative of the Western world. They exhibit great variation in both terminology and emphases, but we have space here for only a brief mention of each approach and the criterion that each one uses to evaluate ideas and actions.

1. *Authoritarianism* (or legalism). The criterion for evaluation is conformity to rules, laws, moral codes, and established systems and customs.
2. *Relativism* (or antinomianism). The criterion for evaluation is the needs of the present situation in the culture of the society concerned.
3. *Situationism*. The criterion for evaluation is "what is fitting" in the situation based on the application of agapeic (God's) love.
4. *Scientific ethics*. The criterion for evaluation is that ideas that are helpful in problem-solving thereby become true. The empirical verification of a hypothesis brings about a union of theory and practice.
5. *The "good reasons" approach*. The criterion for evaluation is whether a given rule or action would be good for everyone alike. Unselfish decisions should be made on the basis of a principle that can be universalized.

**6.** *Emotivism* (analytic philosophy's response to ethical problems). The criterion for evaluation here is whether ethical disputes are resolved on a factual level. Accordingly, value statements must be distinguished from factual ones (Zeigler, 1984).

# DEVELOPING PERSONAL AND PROFESSIONAL ETHICS IN THE WEST

A. Rand in 1960 offered an analysis of what occurs in an individual before any semblance of a rational philosophy develops. According to Rand, the individual possesses a "psychological recorder" that functions as the person's subconscious integrating mechanism. This so-called sense of life "is a pre-conceptual equivalent of metaphysics, an emotional, subconsciously integrated appraisal of man and existence. It sets the nature of a man's emotional responses and the essence of his character."[31]

Granting the apparent truth of this statement, those who are interested in the educational process must hope that all young people will have the chance to develop their rational powers through the finest possible educational experience. Reason should begin early on to act as the programmer of the person's "emotional computer." Unfortunately, the typical child or young person tends to learn to make rational ethical decisions in a poor and inadequate manner. Thus our major concern must be to help young people develop conscious convictions in which the mind leads and the emotions follow. As the person gradually learns what values are important, "the integrated sum of these values becomes that person's sense of life."[32]

What the young person really needs is an intellectual roadbed that provides a course for his or her life to follow. The eventual goal should be the development of a fully integrated personality, a person whose mind and emotions are in harmony a great deal of the time. When this occurs, the individual's sense of life matches his or her conscious convictions. It is important, of course, that the young person's view of reality be carefully defined and reasonably consistent. If ethical instruction were planned more carefully and explicitly, the quality of living would probably be greatly improved for all.

There seems to be agreement that young people in our society should be so educated that they develop rationality as a life competency. It should also be considered essential for them to learn to use their rational powers to address the many ethical problems that arise in daily life. The specific concern in this discussion is that individuals be able to apply such rationality to the ethical problems that arise in sport and physical activity.

Professionals in the field of sport and physical education are no better or worse than those in other professions when it comes to applied ethics. The entire Western culture is confused in this matter. The tangle of ethics has developed because of a diversity of customs and mores within various societies throughout the world. Those of us in Canada and the United States have simply added our own brand of confusion to an ill-suited mixture of moral systems.

Where does that leave the profession of sport and physical education? The answer at this point must be, "In trouble!" We need to take a hard look at ourselves and our ethical behavior—admittedly a difficult assignment. Responding to heavy criticism of highly competitive athletics is a humbling experience.

In some ways we are part of the teaching profession, and yet ideally the field of sport and physical education has a broad mission that extends from infancy to very old age, and to all segments of the population, be they "normal," "special," or "accelerated."

According to M. D. Bayles (1981), we have many of the attributes of a profession, namely (1) an extensive training period; (2) a significant intellectual component to be mastered; and (3) some recognition that the trained person can provide a basic and important service to society.[33] However, the profession of sport and physical education has not done as well as some of the highly recognized professions in developing and enforcing carefully defined professional obligations that the practitioner must follow to remain in good standing.

## ETHICAL CREEDS, CODES, AND STUDIES

In considering professional ethics, initially we must distinguish between a *creed*, or statement of professional beliefs, and a *code*, or set of detailed regulations of a more administrative nature.[34] In competitive sport, for example, the National High School Athletic Coaches Association developed what might be called an embryonic code. A similarly brief code—with some overlap—has been adopted by the Minnesota High School Coaches Association.

In Canada, the Coaching Association, as part of the National Coaching Certification Program, has adopted what is called a coaching creed. It too is very brief and contains elements that might more appropriately appear in a code. However, that is the extent of this type of development, and there is probably no coach at any level who could repeat even the essence of these statements.

In the field of physical education, which is unfortunately usually viewed only within the domain of education, several efforts have been made over the years to define what our ethical concerns should be. In 1992 the Philosophy Academy of the National Association for Sport and Physical Education, which is an association of the American Alliance for Health, Physical Education, Recreation and Dance, developed a workable code of ethics. This represented a firm beginning.

Several texts on ethics in sport and physical education have been written. Among them are works by Shea (1978), Fraleigh (1984), Zeigler (1984), Simon (1991) and Lumpkin, Stoll, and Beller (1995). Kretchmar (1994) included in his book on personal ethics a chapter entitled "Making Sound Ethical Decisions." Similarly, Eitzen (1993) devoted several chapters to issues relating to sport ethics. However, despite these textbooks, very few courses are offered in sport and physical education ethics, and practically none that treat the subject of professional ethics for the teacher or coach.

For sport and physical activity management, Zeigler's monograph on professional ethics for sport managers (1992) provides a theoretical base and laboratory experiences. Another monograph two years later (Zeigler, 1994) treated the subject of critical thinking with a strong relationship to personal and professional ethics. Finally, a text by DeSensi and Rosenberg (1996) titled *Ethics in Sport Management* offers sound theory and applied material to a field that should make steadily increasing use of such material in professional education programs. In summary, therefore, we can report some promising beginnings in an aspect of the profession that warrants significantly greater attention.

The field of recreation has made some, but not substantive, headway in this area. The American Recreation Society developed a brief code of ethics a generation ago, and the Society of Municipal Recreation Directors of Ontario constructed a code in the 1950s. These codes typically receive lip service, but the societies do not enforce compliance with them.

# A RECOMMENDED APPROACH
# FOR WESTERN CULTURE

One is tempted to ask, "Where do we go from here?" The best answer might be, "There's nowhere to go but up!" Many professionals in the field strongly believe that a course in professional ethics should be required for all teachers and coaches in their respective programs of professional preparation. A strong case can be made for this recommendation if we remind ourselves that without ethical behavior a teacher/coach can become "nothing" overnight, professionally speaking. Just one lapse from accepted ethical behavior can put a large dent in—or even ruin—what was otherwise a fine professional career.

For the teaching of ethics to undergraduates in this culture, we would do well to amalgamate three great ideas about ethics, those of Kant, Mill, and Aristotle. The ideas can be arranged in a progression that can be used for determining what's good and bad, or right and wrong. This three-step approach to ethical decision-making moves from the application of Kant's test of universalizability or *consistency,* to Mill's test of *consequences,* and then to Aristotle's test of *intentions.*

An ethical dilemma begins whenever an athlete or coach is faced with an ethical choice. The question becomes, "What should I do about this problem that has come up?" The three-step approach applied to a dilemma would be as follows.

Step 1. *Kant's Test of Consistency.* Kant's test of consistency asks the question, "Is it possible to universalize the action that we are judging to all people on earth?" Kant said, "So act that you could wish the maxim of your action to become a universal law of human conduct." This approach is similar to the Golden Rule and other maxims. It does, of course, have some imperfections.

Step 2. *Mill's Test of Consequences.* After we have determined that the question posed by Kant can be answered either affirmatively or negatively, the next step involves Mill's test of consequences. Here Mill would say something like this: "Have you acted so as to bring about the greatest (net) good or happiness that is possible in this situation?" Accordingly, one should be able to say that he or she has acted on the basis of the best evidence available at the time, and that such an action is right because it produced the maximum amount of net, not gross, happiness. It helps at this stage in making a judgment to keep such principles as autonomy, justice, and beneficence firmly in mind.

Step 3. *Aristotle's Test of Intentions.* This step is derived from the philosophic thought of the legendary Aristotle of ancient Greece, the man who tutored Alexander the Great. It takes the focus away from the results of the action itself by reverting to what the (presumed) perpetrator of the act had in mind when he or she carried it out. In his *Nicomachean Ethics* (1943, Book III, Chapter 1), Aristotle asked, "What were the conditions under which the act was performed?"

## MERGING WITH A JURISPRUDENTIAL (LAW-COURT) ARGUMENT FORMAT

Once the tests of consistency, consequences, and intentions have been applied in sequential order to a problem in ethical decision-making, an individual may decide that the answer to the ethical problem is quite clear. Many people, however, will want additional substantiation for any decision made. Thus it is further recommended that the the tests of consistency, consequences, and intentions be superimposed on what Toulmin (1964) has called his "layout for a jurisprudential argument."[35] This is a formally valid argument that is similar in form to arguments employed daily in jurisprudence (the law courts) and in mathematics. (See Figure 8.1.)

With this approach we can move forward gradually, steadily, and reasonably from *data* (D) to what seems like a reasonable *conclusion* (C) (step no. 1). The next step (no. 2) in the Toulmin argument layout, the *warrant* (W), involves the creation of a general hypothetical statement that acts as a bridge to lend support to the (tentative?) conclusion that has been reached. It typically answers the question, "How do you get there?" The third step (no. 3) in Toulmin's argument layout has two parts—the introduction of a *modal qualifier* (Q) followed by consideration of possible *conditions of exception,* or *rebuttal* (R). Thus, depending on the intensity or force of the warrant, the qualifying term (Q) may be "necessarily," "presumably," "probably," or similar term. This leads directly to the second part of step no. 3, the condition(s) of exception or rebuttal that can introduce particular circumstances of greater or lesser import that might negate or even refute the authority of the warrant (W).

Toulmin's final step involves the introduction of *backing* (B). The backing (B) serves the purpose of strengthening or supplementing the warrant (W) even further. Thus the backing is closely associated with the nature of the warrant (W).

It is possible to merge the tests of Kant, Mill, and Aristotle and Toulmin's jurisprudential argument and apply them to ethical situations in sport and physical education. Toulmin's argument layout can be used to resolve just about any type of argument, theoretical or practical, in any field of endeavor. However, keeping in mind that our primary concern is with *ethical* decision-making, we must be certain to determine the ethical *merits* or *demerits* of the situation at hand. To assist in these deliberations, consider as an example the hypothetical situation described later.

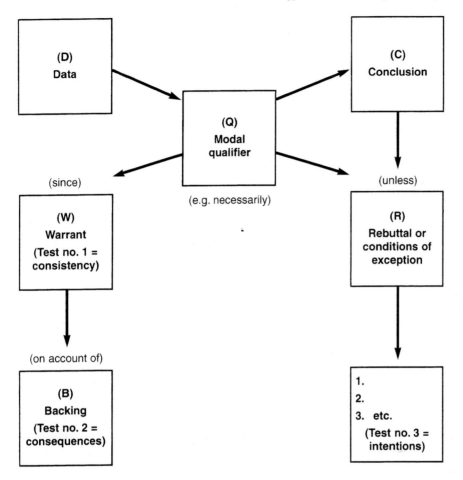

**Key to Jurisprudential Argument Terms**

D  =  Data (a statement of a situation that prevails, including evidence, elements, sources, samples of facts)

C  =  Conclusion (claim or conclusion that we are seeking to establish)

W  =  Warrant (practical standards or canons of argument designed to provide an answer to the question, "How do you get there?")

Q  =  Modal qualifier (adverb employed to qualify conclusion based on strength of warrants (e.g., necessarily, probably)

B  =  Backing (categorical statements of fact that lend further support to the bridge-like warrants)

R  =  Conditions of exception [(arguments, rebuttal, or exceptions that tend to refute or soften the strength of the conclusion (C)]

**FIGURE 8.1  Merging of Three-Step Approach and Jurisprudential Argument Format.**

Adapted from S. Toulmin, *The Uses of Argument* (New York: Cambridge, 1964), 94–145. Reprinted with the permission of Cambridge University Press.

## A SAMPLE CASE: DRUG-TAKING AT A LARGE UNIVERSITY

The head football coach at a large midwestern university is facing a difficult predicament. Moments before his team is scheduled to take the field for the final game of what has been a most successful season, the coach learns that his cocaptains may have been involved with drug-taking throughout the season. What should he do?

Toulmin's jurisprudential argument layout offers one approach to rational analysis (see Figure 8.2). Some might argue, however, that this layout does not put sufficient emphasis on the ethical aspects of the situation. Therefore, it is recommended that the three tests of consistency, consequences, and intentions be superimposed on Toulmin's argument layout to serve as a double-check, so to speak, for the warrant, backing, and rebuttal. For example, if the warrant and the test of consistency (universalizability) clash violently or "contradict" each other, further rationalization seems required. What we are looking for, one might say, is the best possible "fit" between the argument layout and the three tests.

In this situation, then, the following points may be made: (1) With reference to the test of *consistency (universalizability)*, the coach would certainly not wish to universalize a situation in which drug-taking by athletes is condoned. He knows that society expects its so-called amateur athletes to be paragons of virtue. In reference to the second test of *consequences*, the coach is aware that indiscriminate drug-taking has become a significant problem threatening the nation's health and well-being. This situation would become worse if the coach lets the athletes off scot-free, because youth tend to copy practices of top athletes. And lastly, applying the test of *intentions*: if the athletes have some sort of an acceptable explanation for their actions (assuming the report is true), then the coach must assess their present attitude in light of the severity of the claimed infraction of established rules.

## CROSS-CULTURAL APPLICABILITY OF THE PROPOSED APPLIED ETHICS MODEL

As this chapter draws to a close, it is time to broaden our perspective by considering a cross-cultural application of the proposed applied ethics model. In so doing, keep in mind the discussion earlier in the chapter of the means whereby people in both East and West try to "get beyond" what are called normative ethics.

What arguments can be mustered to show that the proposed ethics model might have direct application to the world scene? Consider the following points:

1. People in the cultures of the East and the West are being brought up in similar ways. For example, each develops an implicit sense of life and typically receives very little explicit ethical instruction.
2. Cultures and countries have been steadily and increasingly interacting as a result of advances in communications technology.

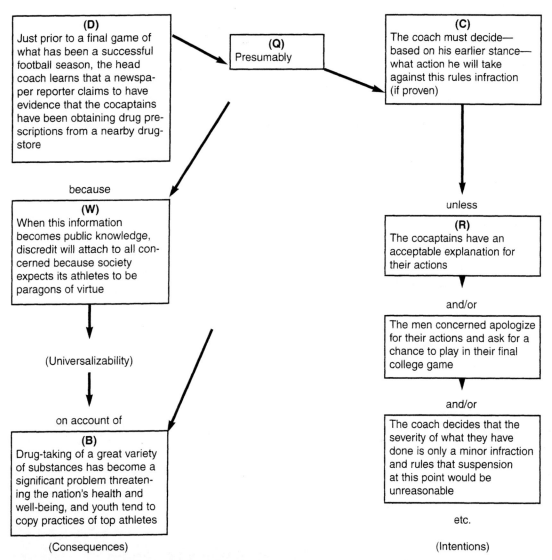

**(D)**
Just prior to a final game of what has been a successful football season, the head coach learns that a newspaper reporter claims to have evidence that the cocaptains have been obtaining drug prescriptions from a nearby drugstore

**(Q)**
Presumably

**(C)**
The coach must decide—based on his earlier stance—what action he will take against this rules infraction (if proven)

because

**(W)**
When this information becomes public knowledge, discredit will attach to all concerned because society expects its athletes to be paragons of virtue

unless

**(R)**
The cocaptains have an acceptable explanation for their actions

(Universalizability)

and/or

The men concerned apologize for their actions and ask for a chance to play in their final college game

on account of

and/or

**(B)**
Drug-taking of a great variety of substances has become a significant problem threatening the nation's health and well-being, and youth tend to copy practices of top athletes

The coach decides that the severity of what they have done is only a minor infraction and rules that suspension at this point would be unreasonable

(Consequences)

etc.

(Intentions)

**FIGURE 8.2  Drug-Taking at "Big-Time" University, Based on a Jurisprudential Argument Layout.**

3. Thus, when confronted with an ethical issue in international sport, both the East and the West employ some version of the Golden Rule. This means that Kant's test of consistency can be generally accepted at this time.
4. All countries have developed formal (legal) and/or informal (ethical) ways of assessing the consequences of an action that has ethical import. The East's *retributive* justice often seems harsh to the West, where the focus in recent decades has been on *distributive* justice. Nevertheless, consideration of the *net*

consequences of an act (that is, Mill's test of consequences) should receive fairly general acceptance in both the West and the East. Further, since all countries have both legal and ethical ways of assessing actions, the informal logic of Toulmin's jurisprudential argument layout represents at least a starting point for the "international courts of sporting justice."

5. Punishments meted out in the past few years to aspiring international athletes appear to have been tempered by an understanding of the athletes' almost involuntary urge to achieve status for self or country as medal winners. This tendency means that the adjudicating groups are already employing Aristotle's test of intentions as they assess the voluntary or involuntary nature of rule infractions.

## SOME REASONABLE CONCLUSIONS

What reasonable conclusions can we draw from this effort to place sport ethics in world perspective? First, the time is ripe for the development of an international code of ethics for both the athlete and the coach (a code is more detailed than a shorter, merely hortatory creed). Second, we should be aware of the means whereby athletes, officials, and coaches in the cultures of both East and the West seem able to "get beyond ethics" both ethically and legally. A third reasonable conclusion is that we are fortunate in having innumerable examples in the cultures of both East and West of the longstanding concept of fair play, upon which we can build.

A fourth reasonable conclusion is that life presents everyone, in whatever culture, with many situations in which (a) established principles of ethical duty and (b) what seems to be good or valuable are incompatible. Here we encounter the great distinction in the history of moral philosophy between respect-for-law (deontic) theories as opposed to value-realization (axiological or telic) theories. When an athlete consciously takes anabolic steroids in hopes of setting new records of achievement for the sake of self, country (including its political ideology), or "world accomplishment," we are facing a similar dilemma between rules and values.

A fifth conclusion is that the world obviously needs a recognizable, reasonable, acceptable concept of duty and responsibility that will help us all live in peace and harmony. Such an understanding could guide our actions in personal life and in our societal undertakings—including sport. Thus we should probably work for increasing *consensus* on ethical values and ethical decision-making, while trying to eliminate the "escape routes" that are used to "get beyond" societies' well-established normative ethics.

A sixth reasonable conclusion is that in competitive sports, as in life, the West should learn from the East how to gain *inner freedom* through personal mind control. The East should learn from the West's science and technology that *outer freedom* is available to all through intelligent planning.

Finally, we can reasonably conclude—or at least hope—that competitive sports, carried out in accordance with high ethical standards, can make a significant contribution toward the achievement of world peace and harmony.

# SUMMARY

At the present time, the world of competitive sport and physical activity is facing a crisis in integrity. Problems of drug use, athlete and spectator violence, cheating, gambling, the bending of the rules, and numerous other ethically questionable practices have become common themes associated with sports. As we enter the new millennium, there is an urgent need for professionals in the field of sport and physical education to understand and develop a better approach toward ethics applied to sport. If the field of sport and physical education is to make a significant contribution to society, it must be in harmony with the values deemed important in the culture. Unless sport serves society in a positive and useful way, people in an ethical society will, over time, do away with it.

From a global perspective, differences exist in the moral mentality of Eastern and Western cultures. A tangle of ethics has developed because of the diversity of customs and mores found in various societies. Through religion, philosophy, psychology, and a variety of social processes, individuals in both the East and the West have figured out ways to "get beyond" or find reasons for ignoring normative ethics. In the Western world, ethical decisions are often arrived at through authoritarianism, relativism, situationism, scientific analysis, good reasoning, or emotivism.

The field of sport and physical education falls short in the development and enforcement of clearly delineated ethical obligations. The merger of the ideas of Kant, Mill, and Aristotle with a jurisprudential argument format offers a viable model for ethical decision-making in competitive sport and physical education. A cross-cultural application of this model would encourage Eastern and Western societies to get beyond typically normative ethics and develop a truly multicultural approach to ethical agreement and decision-making. Finally, the field of sport and physical education should develop a global code of ethics for athletes and coaches.

# STUDY QUESTIONS

1. Did the number of sport ethics problems summarized at the outset of the chapter surprise you? Judging from your own experience, as well as current reports of ethically questionable practices, do you believe the situation is improving or worsening?
2. Explain briefly the "moral mentality" of the East as opposed to that of the West (as postulated by Northrop). As you understand the world situation, which makes more sense today?
3. Reviewing the six Western approaches to ethical decision-making that are listed in the chapter, relate any one or more of these to your personal educational background and development in ethics and morality.
4. Do you agree that ethical instruction for the young is typically not handled well in the United States and Canada?
5. What do you think of Rand's assessment of the moral development of children and youth in our culture?

**6.** To what extent do you believe our culture provides an "intellectual roadbed," a course in life that young people can follow?

**7.** Develop one example from your own life (or that of a friend or associate) of the three-step approach (or progression) recommended for ethical decision-making. Then show how this could be merged with a (standard) jurisprudential (law-court) argument format such as that recommended by Toulmin.

**8.** Do you agree with the text that this conjoined approach could work in the milieu of global sport ethics?

## RECOMMENDED READINGS

Aristotle. "Nicomachean Ethics." In *Aristotle*, edited by L. R. Loomis and translated by J. E. C. Weldon. New York: W. J. Black, 1943.

Asimov, I. "The Fourth Revolution." *Saturday Review* (October 24, 1970): 17–20.

DeSensi, J. T., and D. Rosenberg. *Ethics in Sport Management.* Morgantown, WV: Fitness Information Technologies, 1996.

Eitzen, D. Stanley. *Sport in Contemporary Society.* New York: St. Martin's Press, 1993.

Fraleigh, W. P. *Right Actions in Sport.* Champaign, IL: Human Kinetics, 1984.

Glasser, W. *The Identity Society.* New York: Harper and Row, 1972.

Kaplan, A. *The New World of Philosophy.* Boston: Houghton Mifflin, 1961.

Kretchmar, R. S. *Practical Philosophy of Sport.* Champaign, IL: Human Kinetics, 1994.

Lumpkin, Angela, Sharon K. Stoll, and Jennifer M. Beller. *Sport Ethics: Applications for Fair Play.* St. Louis: Mosby and NASPE, 1995.

Northrop, F. S. C. *The Meeting of East and West.* New York: Macmillan, 1946.

Shea, E. J. *Ethical Decisions in Physical Education and Sport.* Springfield, IL: C. C. Thomas, 1978.

Simon, Robert L. *Fair Play: Sports, Values and Society.* Boulder, CO: Westview, 1991.

Skinner, B. F. *Beyond Freedom and Dignity.* New York: Alfred A. Knopf, 1971.

Zeigler, Earle F. *Ethics and Morality in Sport and Physical Education.* Champaign, IL: Stipes, 1984.

Zeigler, Earle F. *Professional Ethics for Sport Managers.* Champaign, IL: Stipes, 1992.

Zeigler, Earle F. *Critical Thinking for the Professions of Health, Sport, Physical Education, Recreation, and Dance.* Champaign, IL: Stipes, 1994.

## NOTES

1. M. Goodwin, "Blood-Doping Unethical, U.S. Olympic Official Says," *New York Times* (January 13, 1985): 25.

2. B. Rostaing and R. Sullivan, "Triumphs Tainted With Blood," *Sports Illustrated* 62, no. 3 (1985): 12–17.

3. W. Brubaker, "A Pipeline Full of Drugs," *Sports Illustrated* 62, no. 3 (1985): 19–21.

4. W. Goodman and K. Roberts, "Coaches Indicted in Drug Scandal," *New York Times* (March 10, 1985).

5. M. Goodwin, "Athletes Polled on Drugs," *New York Times* (March 17, 1985).

6. M. Goodwin, "Athletes to Face Drug Tests under U.S. Olympic Plans," *New York Times* (March 25, 1985): 19.

7. W. C. Rhoden, "A Betting Scandal Gives Basketball a Black Eye," *New York Times* (March 31, 1985): E7.

8. "Tulane Coach Resigns," *Toronto Globe and Mail* (April 5, 1985): 18.

9. "Tulane Ends Sport," *New York Times* (April 19, 1985): 22.

10. Scott Disher, "Media Draws Criticisms at Violence Symposium," *Toronto Globe and Mail* (April 5, 1985).

11. Ibid.

12. "NCAA Group Backs New Penalties," *New York Times* (April 18, 1985): 23.

13. W. N. Wallace, "One Piece of Bad News Leads to Another for Arizona State," *New York Times* (April 7, 1985): 19.

14. J. Di Paola, "Elsewhere," *USA Today* (April 22, 1985): 11C.

15. "Memphis State Inquiry," *New York Times* (April 30, 1985): B10.

16. S. Goldaper, "Reed Quits in Protest," *New York Times* (May 2, 1985): B13.

17. I. Berkow, "How Creighton's Dreams of Glory Came Apart," *New York Times* (May 19, 1985): 19.

18. D. L. Moore, "Steroids Inquiry," *USA Today* (May 3, 1985): 1C

19. S. Wieberg, "Illinois State Coach Turns in Suspects," "Tulane Leaves Metro," and "Rule Change Proposed," *USA Today* (May 3, 1985): 8C.

20. D. Barry, "Not Sweet, and Not a Science," *New York Times* (November 26, 1995): Sports Section 11.

21. "U.S. Requires Colleges to List Sport Costs," *New York Times* (December 3, 1995): Sports Section.

22. I. Berkow, "The Louts Get Their Just Reward from the Giants," *New York Times* (December 28, 1995): B7.

23. A. Barra, "Sentenced to Play Football," *New York Times* (December 29, 1995): A11.

24. "The N.C.A.A. Gets It Right," *New York Times* (January 23, 1996): A12.

25. N. Bernstein, "Civil Rights Lawsuit in Rape Case Challenges Integrity of a Campus," *New York Times* (February 11, 1996): 1.

26. L. Dorman, "More Than a Drop of Integrity for Sluman," *New York Times* (March 30, 1996): 19.

27. Henry Aaron, "When Baseball Mattered," *New York Times* (April 13, 1997): E15.

28. M. Bamberger and D. Yaeger, "Over the Edge," *Sports Illustrated* 86, no. 15 (1997): 61–70.

29. M. Bamberger, "Under Suspicion," *Sports Illustrated* 86, no. 15 (1997), 73–85.

30. Joyce C. Oates, "Fury and Fine Lines," *New York Times* (July 3, 1997): A15.

31. A. Rand, *The Romantic Manifesto* (New York and Cleveland: World, 1960): 31.

32. Ibid., 35.

33. M. D. Bales, *Professional Ethics* (Belmont, CA: Wadsworth, 1981): 7.

34. Ibid., 24.

35. S. Toulmin, *The Uses of Argument* (New York: Cambridge, 1964): 95.

# CHAPTER NINE

# QUO VADIS?
# A PLEA FOR REFORM

## J. RICHARD POLIDORO

During the nineteenth and twentieth centuries, the world experienced a dramatic modernization of sport and physical activity. As witnessed by events in mainland Europe, North America, and elsewhere, competitive sports mushroomed on the international as well as the national level. At the end of the nineteenth century, the global community saw the rebirth of the modern Olympics, and the world of international sports has not been the same since. Beginning in the late 1800s, competitive sports took on an element of seriousness that continued throughout the 1900s. Nations invested heavily in their systems of sport, for reasons ranging from the need to reinforce political ideology and nationalism to the need to promote individual health benefits. Competitive sport for men grew on all amateur levels as well as on the professional level. In the United States, college and university athletic programs expanded dramatically. Although not as extensive as the programs that developed for men, women's programs grew in both size and status. Compulsory physical education became a commonly required subject in the school curriculum. Sports opportunities were extended to individuals of all ages. Youth sport programs mushroomed in many countries. Similarly, organized programs of sport developed for individuals with special needs, as well as for the aging. Today the world of sport has grown to enormous proportions. There are more opportunities to participate in a wider variety of sporting activities than ever before in history. Programs exist for everyone, regardless of age, race, religion, or sex. Yet, despite this impressive growth, competitive sports and physical education face major problems and issues.

## PROBLEMS IN PHYSICAL EDUCATION AND SPORTS

As we enter the new millennium, it is apparent that while youth sports are expanding, compulsory physical education in the schools is on the decline. Despite widespread public acceptance of the need for physical activity, public support for physical education is rapidly eroding. Despite major advances in the body of knowledge encompassing physical education, the field continues to be plagued with lack of definition, confusion over purpose, questions of accountability, and concerns for quality of education. In many instances, these problems have led to the curtailment of programs, the absence of physical education specialists, budget cutbacks, inadequate and aging facilities, a reduction in instructional time, increased class size, and an overall deterioration of the quality of the program. While most seriously felt in the United States and Canada, the downward trend in physical education is apparent also in many other countries throughout the world. The 1992 Annual Report of the European Physical Education Associations (EUPEA) said that physical education was in danger in many European countries and appeared to be on the decline.[1] In 1998 twenty-six countries were affiliated with EUPEA.[2]

Unlike the current trend in physical education, the popularity of competitive sports has never been higher, nor have competitive sports ever before been so pervasive and influential in the lives of so many people. Yet, despite this popularity, competitive sports are rife with problems and controversies. Throughout the world they are being driven by a "win at all costs" philosophy that has led to the development of numerous questionable, if not unacceptable, practices and concerns. This obsession with winning has led, directly or indirectly, to the use of illicit drugs, increased player violence, financial greed among players and management, gambling, giantism, commercialization, increased professionalization, and the complete contamination of sport ethics. These problems permeate not only the world of professional sports but all levels of amateur sports as well. Unlike the sporting events of the past, which focused primarily on playful activity, competitive sports at the dawn of the new millennium are a combination of business, entertainment, and politics. In the eyes of many, the "win at all costs" philosophy has led to a situation in which competitive sports are completely out of control.

## WHERE DO WE GO FROM HERE?

If the present situation is as bad as all this, what steps if any should we take to improve the situation? Before we attempt to answer this question, we should remember that the roles played by physical education and sports in a society are directly related to the needs and values of that society. That is, physical education and competitive sports reflect the way people in society view the world, and the way people view the contributions made by sport and physical education. The position of physical education in the schools is a direct manifestation of the value society places on it in comparison to other academic subjects. Similarly, competitive sports are viewed in light of their contributions to those elements of society that are deemed important. Many of the problems found in competitive sports are rooted in the values that society applauds, such as power, reward, recognition, and entertainment.

Although society plays a major role in determining the status of physical education and sports, the direction they take at any given time is determined essentially by a select few who hold decision-making power. The prevailing philosophy and the ultimate direction that programs take reflect the motives and desires of these powerful individuals (the establishment).

There is little question that the current directions of competitive sport and physical education are direct manifestations of the self-serving motives of the few who hold the power. These persons are found in the IOC, the NCAA, the sport federations, the sports media, and among educational decision-makers. In most instances, these are self-interested groups that are not concerned with what is good for sports. They are often driven by motives of profit, power, and greed. For the most part, society at large is either ignorant of the real situation in physical education and competitive sports, or it just doesn't care. Recognition of this ignorance or nonchalant attitude helps explain how the public can recognize the need for physical activity while, at the same time, allowing the erosion of school physical education. The public's ignorance of the real situation in competitive sport also helps explain why abuses continue unabated. The public still associates sports with play and appears somewhat oblivious to its commercial and unethical realities. Furthermore, society hears only what the sports establishment wants it to hear.

With this understanding, it appears that society has three options in dealing with problems associated with physical education and sports. First, it can opt to do nothing and maintain the status quo. Under this option, physical education would gradually fade from the school curriculum and competitive sports would continue to grow ever larger and ever more rife with corruption and greed. This option is a very plausible scenario.

The second option would be to completely eliminate competitive sports and physical education. Instead of allowing physical education to undergo a slow and painful death, society could immediately cut it out of the curriculum. Similarly, society might attempt to eliminate, or at least severely curtail, competitive sports everywhere in the world, though this would be a most difficult if not impossible task. Competitive sports are so deeply ingrained in the fabric of society, and the economic aspects of sports are so great, that such a suggestion is totally unrealistic. However, the same cannot be said for school physical education.

The third option that society might consider would be to take steps to eliminate the problems confronting physical education and competitive sports. This would require a transfer of power and control from the elite sports establishments to the participants. Such a move would require either the radical restructuring of contemporary sport or the establishment of controls and regulations over all organized sport activity. Realistically, the radical restructuring of contemporary sport is highly unlikely since the dominant values of sport—winning, commercialization, and competition—are continually reinforced by the values found in society at large. Such changes would require the complete restructuring of society as well. On the other hand, the establishment of regulations and controls appears a more viable and realistic option. The elite sports establishments must be held more accountable for their actions and must become more focused on what is good for sport. The need for regulation of international sports was noted as early as 1913 when, following the meeting of the Olympic Congress, Maurice Millioud stated:

We should not ask ourselves what sports are. We should rather ask ourselves what we want them to be. They are what they are: we need not create them but regulate them.[3]

As we enter the twenty-first century, a few small signs are beginning to appear indicating that the world community is becoming more sensitive to the abuses associated with the "win at all costs" philosophy. A slow but growing unrest is emerging with the violence, the drugs, the scandals, and complete lack of ethics associated with today's competitive sports. Despite the value society has placed on such factors as success, reward, power, and entertainment, a perception is growing that perhaps competitive sports have gone too far. If this is the case, then the world community is awakening to the need to determine for itself the future course of sports and physical education. To be sure, the road to reform is not an easy route to follow. It may require major social change. The challenges are great, but if sport and physical education are to provide positive benefits for society, then reform and regulation are essential. As succinctly stated by Zeigler (1988):

Somehow we must bring ourselves to an assessment that may rock our very social foundations, while causing us to reaffirm what is sound in the traits that make up our nation's character. . . . Have we the energy, the intellect, the foresight, the attitudes, the concern . . . to change our course the required number of degrees so that the ship of state will follow the correct course at a critical juncture in the world's history?[4]

## STUDY QUESTIONS

1. What steps can a society take to regulate and control sports?
2. What can the world community do to improve the present situation in physical education and competitive sports on the global level?
3. What suggestions do you have to rectify the abuses currently found in competitive sports?
4. What are some of the positive values associated with competitive sports?
5. Should physical education be considered a priority in the public schools? If so, why? If not, why not?

## RECOMMENDED READINGS

Beisser, Arnold. *The Madness in Sports.* New York: Appleton-Century-Crofts, 1967.

Cosell, Howard, and Shelby Whitfield. *What's Wrong with Sports.* New York: Simon and Schuster, 1991.

Duffy, Pat, and Liam Dugdale, eds. *HPER—Moving toward the 21st Century.* Champaign, IL: Human Kinetics, 1994.

Hoch, Paul. *Rip Off the Big Game.* Garden City, NY: Anchor Books, 1972.

Lupica, Mike. *Mad as Hell.* New York: G. P. Putnam's Sons, 1996.

Nixon, Howard L. *Sport and Social Organization.* Indianapolis: Bobbs-Merrill, 1976.

Scott, Jack. *The Athletic Revolution.* New York: Free Press, 1971.

## NOTES

1. European Physical Education Associations, *Annual Report of the European Physical Education Associations* (Ghent, Belgium: June 1992).

2. LaPorte, Wily, ed., *The Physical Education Teacher for Secondary Schools in the European Union* (Ghent, Belgium: European Observatory of Sports Occupations, June 1997).

3. Maurice Millioud, *Gazette de Lausanne* (May 18, 1913).

4. Earle F. Zeigler. *History of Physical Education and Sport* (Champaign, IL: Stipes, 1988), 302.

North American Gymnastic Union, 69
North American Society for Sport History
    (NASSH), 171
North American Society for the Sociology of Sport
    (NASSS), 171
North American Society for the Sport
    Management (NASSM), 171
Northrup, F. S. C.,192
Nurmi, Paavo, 107

Oates, Joyce Carol, 190
*Odyssey*, 3
Olympiad, 6
Olympic Games
    ancient, 4–10
    under Brundage, 107–110
    Cold War period, 103, 107
    early 20th century games, 97–99
    first modern, 91–93
    under Killanin, 111–112
    in the 1990s, 116–117
    under Samaranch, 113–116
    summary of modern, 104–106
Olympic movement, German, 49
O'Ree, Willie, 78
Oslo Olympics, 137
Otto, Kristin, 146
Outer freedom, 200
Outerbridge, Mary, 128
Owens, Jesse, 101–102

Palango, Paul, 188
Palmer, Gladys, 140
Pan-American Games, 110, 140
Panhellenic Games, 92
Pankration, ancient Greek, 15–16
Paralympics, 85
Paris Olympics, 97, 133–134
Patoulidou, Paraskevi, 148
Pausanias, 7
Paxson, Frederick L., 75
Pee Wee hockey, 79
Pele, 110
Penn, William, 55
Penny, D., 165
Pentathlon, ancient Greek, 14
Perec, Marie-Jose, 148
Persuasive approach, 181
Petrow, Alexei, 120

Phayllus, 14, 19
Philip, King, 6
Philosophic issues
    in colonial U.S., 55
    in physical education, 82–83
    professional, 172–180
Philosophic Society for the Study of Sport
    (IPSSS), 171
Philostratus, 14, 17
Physical education
    ancient Greek, 18
    in Canada and U.S., 165–168, 170–172
    colleges and universities and, 71–72
    curriculum for, 160–163
    disabilities and, 84–85
    English, 35–37
    eroding support for, 204–207
    gender issues in, 83–84
    German Democratic Republic, 46
    goals of, 82–83
    1990s U.S., 85–86
    19th century U.S., 68–71
    professional concerns for, 169–170
    research in, 163–165
Pindar 17, 16
Pittsburgh Athletic Club, 68
Plato, 4
Playground Association of America, 79
Politics
    German Democratic Republic and, 49–50
    global issues and, 182
    Irish sports and, 41–42
    Olympic Games and, 101–102, 107–110,
        111–112, 113–116
    women's participation and, 145
Pop Warner football, 79
Posse, Nils, 71
Prizefighting, 61, 67
Problem-solving approach, 181
Profession, goals for, 174–180
Professional Golf Association (PGA), 75
Professional players, and Olympic Games, 115
Professional sports, 169
    19th century development of, 67–68
    in 20th century U.S., 75–76
    women and, 151–153
Professionalism, creeping, 109
*Proposals for the Education of Youth in
    Pennsylvania*, 58